Facebook®

FOR

DUMMIES®

4TH EDITION

Facebook® FOR DUMMIES® 4TH EDITION

by Carolyn Abram

WILEY

John Wiley & Sons, Inc.

Facebook® For Dummies,® 4th Edition

Published by
John Wiley & Sons, Inc.
111 River Street
Hoboken, NJ 07030-5774

www.wiley.com

Copyright © 2012 by John Wiley & Sons, Inc., Hoboken, New Jersey

Published by John Wiley & Sons, Inc., Hoboken, New Jersey

Published simultaneously in Canada

For general information on our other products and services, please contact our Customer Care Department within the U.S. at 877-762-2974, outside the U.S. at 317-572-3993, or fax 317-572-4002.

For technical support, please visit www.wiley.com/techsupport.

Wiley also publishes its books in a variety of electronic formats and by print-on-demand. Not all content that is available in standard print versions of this book may appear or be packaged in all book formats. If you have purchased a version of this book that did not include media that is referenced by or accompanies a standard print version, you may request this media by visiting http://booksupport.wiley.com. For more information about Wiley products, visit www.wiley.com.

Library of Congress Control Number: 2011938580

ISBN 978-1-118-09562-1 (pbk); ISBN 978-1-118-17825-6 (ebk); ISBN 978-1-118-17826-3 (ebk); ISBN 978-1-118-17828-7 (ebk)

Manufactured in the United States of America

10 9 8 7 6 5 4 3 2 1

WILEY

About the Author

Carolyn Abram: Originally from Ardsley, New York, Carolyn migrated out to the left coast to attend school at Stanford (Class of 2006). While there, she studied English and became the first Facebook user at Stanford. After graduation, the most logical choice was to get paid to be on Facebook all day long, which she did from 2006 to 2009. Carolyn is currently studying fiction writing at California College of the Arts in San Francisco. Her hobbies include hiking, writing, enjoying sunshine, mocking her friends, and playing Ultimate Frisbee. She lives in San Mateo with her husband, a Roomba, and a sourdough starter.

Author's Acknowledgments

I have to start by thanking two people who made this (and every prior) edition possible: Blake Ross and Leah Pearlman, my former partners in Dummy crime. This book would not exist without the help of everyone listed on the other side of this page, especially Steve Hayes, Linda Morris, and Amy Karasavas.

On the home front, I have to thank Eric, who still lets me use *his* ergonomic chair when I'm working. (Who says chivalry is dead?) My whole family (grandmas, parents, sisters, and in-laws) and all of my friends deserve a big acknowledgement. They consistently post the best photos, leave the funniest comments, and are the biggest dummies I know.

In closing, I'd like to thank the millions of Facebook users around the world who are busy connecting, sharing, and generally having fun on Facebook. Keep on signin' on.

Publisher's Acknowledgments

We're proud of this book; please send us your comments at http://dummies.custhelp.com. For other comments, please contact our Customer Care Department within the U.S. at 877-762-2974, outside the U.S. at 317-572-3993, or fax 317-572-4002.

Some of the people who helped bring this book to market include the following:

Acquisitions and Editorial

Project Editor: Linda Morris

Acquisitions Editor: Steve Hayes

Copy Editor: Linda Morris

Technical Editor: Amy Karasavas

Editorial Manager: Jodi Jensen

Editorial Assistant: Amanda Graham

Sr. Editorial Assistant: Cherie Case

Cover Photo: ©istockphoto.com/ Stigur Karlsson (lady on laptop); ©istockphoto.com/Ozgur Donmaz (all faces)

Cartoons: Rich Tennant (www.the5thwave.com)

Composition Services

Project Coordinator: Nikki Gee

Layout and Graphics: Carl Byers, Joyce Haughey, Lavonne Roberts, Corrie Socolovitch

Proofreaders: Laura Albert, Lindsay Amones, ConText Editorial Services, Inc.

Indexer: Ty Koontz

Publishing and Editorial for Technology Dummies

Richard Swadley, Vice President and Executive Group Publisher

Andy Cummings, Vice President and Publisher

Mary Bednarek, Executive Acquisitions Director

Mary C. Corder, Editorial Director

Publishing for Consumer Dummies

Kathy Nebenhaus, Vice President and Executive Publisher

Composition Services

Debbie Stailey, Director of Composition Services

Contents at a Glance

Table of Contents

Introduction

Facebook connects you with the people you know and care about. It enables you to communicate, stay up-to-date, and keep in touch with friends and family anywhere. It facilitates your relationships online to help enhance them in person. Specifically, Facebook connects you with the *people* you know around *content* that is important to you. Whether you're the type to take photos or look at them, or write about your life, or read about your friends' lives, Facebook is designed to enable you to succeed. Maybe you like to share websites and news, play games, plan events, organize groups of people, or promote your business. Whatever you prefer, Facebook has you covered.

Facebook offers you control. Communication and information sharing are powerful only when you can do what you want within your comfort zone. Nearly every piece of information and means of connecting on Facebook comes with full privacy controls, allowing you to share and communicate exactly how — and with whom — you desire.

Facebook welcomes everyone: students and professionals; grandchildren (as long as they're at least age 13), parents, and grandparents; busy people; socialites; celebrities; distant friends; and roommates. No matter who you are, using Facebook can add value to your life. Results are typical.

About Facebook For Dummies

Part I of this book teaches you all the basics to get you up and running on Facebook. This information is more than enough for you to discover Facebook's value. Part II teaches you about friends and how you can communicate with them on Facebook. Part III explores all the powerful ways of mingling what happens in your life with what you're sharing and planning on Facebook. Part IV does a deep dive into some of the more advanced ways of using the site that can be of great additional value, depending on your needs. Finally, Part V explores the creative, diverse, touching, and even frustrating ways people have welcomed Facebook into their lives.

Here are some of the things you can do with this book:

- **Find out how to represent yourself online.** Facebook lets you create a profile that you can share with friends, co-workers, and the people-you-have-yet-to-meet.

- **Connect and share with people you know.** Whether you're seeking close friends or long-lost ones, family members, business contacts, teammates, businesses, or celebrities, Facebook keeps you connected. Never say, "Goodbye" again . . . unless you want to.

- **Discover how the online tools of Facebook can help enhance your relationships offline.** Event and group organizational tools, photo-sharing, and direct and passive communication capabilities all enable you to maintain an active social life in the real world.

- **Bring your connections off Facebook and on to the rest of the web.** Through Facebook Platform and Connect, you see how many services you already use can be made more powerful by using them in conjunction with your Facebook friends.

- **Promote a business, cause, or yourself to the people who can bring you success.** Engaging with people on Facebook can help you ensure that your message is heard.

Foolish Assumptions

In this book, we make the following assumptions:

- You're at least 13 years of age.

- You have some access to the Internet, an e-mail address, and a web browser that is not Internet Explorer 6 (Internet Explorer 7, Safari, Chrome, Firefox, and so on are all good).

- There are people in your life with whom you communicate.

- You can read the language in which this sentence is printed.

Conventions Used in This Book

In this book, we stick to a few conventions to help with readability. Whenever you have to type text, we show it in **bold**, so it's easy to see. `Monofont` text denotes an e-mail address or website URL. When you see an *italicized* word, look for its nearby definition. Facebook pages and features — such as the

Friends box or the Privacy Overview page — are called out with capital letters. Numbered lists guide you through tasks that must be completed in order from top to bottom; bulleted lists can be read in any order you like (from top to bottom or bottom to top).

Finally, I often state my opinions throughout this book. Though I have worked for Facebook, the opinions expressed here represent only my perspective, not that of Facebook. I am an avid Facebook user and became one long before I worked for Facebook.

What You Don't Have to Read

This book is written with the new Facebook user in mind. If you already have an account and are looking for some help or advice, check the Table of Contents for the parts of the site that you want to learn more about. Sprinkled throughout the book, sidebars cover many bits of extra information; these are simply added points of interest that can be skipped without detriment to your Facebook experience.

How This Book Is Organized

Facebook For Dummies, 4th Edition, is split into five parts. You don't have to read it sequentially, and you don't even have to read all the sections in any particular chapter. We explain the most generalized functionality — that which applies to just about everyone — in the first two parts. There's a small introduction at the beginning of each section that explains what it will talk about, as well as an introduction at the beginning of each chapter. If you're unsure about a particular chapter, try reading its introduction to decide.

Topics in this book are covered mostly in the order in which most people use each particular feature, though Parts 1 and 2 go together like rice and beans, or cookies and milk, or some other really tasty combination. The point is that if you want to read one, you should read the other as well. As the book progresses, I dive deeper into specialized functionality that may be relevant only to certain audiences.

Don't forget about the Table of Contents and the Index; you can use these sections to quickly find the information you need. Here's what you find in each part.

Part I: Getting Started with Facebook

Chapter 1 introduces you to Facebook and gives you all the information you need to get started. This includes learning about what Facebook is and is not for, setting up an account, navigating the site, and creating a profile. Additionally, this section covers privacy. Privacy is an aspect of Facebook that can get quite confusing, so even if you're a seasoned user, you may want to check out Chapter 5.

Part II: Connecting with Friends on Facebook

After you've got your own stuff set up, it's time to start interacting. It's what makes Facebook so great. This section will help you find your friends, add them, and then stay in touch with them. Facebook has a lot of cool features that help you keep up with lots of people, from all parts of your life.

Part III: Out to the Real World and Back Again

Part III covers how Facebook can enhance what's going on in the real world. Facebook isn't just about connecting with friends online; it has a whole set of tools to help connect you around what's happening with your friends offline. This section covers Facebook's incredibly popular photo-sharing system as well as Events and Pages.

Part IV: Pages, Games, and Mobile

Obviously, one needs to get the basics down at some point, but some of the most popular ways to use Facebook involve things like playing games and using Facebook on your mobile device. This section covers these two more advanced features in depth. It also covers Pages, which are to public figures and entities what a Profile is to a regular Joe or Jane.

Part V: The Part of Tens

The final section of this book gives fun-to-read and easy-to-digest views on the creative ways people use Facebook. We highlight ten very different games and apps that other companies have integrated into the Facebook environment. Next, you get the answers to ten of the questions I hear most often about how to use Facebook. Ten real-world scenarios provide you a perspective on the value of integrating Facebook with your lifestyle. Finally, I share ten tips for parents of teens who use Facebook.

Icons Used in This Book

What's a *For Dummies* book without icons pointing you in the direction of great information that's sure to help you along your way? In this section, we briefly describe each icon we use in this book.

The Tip icon points out helpful information that is likely to improve your experience.

The Remember icon marks an interesting and useful fact — something that you may want to use later.

The Warning icon highlights lurking danger. With this icon, we're telling you to pay attention and proceed with caution.

Where to Go from Here

Whether you've been using Facebook for years or this is your first time, I recommend you start by reading Chapter 1, which sets the stage for most of what we describe in detail in the rest of this book. After reading the first chapter, you may have a better sense of which topics in this book will be more relevant to you, and you can, therefore, flip right to them. However, I recommend that *everyone* spend some quality time in Chapter 5, which covers privacy on Facebook. Facebook is an online representation of a community, so it's important that each person understand how to operate in that community to ensure a safe, fun, and functional environment for everyone.

If you're new to Facebook and looking to use it to enhance your own personal connections, I recommend reading this book from Part I straight through Part III.

You may already be quite familiar with Facebook when you pick up this book. But because the site is constantly growing and changing, there is always more to know. Parts III and IV will keep you ahead of the curve.

No matter which category you fall into, it's time to get started: Let one hand flip the pages of this book, the other drive your computer mouse, and let your mind open up to a revolutionary way to enhance and experience your real-world relationships.

Occasionally, we have updates to our technology books. If this book does have technical updates, they will be posted at dummies.com/go/facebookfd4eupdates.

Part I

Getting Started with Facebook

The 5th Wave   By Rich Tennant

"Hello—forget the company's financials, look at the CEO's Facebook page under '25 Things the SEC Doesn't Know About Me.'"

In this part . . .

So, you've been persuaded to read beyond the Introduction. Well done! (You can't see it, but I am patting myself on the back now.) This part starts at the very beginning of Facebook, explaining what Facebook is and some rules about how you can (and cannot) use it.

After that, this is all about you: creating your account, navigating your way through the site, setting up and using your Profile, and, importantly, getting your privacy settings in place. The more you understand the basics of these chapters, the easier it will be for you to continue to use Facebook.

Chapter 1

The Many Faces of Facebook

Think about the people you interacted with throughout the past day. In the morning, you may have gone to get the paper and chatted with the neighbor. You may have asked your kids what time they'd be home and negotiated with your partner about whose turn it is to cook dinner. Perhaps you spent the day at the office, chatting, joking, and (heaven forbid) getting things done with your co-workers. In the evening, you may have shot off an e-mail to an old college roommate, called your mom (it's her birthday, after all), and made plans to have dinner with some friends this weekend. At the end of the day, you unwound in front of your favorite newscaster telling you about the various politicians and celebrities whose lives may (or may not) interest you. You may have, at various points in the day, asked someone to recommend a plumber to unclog your drain or had a full conversation of grunts with your dentist.

That's a one-foot view of the world in which you're the center.

Pan the camera back a ways (farther . . . farther . . . even farther), and you see that each person you interact with — family, friends, the newspaper delivery guy, the lunch lady, your favorite musician, and even me, your dedicated author — are at the center of their own realities. So is each person *they* know. The connections between every single person in the world intertwine, interplay, and interlock to form a sort of network. In the network of people you interact with — your friends, acquaintances, and loved ones — all these people exist online and represent themselves through Facebook, just like you're about to do. Facebook is the online representation of the web of connections between people in the real world. Facebook (and other Internet companies) like to call this network the *social graph*.

Now, you may be asking, if this graph or network exists in the real world, why do I need it online, too? Good question (gold stars all around). The answer is that having it online facilitates and improves all your social relationships. In other words, Facebook makes your life easier and your friendships better. It can help with the very practical, like remembering a friend's birthday, to the more abstract, like staying close with family you aren't physically near.

Getting set up and familiar with Facebook does take a little work (which you know, or else you wouldn't be starting out on this book-length journey). It may feel a little overwhelming at times, but the reward is worth it, I promise you.

So . . . What Is Facebook, Exactly?

Yes, Carolyn, you're saying, I know it's going to help me stay in touch with my friends and communicate with the people in my life, but what *is* it?

Well, at its most basic, Facebook is a website. You'll find it through a web browser like Safari, Firefox, or Internet Explorer, the same way you might navigate to a search engine like Google or to an airline's website to book tickets. Figure 1-1 shows what you will probably see when you navigate to www.facebook.com.

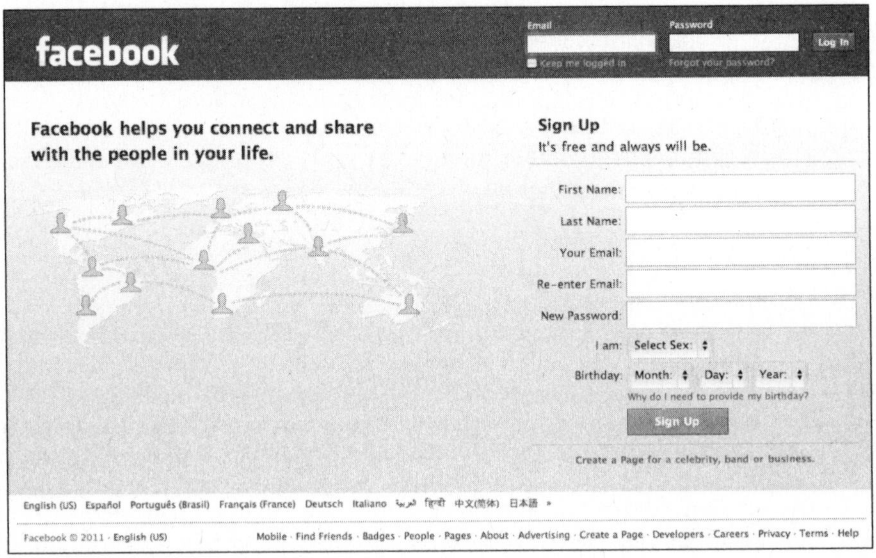

Figure 1-1:
Welcome to
Facebook.
Would you
like fries
with that?

Facebook is a website where you go to accomplish certain tasks. These tasks usually fall under the umbrella category of *social maintenance*. For example, you may go to Facebook to

- ✔ Find the phone number of an old friend
- ✔ Check out what your friends are up to today
- ✔ Make a contact in a city you're moving to or at an office where you're applying for a job
- ✔ Plan an event
- ✔ Garner support for a cause
- ✔ Get recommendations from friends for movies, books, and restaurants
- ✔ Show off the pictures from your latest vacation
- ✔ Tell your friends and family about your recent successes, show them your photos, or let them know you're thinking of them
- ✔ Remember everyone's birthday

So what Facebook *is,* exactly, is a website built to help you represent yourself online and share with your real-world friends online. The rest of it — how that's accomplished, what people typically share on Facebook, and how it all works — is what this book is all about.

Discovering What You Can Do on Facebook

Now that you know that Facebook is a means by which you can connect with people who matter to you, your next question may be, "How?" More gold stars for you! In the next few sections, I give you an overview.

Establish a Profile

When you sign up for Facebook, one of the first things you do is establish your *Profile.* A Profile on Facebook is a social résumé — a page about you that you keep up-to-date with all the information you want people to know.

If you were handing out résumés in the real world, you'd probably give different documents to different people. Your social résumé may have your phone number, your favorite quotes, and pictures from that crazy night in you-know-where with you-know-who. Your résumé for a potential employer would probably share your education and employment history. Your résumé for your family may include your personal address as well as show off your recent vacation photos and news about your life's changes.

You show different slices of your life and personality to different people, and a Facebook Profile, shown in Figure 1-2, allows you (no, *encourages* you) to do the same. To this end, your Profile is set up with all kinds of privacy controls to specify *who* you want to see *which* information. Many people find great value in adding to their Profile just about every piece of information they can and then unveiling each particular piece cautiously. Facebook is now organizing that information into a timeline format, which I cover more in Chapter 2. The safest rule here is to share on your Profile any piece of information you'd share with someone in real life. The corollary applies, too: Don't share on your Profile any information that you wouldn't share with someone in real life. I provide more detail about the Profile in Chapter 2. For now, think of it like a personal web page with privacy controls for particular pieces of information. This page accurately reflects you so that you hand the right social résumé to the right person.

Figure 1-2:
An example of a Facebook Profile.

The motivations for establishing a Profile on Facebook are twofold. First, a Profile helps the people who know you in real life find and connect with you on Facebook. Each individual is actively (or actively trying) to keep track of the people she knows. If your name is something relatively common, such as James Brown or Maria Gonzales, it's difficult for people to find you without additional identifiers. Information about you, such as your hometown, your education history, or your photos, helps people find the right James or Maria.

The second (and way cooler) reason to establish an accurate Profile is the work it saves you. Keeping your Profile detailed and relevant means that your friends and family can always get the latest information about where you live, who you know, and what you're up to. You no longer have to read your phone number to someone while he fumbles to find a pen. Just tell him, "It's on Facebook." If a cousin wants to send you a birthday present, he doesn't have to ruin the surprise by asking you for your address. When your Profile is up-to-date, conversations that used to start with the open-ended, "How have you been?" can skip straight to the good stuff: "I saw your pictures from Hawaii last week. *Please* tell me how you ended up wearing those coconuts."

Connect with friends

Now that you know about Profiles, you should know that there are ways to connect your Profile to the Profiles of people you know. These connections are called *friendships*. On Facebook, it's pretty common to refer to *friending* people you know. This just means establishing the virtual connection. Friending people allows you to communicate and share with them more easily. Friends are basically the reason Facebook can be so powerful and useful to people. After all, you can only sit and stare at your own Profile for so long. Facebook offers the following tools to help you find your friends:

✔ **Facebook Friend Finder:** Allows you to scan the e-mail addresses in your e-mail address book to find whether those people are already on Facebook. Selectively choose among those with whom you'd like to connect.

✔ **People You May Know:** Shows you the names and pictures of people you likely know. These people are selected for you based on various signals like where you live or work or how many friends you have in common.

✔ **Search:** Helps you find the people who are most likely already using Facebook.

After you establish a few connections, use those connections to find other people you know by searching through their connections for familiar names. We explain how to find people you know on Facebook in Chapter 6.

Communicate with Facebook friends

As Facebook grows, it becomes more likely that anyone with whom you're trying to communicate can be reached. These days it's a fairly safe assumption that you'll be able to find that person you just met at a dinner party, an old professor from college, or the childhood friend you've been meaning to catch up with. Digging up a person's contact information could require calls to mutual friends, a trip to the white pages (provided you know enough about that person to identify the right contact information), or an e-mail sent to a potentially outdated e-mail address. You may have different methods of reaching people depending on how you met the person, or what limited information you have about him or her.

Facebook streamlines finding and contacting people in a reliable forum. If the friend you're reaching out to is active on Facebook, no matter where she lives or how many times she's changed her e-mail address, you can reach one another.

Share your thoughts

You have something to say. I can just tell by the look on your face. Maybe you're proud of the home team, maybe you're excited for Friday, or maybe you can't believe what you saw on the way to work this morning. All day long, things are happening to all of us that make us just want to turn to our friends and say, "You know what? . . . That's what." Facebook gives you the stage and an eager audience. In Chapter 7, I explain how you can make short or long posts about the things happening around you, and how they're distributed to your friends in an easy way.

Share your pictures

Since the invention of the modern-day camera, people have been all too eager to yell, "Cheese!" Photographs can make great tour guides on trips down memory lane, but only if we actually remember to develop, upload, or scrapbook them. Many memories fade away when the smiling faces are stuffed into an old shoe box, remain on undeveloped rolls of film, or are forgotten in some folder on a hard drive.

Facebook offers three great incentives for uploading, organizing, and editing your photos:

- **Facebook provides one easy-to-access location for all your photos.** Directing any interested person to your Facebook Profile is easier than e-mailing pictures individually, sending a complicated link to a photo site, or waiting until the family reunion to show off the my-how-the-kids-have-grown pics.

- **Every photo you upload can be linked to the Profiles of the people in the photo.** For example, you upload pictures of you and your sister and link them to her Profile. Whenever someone visits her Profile, he sees those pictures; he doesn't even have to know you. This is great because it introduces a longevity to photos that they've never had before. As long as people are visiting your sister's Profile, they can see those pictures. Photo albums no longer have to be something people look at right after the event and maybe then again years later.

✔ **Facebook gives you the power to control exactly who has access to your photos.** Every time you upload a photo or create a new photo album on Facebook, you can decide whether you want everyone on Facebook to see it, just your friends, or even just a subset of your friends based on your comfort level. You may choose to show your wedding photos to all your friends, but perhaps only some friends see the honeymoon. This control enables you to tailor your audience to those friends who might be most interested. All your friends might enjoy your baby photos, but maybe only your co-workers will care about photos from the recent company party.

Plan Events, join groups

Just about anything you do with other people is easier on Facebook . . . except cuddling. Facebook isn't meant to be a replacement for face-to-face interaction; it's meant to facilitate interactions when face time isn't possible or to facilitate the planning of face time. Two of the greatest tools for this are Facebook Events and Facebook Groups.

Events are just what they sound like: a system for creating Events, inviting people to them, sending out messages about them, and so on. Your friends and other guests RSVP to Events, which allows the Event organizers to plan accordingly and allows attendees to receive Event reminders. Facebook Events can be used for something as small as a lunch date or something as big as a march on Washington, D.C. Sometimes Events are abstract rather than physical. For example, someone could create an Event for Ride Your Bike to Work Day and hope the invitation spreads far and wide (through friends and friends of friends) to promote awareness. I use Events to plan barbecues for my friends as well as to put together a larger reading series. I cover Events in detail in Chapter 11.

Groups are also what they sound like: groups of people organized around a common topic or real-world organization. One group may be intimate, such as five best friends who plan several activities together. Another group could be practical, for example, PTA Members of Denver Schools. Within a group, all members can share relevant information, photos, or discussions. My groups include one for my family where we might post photos we don't want to share with the world at large, one for my Dummies editorial team so we can update each other on how the writing is going, and one for a group of friends who are all planning to take a trip together next year. Groups are covered in detail in Chapter 9.

Facebook and the web

Facebook Photos, Groups, and Events are only a small sampling of how you can use Facebook to connect with the people you know. Throughout this book, you'll find information about how Facebook interacts with the greater Internet. You might see articles recommended by friends when you go to *The New York Times* website, or information about what music your friends like when you go to Pandora, an Internet radio website. Additionally, in Chapter 14, I explain in detail the Games and Applications that you can use with your Facebook information.

Many of these websites and applications have been built by *outside developers,* people who don't work for Facebook. They include tools to help you edit your photos; create slideshows; play games with friends across the globe; divvy up bills among people who live or hang out together; and exchange information about good movies, music, books, and restaurants. After you get a little more comfortable with the Facebook basics, you can try some of the thousands of applications and websites that allow you to interact with your Facebook friends through their services.

Promote a cause or business

In addition to your friends and family, you interact with tons of other things or entities every day. These may be a newspaper or magazine, a celebrity whose marriage travails you can't help but be fascinated by, a television show that has you on the edge of your seat, or a cause that's near and dear to your heart. All these entities can be represented on Facebook through Pages (with a capital P). These Pages look almost exactly like Profiles, just for the not-quite-people among us. Instead of becoming "Friends" with Pages, you can "Like" them. So when you Like a television show (say, *The Daily Show with Jon Stewart*), you'll start to see updates from *The Daily Show* on your Home page. Liking Pages for businesses or causes helps you stay up-to-date with news from them.

If you're the one managing something like a small business, a cause, or a newsletter, you can also create a Page. After you've created that page, your users/customers/fans can like it and then you can update them with news about whatever's going on in the world of your store/cause/thing. We'll talk about all the ins and outs of Pages in Chapter 13.

Keeping in Mind What You Can't Do on Facebook

Facebook is meant to represent real people and real associations; it's also meant to be safe. Many of the rules of participation on Facebook exist to uphold those two goals.

Note: There are things you can't do on Facebook other than what we list here. For example, you can't send multiple unsolicited messages to people you're not friends with; you can't join the school network of a school you didn't attend (or a workplace network of a company you don't work for); and you can't spin straw into gold. These rules may change how you use Facebook, but probably won't change *whether* you use it. The following four rules are highlighted in this section because, if any are a problem for you, you probably won't get to the rest of the book.

You can't lie

Okay, you can, but you shouldn't, especially not about your basic information. Lying about your identity is a violation of the Statement of Rights and Responsibilities and grounds for your Profile being disabled. Although many people try, Facebook doesn't let anyone sign up with an obviously fake name like Marilyn Manson or Fakey McFakerson. Those who do make it past the name checks will likely find their account flagged and disabled.

You can't be twelve

Or younger. Seriously. Facebook takes very seriously the U.S. law that prohibits minors under the age of 13 from creating an online Profile for themselves. This rule is in place for the safety of minors, and it's a particular safety rule that Facebook takes extremely seriously. If you or someone you know on Facebook is under 13, deactivate (or make them deactivate) the account now. If you're reported to the Facebook user operations team and they confirm that you are underage, your account will be disabled.

You can't troll or spam

On the Internet, *trolling* refers to posting deliberately offensive material to websites in order to get people upset. *Spamming* refers to sending out bulk promotional messages. If you do either of these things on Facebook, there's a good chance your account will get shut down.

The logic for this is that Facebook is about real people and real connections. It is one thing to message a mutual friend or the occasional stranger whose Profile implies being open to meeting new people if the two of you have matching interests. However, between Facebook's automatic detection systems and user-generated reports, sending too many unsolicited messages is likely to get your account flagged and disabled.

Similarly, Facebook aims to be a "trusted" environment for people to exchange ideas and information. If people deliberately disturb the peace with pornographic, hateful, or bullying content, that trust is pretty much broken.

Chances are, you have no intention of spamming or trolling, so keep in mind that if you see either of these things happening, you can report the content or person to Facebook (you can learn how to report a photo, for example, in Chapter 12), and its User Operations team investigates the report.

You can't upload illegal content

Facebook Users live in virtually every country in the world, so Facebook is often obligated to respect the local laws for its users. Respecting these laws is something Facebook has to do regardless of its own position on pornography (where minors can see it), copyrighted material, hate speech, depictions of crimes, and other offensive content. However, doing so is also in line with Facebook's value of being a safe, happy place for people 13 and older. Don't confuse this with censorship; Facebook is all about freedom of speech and self-expression, but the moment that compromises anyone's safety or breaks any law, disciplinary action is taken.

Realizing How Facebook Is Different from Other Social Sites

Several social sites besides Facebook try to help people connect. Some of the most popular sites are Twitter, MySpace, Friendster, Orkut, LinkedIn, Windows Live Spaces, Bebo, Meebo, Match.com, and QQ.

In some cases, these sites have slightly different goals than Facebook. LinkedIn, for example, is a tool for connecting with people specifically for career networking. MySpace (www.myspace.com) is a way for people to connect to lots of people outside their real-world experience, especially for people to connect with their favorite musicians and bands. Match.com (www.match.com) is a social networking site specifically geared toward people looking to date. Alternatively, other sites have the same goals as Facebook;

they just have different strategies. MySpace gives users complete customization over the look and feel of their Profile, whereas Facebook maintains a pretty consistent design and expects users to differentiate their Profiles by uploading unique content. On the other extreme, Twitter allows its members to share very short bits of text and photos to achieve super-simple and consistent information sharing, whereas Facebook allows more flexibility with respect to sharing complete photo albums, videos, and more. That's not to say one model is better than another; different models may appeal to different people.

How You Can Use Facebook

Originally, Facebook was created as a way for students at a particular college or university to find and connect with each another. In fact, when Facebook launched, only those people with a verified college e-mail address were permitted to sign up.

After a few years of being "that site for college kids," Facebook knocked down its walls and invited everyone to sign up. Now, Facebook Nation is 800 million strong and growing every day the world over. This means that all sorts of different people are using Facebook with all sorts of different goals in mind. Here are a few common ways people use Facebook. You might see yourself here multiple times. If you don't see yourself at all, don't worry; there's plenty of room for someone like you on Facebook, too.

Eight hundred million people use Facebook, but not all of them can see your whole Profile. You can share as much or as little with as many or as few people as you so desire. Put under lock and key the parts of your Profile you *don't* want to share with everyone. Chapter 5 goes into much greater detail on how to protect yourself and your information.

The following list is by no means comprehensive, and I've left out some of the things already mentioned in this chapter (things like sharing photos and Events and groups). These are more specific use-cases than an advertisement for Facebook's features.

Getting information

At any age, you may need to find someone's phone number or connect with a friend of a friend to organize something. Facebook can make these very practical tasks a little bit easier. As long as you can search for someone's name, you should be able to find them on Facebook and find the information you're looking for.

Keeping up with long-distance friends

These days, families and friends are often spread far and wide across state or country lines. Children go to college; grandparents move to Florida; people move for their job or because they want a change of scenery. These distances make it hard for people to interact in any more significant way than gathering together once per year to share some turkey and pie (pecan, preferably). Facebook offers a place where you can virtually meet and interact. Upload photos of the kids for everyone to see; write notes about what everyone is up to. Even the more mundane information about your life ("I'm at jury duty") can make someone across the world feel like, just for a second, they are sitting next to you and commiserating with you about your jury summons.

Flirting

Throughout this book, you will read about ways to communicate: messages, chatting, poking, liking, and commenting. These fairly neutral activities will stay neutral, but between two people interested in each other, they can take on a whole new meaning and spark.

Your Profile has the ability to inform people who you're looking to meet (women, men, or both) and for what purpose (relationship, dating, friendship, and so on). Those already in a relationship can link to their significant other's Profile for the world to see.

Moving to a new city

Landing in a new city with all your worldly belongings and an upside-down map can be hugely intimidating. Having some open arms or at least numbers to call when you arrive can greatly ease the transition. Although you may already know some people who live in your new city, Facebook can help connect with all the old friends and acquaintances you either forgot live there or have moved there since you last heard from them. These people can help you find doctors, apartments, hair stylists, Frisbee leagues, and restaurants.

As you meet more and more new friends, you can connect with them on Facebook. Sooner than you thought possible, when someone posts about construction slowing down their commute, you know exactly the street they mean and you may realize, *I'm home.*

Getting a job

Plenty of people use Facebook as a tool for managing their careers as well as their social lives. If you're looking at a particular company, find people who already work there to get the inside scoop or to land an interview. If you're thinking about moving into a particular industry, browse your friends by past jobs and interests to find someone to connect with. If you go to a conference for professional development, you can keep track of the other people you meet there as your Facebook friends.

Facebook reunion

Thanks to life's curveballs, your friends at any given time may not be the people in your life at another. The memories of people you consider to be most important in your life fade over the years so that even trying to recall a last name may give you pause. The primary reason for this lapse is a legitimate one: There are only so many hours in a day. While we make new, close friends, others drift away because it's impossible to maintain many intense relationships. Facebook is an extremely powerful tool; however, it hasn't yet found a way to extend the number of hours in a day, so it can't exactly fix the problem of growing apart. Facebook can, however, lessen the finality and inevitability of the distance.

Because Facebook is less than seven years old (and because you're reading this book), you probably don't have your entire social history mapped out. Some may find it a daunting task to create connections with everyone they've ever known, which we don't recommend. Instead, build your graph as you need to or as opportunity presents. Perhaps you want to upload a photo taken from your high school graduation. Search for the people in the photo on Facebook; form the friend connection; and then *tag,* or mark, them as being in the photo. Maybe you're thinking about opening a restaurant, and you'd like to contact a friend from college who was headed into the restaurant business after graduation. Perhaps you never told your true feelings to the one who got away — your unicorn. For all these reasons, you may find yourself using the Facebook Search box.

 Frequently, I receive reports from adopted children who connect with their biological parents, or estranged siblings who find each other on Facebook. I once heard from my sixth-grade bully, who found me on Facebook and apologized for his behavior as a kid.

Organizing movements

If you kept up on the news of the "Arab Spring" uprisings in the early part of 2011, you couldn't avoid hearing about the role Facebook played. Young people used Facebook as an organizing tool, letting each other know about protest locations and times. People in geographically distant regions could share ideas about their countries and what they wanted to see outside of the watchful eye of oppressive regimes.

And as the drama unfolded, plenty of people with family in the affected areas turned to Facebook to make sure their loved ones were okay. People unrelated but concerned offered their support through their own status updates and more.

The term *movement*, here, can apply to anything. Whether it's a campaign to raise awareness about gay teen suicides or a campaign to raise money for victims of a natural disaster, Facebook can be used to bring support and spread the word.

The birth of the 'Book

In the old days, say, ten years ago, most college freshmen would receive a thinly bound book containing the names and faces of everyone in their matriculating class. These *face books* were useful for matching names to the students seen around campus or for pointing out particular people to friends. There were several problems with these face books. If someone didn't send his picture in, they were incomplete. They were outdated by junior year because many people looked drastically different, and the book didn't reflect the students who had transferred in or who were from any other class. Finally, they had little information about each person.

In February 2004, Mark Zuckerberg, a sophomore at Harvard, launched an online "book" to which people could upload their photos and personal information; a service that solved many of these problems. Within a month, more than half the Harvard undergraduates had created their own Profiles. Zuckerberg was then joined by others to help expand the site into other schools. I was the first non-Harvard student to receive an account. During the summer of the same year, Facebook moved to Palo Alto, California, where the site and the company kept growing. By December 2004, the site had grown to one million college students. Every time Facebook opened to a new demographic — high school, then work users, then everyone — the rate at which people joined the site continued to increase. At the end of 2006, the site had more than 10 million users; 2007 closed out with more than 50 million active users. At the time of this book's publication in 2011, that final count has grown more than 16-fold, passing 800 million active users logging in each month.

Chapter 2

Adding Your Own Face to Facebook

*I*n Chapter 1, I cover why you want to join Facebook. In this chapter, I actually get you signed up and ready to go on Facebook. Keep a couple of things in mind when you sign up. First, Facebook gets exponentially more useful and more fun when you start adding friends. Without friends, it can feel kind of dull. Second, your friends may take a few days to respond to your friend requests, so be patient. Even if your first time on Facebook isn't as exciting as you hope, be sure to come back and try again over the following weeks. Third, you can have only one account on Facebook. Facebook links accounts to e-mail addresses, and your e-mail address can be linked to only one account. This system enforces a world where people are who they say they are on Facebook.

Signing Up for Facebook

Officially, all you need to join Facebook is a valid e-mail address. When I say *valid,* I just mean that you need to be able to easily access the messages in that account because Facebook e-mails you a registration confirmation. Figure 2-1 shows the crucial part of the sign-up page, which you can find by navigating to www.facebook.com.

Figure 2-1:
Enter infor-
mation here
to create a
Facebook
account.

As you can see, you need to fill out a few things:

- ✓ **First and Last Name:** Facebook is a place based on real identity. It's not a place for fake names or aliases. Numerous privacy settings are in place to protect your information (see Chapter 5), so use your full real name to sign up.

- ✓ **E-mail:** You need to enter your valid e-mail address here. Facebook asks you to enter your e-mail twice to make sure there are no typos and your e-mails will actually get to you.

- ✓ **Password:** Like with all passwords, using a combination of letters and numbers is a good idea for your Facebook password. It's probably not a good idea to use the same password for every site you join, so I recommend using something unique for Facebook.

- ✓ **Gender (I am):** Facebook uses your gender information to construct sentences about you on the site. Especially in other languages, it's weird to see sentences like "Jennifer added a photo of themself." If you want to hide your gender on your Profile, you'll be able to do so after you sign up.

- ✓ **Birthday:** Enter your date of birth. If you're shy about sharing your birthday, don't worry: You'll be able to hide this information on your Profile later.

- ✓ **Security Check:** The security check on Facebook is in the form of a CAPTCHA (see Figure 2-2). A CAPTCHA is that funky-looking word-in-a-box. Computers can't read CAPTCHAs, but humans can. Asking you to type the word in a CAPTCHA is Facebook's way of making sure you're a real person, not a spam-producing computer or robot. You see the CAPTCHA after filling out your information and clicking Sign Up.

Sign Up
It's free and always will be.

Security Check

NQ8U

Can't read the text above?
Try another text: or an audio captcha

Text in the box: | What's this?

◄ Back   Sign Up

By clicking Sign Up, you are indicating that you have read and agree to the Terms of Use
and Privacy Policy.

Figure 2-2:
Security
checks
weed out
robots.

After you've filled out this information, click Sign Up (that's the big green button). Congratulations: You have officially joined Facebook!

When you click Sign Up, you are agreeing to Facebook's Statement of Rights and Responsibilities and Privacy Policy. Most websites have fairly similar Terms and Policies, but if you're curious about just what Facebook's say, you can always follow the links at the bottom of every Facebook page.

Getting Started

While you have this book to help guide you through the ins and outs of Facebook, lots of Facebook users do not. (How sad for them!) That's why Facebook puts all its users through a three-step Getting Started Wizard to help start them out on the right foot. This is one of those places where what I think you should do and what Facebook thinks you should do line up exactly, so I'll go through all three of these steps together: what to enter as well as why they are important to using Facebook.

In certain cases, depending on if you were invited to join Facebook by a friend, or if you joined with an e-mail address from your workplace or school, you may get slightly different steps than those detailed as follows. Don't worry; the same principles will apply.

Step 1: Find Friends

The Find Friends step, shown in Figure 2-3, is first because it is that important to enjoying Facebook. Without friends, Facebook can feel a little bit like going to an amusement park alone. Sure, the rides were fun, and the food was greasy, but no one was there to appreciate it with you.

You have many ways to find friends on Facebook. I go over all of them in Chapter 6, as well as talking more about what friendship really means on Facebook. The method Facebook is highlighting in this step is called the *Friend Finder*.

The Friend Finder works by allowing Facebook access to your e-mail account. Facebook then combs through your e-mail contacts and matches the e-mails it finds with e-mails attached to the Facebook accounts of the people you e-mail. So if Joe Smith, your friend, e-mailed you from `jsmith@email.com`, and also had a Facebook account he created with that e-mail address, the Friend Finder presents you with Joe's Facebook Profile and ask if you want to be friends on Facebook.

To use the Friend Finder, follow these steps:

1. **Select the e-mail provider you are using.**

   This may be Windows Live Hotmail, Gmail, Yahoo!, or another e-mail client. Facebook automatically selects a provider based on the e-mail you used to register, so in Figure 2-3, Gmail is preselected and the e-mail is prefilled.

2. **Enter your e-mail address and e-mail password.**

   Remember to enter your e-mail password, not the password you just created for Facebook.

3. **Click Find Friends.**

   Behind the scenes, Facebook searches your contact list and presents you with the people in your e-mail contact list who are already on Facebook. By default, all of these people are selected to be your friends.

4. **Look through the list and choose the people you want to be friends with on Facebook.**

   I talk more about *who*, exactly, should be your Facebook friends in Chapter 6, but for now, a good rule of thumb is to look for people you are friends with or related to in real life. You can deselect the people you don't want to add by clicking on their face or in the check box.

   This isn't your only opportunity to use the Friend Finder. If you aren't sure about adding a lot of people right away, that's okay. Chapter 6 shows you how to get back to these steps at any point in time.

5. **Click Add as Friends.**

   This sends *Friend Requests* to all the people you've selected in Step 4. On Facebook, all friendships have to be agreed to by both people. A request to your friend needs to be approved by them before you are officially Facebook friends.

   After you've added friends, Facebook looks at the e-mail addresses it didn't find matches for and ask you if you want to invite those people to join Facebook.

6. **Select people you want to invite to join Facebook.**

   Much like selecting friends to add, you can select and deselect friends' e-mail addresses by clicking the check box next to their e-mails.

   If you don't want to invite anyone to join Facebook just yet, look on the bottom right of the screen for a Skip link. It's right next to the Send Invites button.

7. **Click Send Invites to send out invitations to your friends via e-mail.**

   They'll receive e-mails from Facebook letting them know you invited them to join.

The Friend Finder is very useful when you're just getting started on Facebook because it allows you to find a whole bunch of friends all at once. If you had to look for each of your friends by name, it could take a while. Friend Finder allows you to speed that process up.

Step 2: Profile Information

Your *Facebook Profile* is the online representation of who you are. Most likely, you have online Profiles for various websites. Facebook Profiles tend to be a little more comprehensive and dynamic, for reasons that I detail in Chapter 4.

While you're getting started, Facebook only asks for a little bit of Profile Information, the part that I like to call the *bio*. Facebook asks for this bio because this is the information that will help your friends find you. The Profile Information step is shown in Figure 2-4.

Figure 2-4:
Profile
Information
helps
your friends
find you.

There are three fields that Facebook asks for. You can fill out all or none of them, but I definitely recommend filling them all out:

- ✔ **High School:** Enter the high school you attended and your class year. Just enter one for now; you'll be able to add more schools later.

- ✔ **College/University:** If you attended college, enter your school and class year. If you attended more than one school, either because you transferred or because you also attended a graduate program, just pick one school for now. You'll be able to add the rest later.

- ✔ **Employer:** Enter the name of the company you work for. For now, enter wherever you are currently working or where you worked most recently. You'll be able to enter a full work history later on.

You might notice that as you type in the name of your high school or college, a list of names appears below the field where you are typing. Get used to seeing these *auto-complete* menus around Facebook. As you type, Facebook tries to guess the rest of the word you are typing. When you see what you are looking for, use your arrow keys to highlight the correct match and press Enter. You'll find similar menus later when you start using search, tagging photos, and sending messages.

Now that you've entered this information, you've made it easier for old friends to find and identify you. If you have a common name, this is especially important. An old friend might be looking to catch up, but if she can't figure out if you are the Jane Smith from Barnard Class of 1966, she might not be able to reach out at all.

Depending on how many people Facebook finds that it thinks you may want to be friends with, it may show you an "Add People You Know" screen after filling out your info in Step 2. You can click on the people you want to be your friend and then click the Save and Continue button. You can also choose to Skip that part of the step using the Skip link (next to the Save & Continue button).

Step 3: Profile picture

Much like Step 2, Step 3 is more about helping your friends find you, while Step 1 was about helping you find them.

Like your biographical information, the Profile picture helps set you apart from other people with similar names. Step 3 is shown in Figure 2-5.

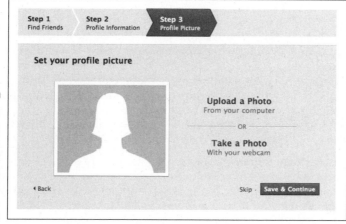

Figure 2-5:
Add a
Profile pic-
ture to get
your own
face on
Facebook.

To add your Profile picture, make sure you have a photo you want to use saved somewhere on your computer's hard drive, and follow these steps:

1. **Click Upload a Photo.**

   This brings up a dialog box similar to the one shown in Figure 2-6.

2. **Click Choose File.**

   Depending on what kind of computer you have, this may say something slightly different, but the gist is the same: Choose a file from your hard drive. This opens a navigation interface.

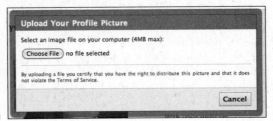

Figure 2-6:
Start here
to navigate
your
computer's
hard drive.

3. **Select your desired photo and click Select or OK.**

   This brings you back to the original screen, except now there's a preview of your new Profile picture.

4. **Click Save & Continue.**

I talk a lot about your Profile picture and the many ways it is used on Facebook in Chapter 4, but here are a few quick tips on selecting a Profile picture:

✔ **Make a good first impression.** Your Profile picture is one of the first ways people interact with your Profile and how you choose to represent yourself. Most people pick pictures that are more or less flattering, or that represent what's important to them. Sometimes, Profile pictures include other people — friends or significant others. Other times, the location matters. If the first photo you see of someone is at the beach versus at a party or sitting at his desk, you may draw different conclusions about that person. What picture represents you?

✔ **Consider who will see your Profile picture.** By default, your Profile picture appears in search results that are visible to all of Facebook and can even be made available to the larger Internet population. So, generally, people who search for your name can see that picture. Make sure it's something you're comfortable with everyone seeing.

✔ **Remember that you're not stuck with it.** After I put all this pressure on you to represent yourself and let people identify you, keep in mind that you can easily change your Profile picture at any time. Is it the dead of winter, and that photo of you on the beach last summer is just too depressing to look at? No problem; simply edit your Profile picture.

Well, that's pretty much the basics of getting started on Facebook. Hopefully by now you've added a few friends, some information about yourself, and a Profile picture.

Your New Home Page

After you've completed your Getting Started Wizard, you arrive at your Home page. This is where Facebook starts to look like the Facebook you'll be happily using for years to come, as shown in Figure 2-7.

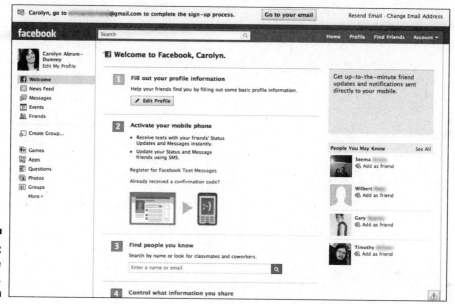

Figure 2-7: Welcome Home.

This page has a lot of links on it: in fact, a whole *For Dummies* book worth of them. For now, focus on what's happening in the center of the page. These numbered steps won't be here forever; soon they'll be replaced with information about what's happening with your friends.

Facebook has four additional steps it wants people to take. These are all relevant to you, but this book doesn't cover all of them right away:

- ✔ **Fill out your Profile information:** Those three things you filled out are just the beginning of what your Profile can say about you. I cover all of that in Chapter 4.

- ✔ **Activate your mobile phone:** Using Facebook on your mobile device is actually considered a bit more advanced, and is covered in depth in Chapter 15. There's an additional reason to do this, however: *Verification,* which is covered in the next section of this chapter.

Am I too old for Facebook?

No. Most emphatically, no. This is a common misconception, mainly because Facebook was originally exclusive to college students. Facebook's origins, even its name, are rooted in college campuses, but its utility and nature aren't limited to being useful to only college students.

Everyone has networks of friends and people with whom they interact on a day-to-day basis. Young or old, in college or working, this is true. Facebook tries to map these real-world connections to make it easier for people to share information with their friends.

If you're reading this section and thinking maybe you're just too old for Facebook, you're wrong. More and more people in older age demographics are signing up for Facebook every day to keep in touch with old friends, share photos, create events, and connect with local organizations. Almost everything I discuss in the book is non-age-specific.

Obviously, how people use the site can be very different at different ages, but you will discover these nuances when you use Facebook more and more. Generally, you should feel confident that you and your friends can connect and use Facebook in a meaningful way.

There are more than 800 million people using Facebook, and that number isn't made up of "a bunch of kids." Rather, it's a bunch of people from every age group, every country, and every walk of life.

✔ **Find people you know:** This might sound a bit redundant at this point, but Facebook is *way* better with friends. Chapter 6 is all about your friends and how to find them.

✔ **Control what information you share:** People share a lot of information on Facebook, and a lot of it is very personal. It's important to understand what you are sharing and with whom, which is why Chapter 5 is dedicated entirely to privacy and safety on Facebook.

Trust Me: Getting Confirmed and Verified

As I say over and over, Facebook is a website for real identity and real people. To protect this fact, Facebook has systems in place to detect any fake Profiles. Fake Profiles may be jokes (for example, someone creating a Profile for her dog), or they may be *spammers* (robots creating accounts to send thousands of fake friend requests). Regardless, they're not allowed on the site.

You, however, aren't fake or a spammer; how does Facebook know that? Facebook figures that out by confirming and verifying you.

Confirmation

Confirmation is Facebook's way of trying to make sure you are really you, and that the e-mail address you used to sign up is really yours. After you finish the three getting started steps, you may see a banner like that shown in Figure 2-8 across the top of your Home page.

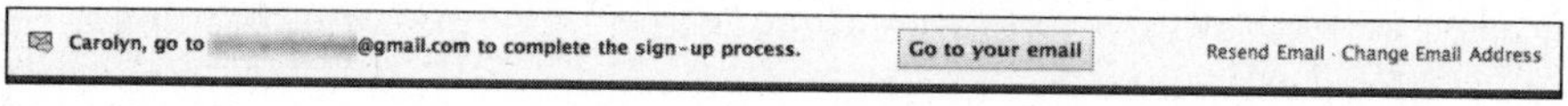

Figure 2-8:
If you see this banner, you need to confirm your e-mail.

✉ Carolyn, go to ▓▓▓▓▓▓▓@gmail.com to complete the sign-up process. | Go to your email | Resend Email · Change Email Address

I know it was a while ago, way back at the beginning of this chapter, that you clicked Sign Up. At that moment, Facebook sent you an e-mail asking you to confirm your account. In other words, Facebook is double-checking that you are the person who owns your e-mail address.

To confirm that you are, in fact, you; and that the e-mail address is, in fact, yours, go to your e-mail, look for that message, and open it. (It will usually have a subject like "Just one more step to get started on Facebook" or "Facebook Confirmation.") That e-mail contains a link. Click the link in that e-mail and you will be confirmed.

You may have already confirmed your e-mail address by using the Friend Finder or other normal activities. If Facebook isn't bugging you about it with banners or follow up e-mails, you can pretty much assume you're good to go.

Verification

Verification is a way to make sure that beyond just owning an e-mail account (which, unfortunately, any evil robot can do), you are a real human being who won't abuse Facebook or post inappropriate content. Unfortunately, Facebook has a bit of a "guilty until proven innocent" attitude about all of this. And Facebook puts you through a series of tests to prove your innocence.

Most of these tests aren't ones you have to actively take. Instead, just use the site as your lovely, non-spamming self, and eventually you'll be verified. If you're concerned about being verified right away, however, you can be verified by activating Facebook Texts:

1. **On your Home page, click Register for Facebook Text Messages.**

   If this link does not appear on your home page, click the Home button in the top-right corner, select Account Settings, choose Mobile from the left menu, and click the Add a Phone button. A pop-up appears, as shown in Figure 2-9. Under the drop-down menus, a line of text reads, Just need to verify your account? Add your phone number here.

2. **Click the Add Your Phone Number Here link.**

   This opens the Confirm Your Phone window, shown in Figure 2-10.

3. **Select your country code.**

4. **Enter your phone number into the Phone number box.**

5. **Click Confirm.**

   This sends a text message containing a code to your phone.

6. **Back at your computer, enter that code into the designated box on the screen and click Confirm.**

   After you've confirmed this code, your account with be verified.

Figure 2-9:
Activate
Facebook
Texts
to verify
yourself.

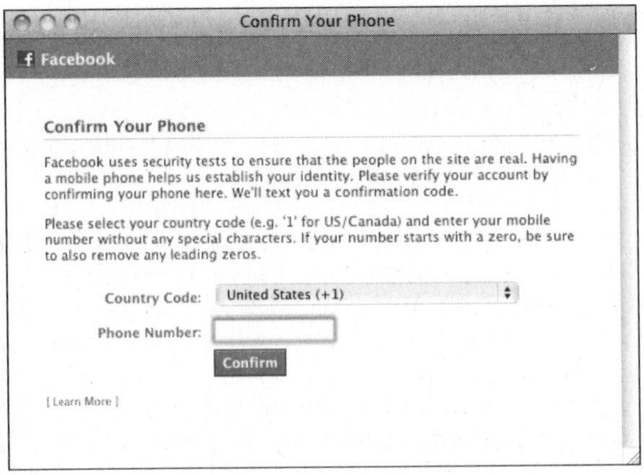

Figure 2-10:
Confirm
your phone
number
to prove
you're real.

Chapter 3

Finding Your Way Around Facebook

*H*ere's the thing about using Facebook: It has a lot of options. Now, this is actually one of the best things about Facebook: You can upload photos, look at photos, chat with a friend, message a friend, read updates from friends . . . the list goes on and on. What does get a little confusing is that there's no one way to do anything on Facebook. Depending on what page you're on, you'll see slightly different things. Depending on who your friends are, you'll see slightly different things. Using Facebook can't exactly be broken down into ten easy steps.

However, there are a few more constant places that you can learn to recognize. Starting from when you log in, you will always start on your *Home page*. The Home page, though continually evolving, has a few constants that are detailed in this chapter. If you ever find yourself lost on Facebook (it happens, trust me), click the Home link or the Facebook logo to go to the Home page, where you'll be able to reorient yourself.

As soon as I log in to Facebook, I see my Home page, which you can see in Figure 3-1. This chapter details the elements of the Home page that you are likely to see, too: menus and links to other parts of the site. Some of these links can be found no matter where you are on Facebook, some appear only when you're on your Home page, and some will be there, well, sometimes. Learning about these links helps you understand how to find your way around Facebook and enables you to learn about some of Facebook's features and options.

Figure 3-1:
Your Home
page may
look a little
like this.

Checking Out the Blue Bar on Top

I happen to spend a lot of time in coffee shops working alongside writers, students, businesspeople, and hobbyists — all drinking steamy beverages and manning laptops. I can always tell at a glance when someone is browsing Facebook by the big blue bar across the top of the page. The blue bar is home to many of the important navigational links on Facebook. And anytime you're looking at a Facebook page, you'll have the blue bar accompanying you, like a really loyal puppy. When you can adequately navigate the blue bar, you might as well kick off your shoes and put up your feet because you'll undoubtedly be feeling right at home on Facebook. Figure 3-2 shows the blue bar links from left to right.

Figure 3-2:
The blue bar
at the top:
link by link.

Here's what you need to know about each one:

✔ **Facebook logo:** The Facebook logo on the left of the blue bar serves two purposes. First, it reminds you what website you're using. Second, no matter where you are on Facebook, if you click this icon, you're back at the Facebook Home page.

✔ **Friend requests:** Next to the Facebook logo is an icon of two people, intended to depict friends. Clicking this icon reveals a menu that shows you any pending friend requests you may have, like that shown in Figure 3-3. Notice in the right corner that there's also a link here that takes you to where you can find friends. Whenever you receive brand new friend requests, a little red number totaling the number of new requests shows up on top of this icon. When you view the new requests, regardless of whether you respond to them, the red flag goes away. Sending and receiving friend requests are covered in more detail in Chapter 6.

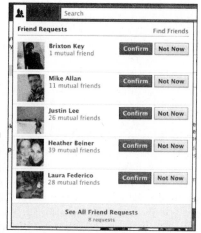

Figure 3-3: Friend requests appear here.

✔ **Messages:** An icon depicting two speech bubbles lets you access your message Inbox. Clicking it shows you snippets from your five most recent messages, as well as links if you want to send a new message or go to your Inbox. As with the friend requests, a little red flag appears to show you how many new messages you have. When you click that flag, you see the new messages, and the flag clears. Facebook Messages are covered in Chapter 8.

✔ **Notifications:** When someone on Facebook has taken an action that involves you or your timeline, you are notified by a red flag on top of the next icon — the globe. Maybe the person has tagged you in a photo, posted to your timeline, or commented after you on a post. Click the globe to see the five most recent notifications, as well as a link to the rest. Figure 3-4 shows a sample of notifications.

Figure 3-4:
Notifications
let you
know what's
happening.

✔ **Search:** This search bar works as a search engine just for Facebook. You can use it to find people, groups, events, and applications on Facebook. As you start typing a search topic, a list of items begins to auto-complete. If you see the person or item you're looking for, scroll down or use your mouse to select it. Pressing Enter automatically takes you to the top item in the list. Most of the time, you'll use search to go directly to a friend's timeline.

People sometimes try queries that the Search box isn't designed to handle. Searching for elements of Facebook itself, such as Account or Privacy, for example, doesn't give you what you're looking for. A better way to discover or navigate to a particular feature of the site is to click the Account menu, represented by a white downward-facing arrow, in the big blue bar on top. This opens a menu of links to certain parts of the site, including Privacy Settings and the Help Center.

✔ **Timeline:** The first link on the right side of the blue bar is your name and a thumbnail version of your timeline photo, which act as a link to your own Facebook timeline. You can get to your timeline by clicking your own name or photo wherever you see them on the site. See Chapter 4 for more on timelines.

✔ **Home:** This link works just like the Facebook logo. Wherever you are on the site, clicking it brings you back to the screen you see when you log in.

If you're paying attention, you might have started noticing duplicate links. The Home link takes you to your Home page, as does clicking the Facebook logo. This happens a lot on Facebook: There's more than one way to get from A to B.

✔ **Find Friends** (not shown; only for new users): This link takes you to a page that will help you find your friends. Once you have reached a certain number of friends, this link will disappear from the big blue bar on top.

✔ **Account menu (downward-facing arrow):** This link gives you access to most of the administrative actions you can take on Facebook. In this book, I reference the *Account menu*. That's the menu that appears when you click this arrow, shown in Figure 3-5. Here's a rundown of all the Account menu options:

Figure 3-5:
The
Account
menu.

- *Help Center:* Takes you to all sorts of tools for finding out how to use the site, how to stay safe on Facebook, and where to report a problem or bug with the site.

- *Account Settings:* Enables you to change your name, your e-mail address or password, your mobile information (which allows you to access the site from a mobile phone), or the language you want to use on the site. This is also where you go to deactivate your account.

- *Privacy Settings:* Enables you to set the visibility of the information in your timeline (see Chapter 5).

- *Credits Balance* (not shown in Figure 3-5): Takes you to a Settings tab where you can see how many credits you have purchased for playing games or buying gifts. Here you can also enter and edit your credit card information and set your preferred currency. This setting only appears if you've started using applications on Facebook that require Facebook credits as a form of payment. Applications and credits are covered in Chapter 14.

  Many Facebook games and applications are written by outside developers (not by Facebook). If you're having trouble using one of these applications, the Facebook Help Center offers methods for contacting the developers directly.

- *Log Out:* Ends your Facebook session. If you share your computer with others, always be sure to log out to ensure that another person can't access your Facebook account.

  If you have the Remember Me option selected when you log in, you won't ever be logged out until you click Log Out. Remember Me keeps you logged in despite closing the browser; therefore, we recommend using the Remember Me option only on a computer you don't share with others.

Moving Down the Left

The left column of your Home page is also very important, and one that will, like a slightly less loyal puppy, occasionally follow you around even when you leave the Home page. Figure 3-6 shows the left column of my account.

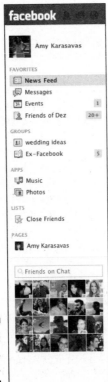

Figure 3-6:
To the left,
to the left.

Here's a summary of these links and what happens when you click them:

- **Name and Timeline Picture:** This is another link that takes you to your own timeline. All things timeline are covered in Chapter 4.

- **News Feed:** You may notice that News Feed is highlighted with a light blue background when you are on your Home page. This is because News Feed, which occupies the central real estate of your screen, is the default view of your Home Page. News Feed is a way to keep up with what your friends are doing as well as see their most recent photos, videos, and activities. The details of just how that works can be found in Chapter 7.

✔ **Messages:** This link opens your Messages Inbox. Facebook's messaging system is actually pretty different than what you may be used to in your e-mail, but very useful. It's covered in detail in Chapter 8.

✔ **Events:** This link brings you the Events page, where you can see upcoming birthdays and events you've been invited to. Events can range from intimate birthday parties to big talks or lectures. They are covered in detail in Chapter 11.

✔ **Bookmarks:** You can bookmark an app, group, list, or page so that it remains in the left column for convenient one-click access. These bookmarks, along with the three previously mentioned links, comprise your Favorites section. Head to Chapter 7 for more information on customizing your News Feed.

✔ **Groups:** Here's where you might notice that my left menu looks different from yours. If you're brand new to Facebook, you may just see a link that says Create Group, whereas I have these enticing links with different icons: Ex-Facebook and Wedding Ideas. Groups are ways to communicate with, you guessed it, groups of related people (in this case, other people who used to work at Facebook and my soon-to-be-hitched pal who created a Group for sharing ideas with members of her wedding party). Any Groups you join appear in this space. Clicking the name of the Group brings you to that Group's main page. Groups are covered in Chapter 9.

✔ **Apps:** Again, my Home page looks different than yours depending on what applications and games you use. Clicking the name of the game or app brings you to it. You can learn all about Apps and Games in Chapter 14.

✔ **Lists:** Lists are an optional way to organize friends by categories relevant to you, such as family or co-workers. There are three types of lists you should know about. Custom lists are Friend Lists you create on your own from the Lists page. Smart lists are automatically created for you and populated with friends based on common timeline information, such as where you attended college. The Close Friends and Acquaintances lists are automatically created, but you select which friends appear there. Learn more about each type of list in Chapter 6.

✔ **Pages:** Again, my Home page looks different than yours depending on whether or not you admin a Facebook Page. For example, a restaurateur who maintains a Page for his café would see the café's Page listed in this section. Facebook Pages and admins are explained in depth in Chapter 13.

✔ **Friends on Chat:** Break out your reading glasses. These tiny pictures represent friends whom you can instant message using Facebook's Chat feature. Chat is actually part of the messaging system covered in Chapter 8. You can click someone's face to start a chat, or type their name into that search box right above these little thumbnail photos. Any chats you start will pop up in the bottom-right corner of the screen, where you may notice a little floating box that says Chat.

Viewing the Main Event: News Feed

This chapter is about navigating Facebook, which is why the blue bar and the left menu are so important. At the same time, these menus aren't really the focus of the Home page. Instead, these menus serve as a bit of a background to the main event: News Feed. As I mentioned earlier, News Feed is what you see by default in the middle of the page when you go to your Home page.

So what is News Feed? Imagine if your morning paper, news show, or radio program included an additional section that featured articles solely about the specific people you know. That's what News Feed is. As long as the people you know are active on Facebook, you can stay up-to-date with their lives via your Facebook Home page. A friend may post photos from his recent birthday party, another may write a Note about her new job, and another may publish a public event for her upcoming art show. These may all show up as stories in your Facebook News Feed. A News Feed bonus: You can often use it to stay up-to-date on current events just by seeing what your friends are talking about or by Liking the Pages of real-world news organizations and getting their updates in your News Feed.

News Feed is possibly one of the best and more interesting things about Facebook, but also one of the hardest to explain. This is because no matter how I describe seeing a photo of my friend and her new baby pop up in my News Feed, it won't be as exciting as when *your* friend posts those photos. I do my best to capture at least a bit of this excitement in Chapter 7.

Discovering the Right Column

On the right side of the Home page, next to the News Feed, you find a somewhat random smorgasbord of what's new, what's now, and what's coming up next on Facebook:

- ✔ **Ticker:** The newest addition to the Home page is Ticker, a stream of updates your friends post in real-time. Just think of Ticker as a lightweight version of News Feed — a continuously scrolling stream of your friends' various activities presented in a concise format. Click any story in Ticker to view the full News Feed version. Ticker is explained in detail in Chapter 7.

- ✔ **Upcoming Events:** Reminders about all Events to which you're invited show in this column — unless you RSVP as Not Attending. Click the Events link to open a pop-up window with details of your upcoming Events. From this window, click See All to see all the Events to which you've been invited. After Events, see all the friends who have birthdays today and click their name to open a pop-up window with a text field for writing a quick birthday message (press Enter to post the message to that friend's timeline). You won't see birthday reminders for those friends who have chosen in their timelines to hide their birthday information.

✔ **Suggested Pages, People, and More:** Going out and finding all the people you know on Facebook would be a lot of work. Same goes for the Pages you like or other things on Facebook you might be interested in viewing. In this space, you see rotating suggestions that might interest you, and the headline of this section will rotate to match. You'll see people, celebrities, and bands that Facebook believes you may know or like. These suggestions are calculated using a number of factors, the most important of which being how many mutual friends you have with the suggested person, or how many of your friends are fans of the suggested brand or celebrity. If you see someone you recognize, click her photo to add that person as a friend. This box may not appear if Facebook doesn't have recommendations for you at this time.

✔ **Sponsored:** Facebook doesn't grow on trees, you know. Nor was it brought into this world hanging from the beak of a magical stork. Facebook is built from pure manual labor (where manual labor equals a lot of typing) and a whole lot of computers storing all the information you and your friends add to the site each day. Labor and technology — these things cost. The ads that appear in this section fund the entire system.

One way to look at the Home page is to divide it into three columns: a skinny one on the right for navigation, a fat one in the middle displaying the most interesting and compelling stories, and a skinny one on the right with scrolling real-time updates and reminders. Keep in mind this layout: You'll see it on a lot of different Facebook pages, including Groups, friendship pages, and Events.

Exploring the Lowest Links: The Footer

In blue type at the very bottom of every Facebook page, you see a set of links collectively called the *Footer,* shown in Figure 3-7. The Footer is the catch-all for important information about Facebook the social network, Facebook for business, Facebook the company, and the Facebook policies.

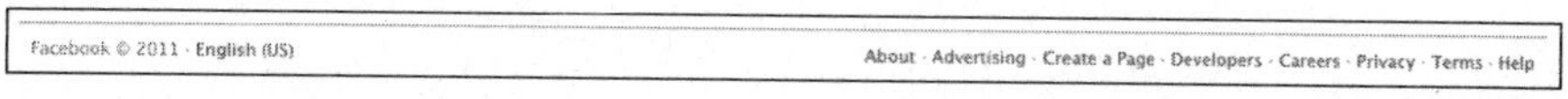

Figure 3-7:
You probably won't need many of these links, but just in case . . .

Facebook © 2011 · English (US)   About · Advertising · Create a Page · Developers · Careers · Privacy · Terms · Help

Here is a description of each link:

- *<Language>*: The first link on the left of the footer shows the name of the language in which you're seeing the rest of Facebook written — English, for example. Click the name of the language to see a drop-down menu with all the languages in which Facebook is available.

- **About:** Takes you to the About Facebook page where you can read about key features of Facebook, see the latest headlines from the Facebook Blog, discover the newest Facebook features, and see links to recent articles written about Facebook.

- **Advertising:** If you are running ads on Facebook, or want to, this is where you'd go to track what's happening with them.

- **Create a Page:** *Pages*, basically timelines for businesses, causes, and other non-people, are how you interact with these entities on Facebook. This link takes you to the Create a Page screen. Pages are covered in detail in Chapter 13.

- **Developers:** Most of the apps and games you can use on Facebook are written by outside developers who don't work at Facebook. If you're interested in creating a new Facebook application, this is your link.

- **Careers:** Wanna work for Facebook? Click this link to find out what jobs are available and all about the working environment.

- **Privacy:** Details the Facebook Privacy Policy, which states

    Facebook is about sharing. Our privacy controls give you the power to decide what and how much you share. Learn how to manage who can see your information on and off Facebook.

- **Terms:** This link takes you to the Statement of Rights and Responsibilities. These are the rules you agreed to when you signed up and that all users agreed to. Facebook can ban you from the site for breaking these rules.

- **Help:** The Help Center gives you all sorts of tools for finding out how to use the site and how to stay safe on Facebook.

Chapter 4

Timelines: The Story of You

· ·

· ·

Your Facebook timeline is more than just a bunch of information —
it's an ongoing, ever-evolving story about you. Did you ever have to
respond to a writing prompt that asked you to write page 73 of your 248-page
autobiography? Your timeline is the page you are working on right now,
except your autobiography is a complete multimedia presentation, pulling
together your words, your photos, your friends' thoughts, and your post-
ings. All of those things together tell the reader both who you are and what's
important to you. Your Facebook timeline is not about altering who you are
but rather representing yourself. Use it to introduce and share yourself with
the people who matter to you. Use it to construct and take note of the important events in your life. What do you want people to know about you? What
do you want your friends to find out about you?

In Chapter 2, I covered getting your timeline set up so your friends could find
you. In the world of Facebook timelines, this information is just the tip of the
iceberg.

Figure 4-1 shows the top of a timeline. This is my own timeline, so it looks
a bit different than when you look at a friend's timeline. The timeline has a
few different portions: the at-a-glance section running across the bulk of the
screen at the top of the page, the navigational markers to the very right of
this, the Share menu or Publisher just below, and the timeline itself, extending from the present back and back and back to the day you were born.

Navigating the Timeline

In this section, I walk you through the parts of the timeline.

Figure 4-1:
A timeline.

Photos

The first impression of any timeline, including your own, is the two photos that greet you when you first arrive. The big background one (in my case, a photo of some Frisbee throwing) is called the *cover photo*. It's meant to be sort of like the cover of a music album. It can be anything you choose. The second, smaller photo is meant to be more like a headshot, your actual *profile photo*. This smaller photo appears on Facebook anywhere your name is: places you comment on posts or where your posts are shared.

At-a-Glance Info

Your profile photo actually juts into an Info section of your timeline, shown in Figure 4-2. This section includes your Name, info about where you work and live, where you went to school, and who you're in a relationship with (assuming you choose to share these facts). The rest of this section hints at the other information that you may have made available and allows you to get to it. For example, clicking the About link takes you to all of your information, not just the basics. The Friends box takes you to a list of your friends; the Photos box previews a recent photo of you and the number of photos there are of you on Facebook. Clicking it lets you check out all of the photos of you.

The Share menu

Just below the At-a-Glance Info section, on the left side of the screen, is the Share menu. This is what you use to post content such as statuses, photos, and more to your timeline (and to your friends' News Feeds). It's also how you add events to your timeline that you want to commemorate. Using the Share menu is covered in the "Sharing" section of this chapter.

The thin blue line

The true meat of your timeline is the line itself. Scrolling down reveals an extended blue line that starts in the present, and if you keep scrolling, it goes all the way back to your birth. At various points in time, bullets call out significant events, statuses, photos, or actions you took on Facebook. This line tells your story.

Jumping around in time

To the right of your cover photo is a condensed timeline, shown in Figure 4-3, which allows you to jump to any point in time you wish to see just by clicking it. More recent time is shown more specifically, so you can choose a month or two ago, or choose a decade and then drill down to the year you want to peruse. Jumping around becomes important as you build out your history on your timeline.

Cover Me

If you're brand new to Facebook, your timeline may seem a little empty compared to that of your friends. That's okay; your timeline will fill up as you start to update your status, post links, and so on (see the upcoming "Sharing" section). But before you do all that, you want to get the basics filled out so that people can find you, recognize you, and learn a little bit about you.

The two photos at the top of your Profile make the initial first impression to all visitors to your Profile. The cover photo is the larger photo that serves as a background to your Profile. People often choose visually striking photos or images that really speak to who they are and what they love — you'll see a lot of nature shots. To change your cover photo, follow these steps:

1. **Hover over your existing cover photo.**

   A Change Cover button appears in the bottom right corner of the photo.

2. **Click the Change Cover button.**

   This opens the Change Cover menu, which has four options: Choose from Photos, Upload Photo, Reposition, and Remove.

3. **Click Choose from Photos to select a cover photo from photos you've already added to Facebook.**

   This opens the Choose from Your Photos window, shown in Figure 4-4. By default, it shows Recent Uploads. You can get to a full list of your photos by clicking View Albums in the upper right corner.

3a. **Choose Upload Photo to select a cover photo from your computer.**

   This opens a window for navigating your computer's files.

4. **Select your cover photo by clicking your desired album and then the desired photo within that album.**

   This brings you back to your timeline, where you should see the new cover photo in place with an overlaid message, "Drag to Reposition Cover."

4a. **Select the photo file you want as your cover and click Open.**

   This brings you back to your timeline, where you should see the new cover photo in place with an overlaid message: Drag to Reposition Cover.

5. **Click and drag your cover photo to position it correctly within the frame of the screen.**

6. **Click Save Changes.**

   Your new cover photo is now in place.

Figure 4-4:
Use the
Choose
from Photos
window to
choose a
cover photo.

If you don't like the way your cover photo is positioned, you can use the same Change Cover Photo to either reposition or remove your cover photo. You can change your cover as often as you want.

Your Profile photo is the smaller photo. This photo is what sticks with you all around Facebook, appearing wherever you comment or post something. For example, your friends may see your status post in their News Feeds, accompanied by your name and Profile photo. Most people use some variation on a headshot for their profile photos. To change your profile photo, follow these steps:

1. **Hover over your existing Profile photo.**

   The Edit Profile Picture button appears.

2. **Click the Edit Profile Picture button.**

   This opens the Profile Picture menu, which has five options: Choose from Photos, Take Photo (only for people with a webcam), Upload Photo, Edit Thumbnail, and Remove.

3. **To choose from the photos of you on Facebook, click Choose from Photos.**

   This opens the Choose from Photos window, which by default shows you all the photos in which you are tagged in Facebook. Page through these photos by clicking the arrows in the bottom-right corner. You can also get to the photos you've added to Facebook by clicking View Albums in the upper-right corner.

4. Select the photo you'd like to be your profile photo by clicking it.

This brings you to the photo with a cropping interface, as shown in Figure 4-5.

Drag the corners of the transparent box below to crop this photo into your profile picture. Done Cropping | Cancel

Figure 4-5:
Crop Profile photos to focus on just you.

5. Choose the portion of the photo you'd like to be your Profile photo using the cropping functions.

Move the transparent box around the photo by clicking and dragging it. Click and drag the corners of the transparent box to include more or less of the original photo.

6. Click Done Cropping when you've finished.

It's a small link right beneath the photo. This brings you back to your timeline. The new profile photo should be visible.

To choose a Profile photo from your computer's hard drive, follow Steps 1 and 2, and then

1. In the Edit Profile Picture menu, click Upload Photo.

This opens an interface for navigating your computer's hard drive.

2. Locate and click the desired photo.

3. Click Open or Choose.

The photo is added and appears in place of your old profile photo.

If you have a camera built into your computer or an external webcam, you can also take a photo to be your Profile picture by following these steps:

1. **In the Edit Profile Picture menu, click Take Photo.**

   This opens an interface for shooting a photo using your computer's webcam.

2. **Click the button at the bottom of the screen to take your photo.**

   Remember to smile!

3. **If you're happy with the photo, click Save Picture.**

   The photo is added and appears in place of your old profile photo.

Much like your cover photo, you can change your profile picture as often as you choose. All the photos you make into your profile picture are automatically added to the "Profile Pictures" album.

All About Me

The at-a-glance box gives you (and your friends) what I like to think of as the dinner party basics: where you live, what you do, where you're from, who you're with. But clicking the About link opens the About section of your timeline, shown in Figure 4-6.

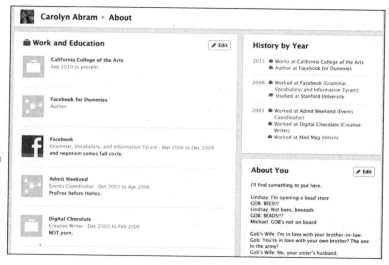

Figure 4-6: The About section of your timeline.

This page houses lots of information about you in a few boxes: Work and Education, Basic Info, Living, Relationships and Family, Contact Info. You can visit the About section to edit this information as well as edit who can see it. In general, you have five basic privacy options to remember:

✔ **Public or Everyone:** This means that anyone who finds your timeline, potentially anywhere on the Internet, can see this piece of information. This is a good setting for the things that are not very personal or are already public knowledge.

✔ **Friends:** This means that only your friends can see that piece of information. This setting is useful for more personal things like your contact information.

✔ **Friends Except Acquaintances:** This option refers to the "acquaintances" smart list that Facebook creates for many users. People who have been added to this list will be unable to see this information.

✔ **Only Me:** This option allows you to keep information on your profile for your own reference, but not show it to anyone else on Facebook.

✔ **Custom:** You can use custom settings to show items to specific groups of people. You can choose a setting like Friends of Friends if you want something to be visible to more than just friends, but not to the public; or you can even choose to show something only to specific friends, or to hide it from specific friends. To learn about these privacy options and how to use them, check out Chapter 5.

All information fields in the About section are optional to fill out. If something doesn't apply to you, or you don't want to share that information, just leave it blank.

Education and Work

In Chapter 2, when you were getting started on Facebook, you were asked to enter your education and work history. If you didn't do that or want to add a more complete online resume, you can add more schools and employers on this page. Remember, this sort of information can really help old friends find you for reunions, recommendations, or reminiscing. From the About section of the timeline, first click the Edit button in the upper-right corner of the Work and Education section. You can then add and edit professional and educational information. When you're done editing, click the Done Editing button in the upper-right corner.

To add an employer, follow these steps:

1. **Click the Where Have You Worked? field.**

2. **Start typing the name of the company where you worked or currently work.**

   Facebook tries to find a match while you type. When that match is highlighted, or when you finish typing, press Enter.

3. **Enter details of your job into the fields that appear.**

   These include

   - **Position:** Enter your job title.

   - **City/Town:** Enter where you physically went (or go) to work.

   - **With:** Here you can enter the names of co-workers by typing their names into this field. This is especially useful if you are using your timeline for business networking and you want people to know those to whom they could look for a referral.

   - **Description:** Provide a more detailed description of what it is you do.

   - **Time Period:** Enter the amount of time you worked at this job. If you select I Currently Work Here, it appears at the top of your timeline.

4. **Click Add Job.**

See the little privacy icon to the right of the Where Have You Worked field? That icon represents who can see this information, and clicking it allows you to change who can see it. This is true of virtually every field in the About section. Look for the privacy icons and adjust according to your comfort levels.

To add a college, follow these steps:

1. **Click into the field that says Where Did You Go to College/University?**

2. **Start typing the name of the college you attended (or attend).**

   Facebook tries to find a match while you type. When that match is high-lighted, or when you finish typing, press Enter.

3. **Enter details of your school into the fields that appear.**

   These include

   - **Class Year:** Select your class year.

   - **Concentrations:** List any majors or minors you had.

   - **Attended for:** Choose whether you attended as an undergraduate or a graduate student.

4. **Click Add School.**

To add a high school, follow these steps:

1. **Click into the High School field, where it says Where Did You Go to High School?.**

2. **Start typing the name of the high school you attended (or attend).**

   Facebook tries to find a match while you type. When that match is high-lighted, or when you finish typing, press Enter.

3. **Enter details of your school into the fields that appear.**

   These include

   • **Class Year**: Select your class year.

4. **Click Add School.**

You can edit any of this information (for example, if you leave your current job or remember that you were actually class of '45, not '46) by clicking the Edit link next to the employer or school you want to edit. The same fields reappear, and you can change any and all information.

When you're done adding and editing your professional and educational history, click Done Editing to save your changes.

Basic Information

Your Basic Information is just what it sounds like: the very basics about you that you might use to identify who you are and where you're from. Click Edit to open a pop-up screen to edit any of these fields and who can see them.

- ✓ **Sex (I Am):** You entered your sex when you signed up for Facebook, and Facebook mirrors your selection here. If you don't want people to see your sex on your timeline, you can deselect the check box opposite this field.

- ✓ **Birthday:** You also entered your birthday when you registered for Facebook. Here, you have the ability to tweak the date (in case you messed up) as well as decide what people can see about your birthday. Some people don't like sharing their age, their birthday, or both. If you're one of these people, use this drop-down menu to select what you want to share.

  Although you can change your birthday and year at will most of the time, Facebook's systems prevent you from shifting to under 18 once you have been listed as over 18. If, through a legitimate mistake, this happened to you, contact Facebook's User Operations team from the Help Center.

- ✓ **Interested In:** This field is primarily used by people to signal their sexual orientation. Some people feel that this section makes Facebook seem like a dating site, so if that doesn't sound like you, you don't have to fill it out.

- ✓ **Languages:** Languages might seem a little less basic than, say, your city, but you can enter any languages you speak here.

- ✓ **Religion:** You can choose to list your religion and describe it.

- ✓ **Political Views:** You can also choose to list your political views and further explain them with a description.

Whenever you edit a section of your information, click Save (a button at the bottom of the page) so you don't lose your work.

Living

This box contains two pins on a map: one to show where you're from, and one to show your current city. Click Edit to change either of these and to control who can see this information. Remember to click Save when you're done.

Relationships and Family

This box provides space for you to list your romantic and family relationships. Additionally, these relationships provide a way of linking your timeline to someone else's timeline, and therefore require confirmation. In other words, if you list yourself as married, your spouse needs to confirm that fact before it appears on both timelines.

You can add a relationship by following these steps:

1. **Click the Edit button in the upper-right corner of the Relationships and Family box.**

   This opens a pop-up window for editing this information.

2. **Click Add a Family Member.**

   This adds a blank box to the list of any existing Family Members.

3. **Start typing your family member's name into the box**

   Facebook tries to auto-complete as you type. When you see your sister's or husband's or whoever's name appear, click to select it.

4. **Select the type of relationship from the drop-down menu.**

   Facebook offers a variety of family relationships ranging from the nuclear to the extended.

5. **Click Save at the bottom of the pop-up window.**

For many couples, the act of changing from Single to In a Relationship on Facebook is a major relationship milestone. There's even a term for it: Facebook official. You may overhear someone saying, "It's official, but is it Facebook official?" Feel free to impress your friends with this knowledge of Facebook customs.

Contact Information

Privacy settings are a very useful part of Facebook because people can share their telephone numbers, e-mail addresses, and other contact information without the whole world seeing it. This enables incredibly useful features (such as Facebook Mobile — see Chapter 15) and the ability to track down someone's e-mail address and phone number — even if you were accidentally left off of his "I'm moving/changing jobs/changing names" e-mail. For your own contact information, share what you're comfortable sharing and try to keep it up-to-date. We talk more about the privacy settings that protect this information in Chapter 5.

If you are editing information as you go, remember to click the blue Save buttons after you make changes on each page. Otherwise, all your hard work will be undone.

Friends

From the at-a-glance box, a smaller box labeled Friends displays tiny previews of a few of your friends' profile pictures. Clicking this box brings you to the Friends section of your timeline, which displays all of your friends in a giant grid. When you're visiting your friend's timeline, this can be a good place to go to find mutual friends that you'd like to add.

Photos

Next to the Friends box is the Photos box, which displays a random photo. Clicking this box takes you to the Photos section of the timeline. The Photos application is covered in depth in Chapter 12, but what's interesting about this section specifically is that, along with photos that you have taken of yourself, it highlights other photos of you posted by other people.

One of the features the Photos application provides you is the ability to *tag* friends. Tagging a friend in a photo means that you establish a link between his timeline and the photo. Any photos that you have been tagged in appear in chronological order on your Photos tab.

The top part of the page focuses on the photos you've added to Facebook, including a special space for the Profile Picture album and the Cover Photo. This is an album that Facebook makes for you automatically. Every time you change your Profile or Cover photos, the new one is added to its respective album.

The bottom part of the page is where you can see all the photos and videos where you've been tagged. If you don't like any of the photos or don't want them to appear here, simply remove the tag from the photo (you can learn how in Chapter 12), and the photo will no longer appear here.

 On Facebook, photos are a really important part of how people communicate and how people learn about each other. Whether it's learning about someone's recent trip, family reunion, or night out with friends, photos provide real insight into a person's life.

Map

Next to the Photos box is the Map box. Clicking this takes you to the Map section of your profile. The map keeps track of any location check-ins you've made, allowing you (and your friends) to see where you spend your time.

Likes

Next to the Map box is the Like box. Clicking this takes you a list of all the Pages you've liked on Facebook. Pages are sort of like timelines, but for non-people: brands, products, bands, books, and so on. Most of these categories (Music, Books, Movies, Television) will get filled out naturally as you click the Like button that you find all around Facebook. If you want to add a bunch of favorites right away, click the Edit button in the top right of the Favorites box. This shows you all the possible categories for your favorites. Start typing your favorite artist or book into the appropriate box. Facebook will auto-complete as you type.

Also keep in mind that you can come here to control who can see your Favorites or other likes. Again, click the Edit button in the upper-right corner; then look for the audience icons next to each type of favorite. Click the icon to change your audience.

Sharing

Getting back to the main focus of your timeline, take a look at the thin blue line running down the center of the screen. Popping out from either side of the line are boxes that represent Events. These Events might be something you've added to Facebook, like a status or a photo; something someone has added to Facebook about you, like a photo tag; or something you've done on Facebook, like becoming friends with someone. These Events constitute your timeline, what tells the story of you. You can even go back in time and add life events that Facebook might not have been around to commemorate (Christmas 2003, anyone?). These events are the things you share with friends. So start with the basics: sharing.

The Share menu

The Share menu, also known as the Publisher, is the text field just below your cover photo and at-a-glance info that says "What's on your mind?" (You can match it to the Share menu in Figure 4-7.)

Figure 4-7:
The Share
menu on the
timeline.

The Share menu is what you use to post information — statuses, photos, check-ins, links, and so on — to your timeline. When you post information, you can also choose who can see that information. Friends and subscribers then may see these posts in their News Feeds when they log in (for more information on News Feed, check out Chapter 7).

Status

The most common type of post that you see people make from the Share menu is a basic text update that answers the question, "What's on your mind?" On Facebook, people refer to this type of post as a *status update* or just as their *status*. Status updates are quick, short, and completely open to interpretation. People may update them with what they may be doing at that moment ("Eating a snack"), offer a random observation ("A cat in my backyard just caught a snake!"), or request info ("Planning a trip to India this summer. Anyone know where I should stay?") It's very easy for friends to comment on statuses, so a provocative update can really get the conversation going. We comment on commenting in Chapter 7.

Status updates sound small and inconsequential, but when they are added together, they can tell a really big story for one person or for many people. For close friends, they let you keep up-to-date on their daily lives and share a casual laugh over something that you might never hear about otherwise. As a collective, statuses are how news spreads quickly through Facebook. Because your posts go into your friends' News Feeds, a single update can have a big impact and is somewhat likely to be repeated in some way or another. For example, news of a minor earthquake in my area of California spread faster on Facebook than it did on news sites. A status about a very important event may become a post you wish to feature on your timeline in perpetuity, but more about that in the timeline Maintenance section.

To update your status, follow these steps:

1. **Click in the What's on Your Mind? field of the Share menu.**

   This expands the Share menu.

2. **Type your comment/thought/status.**

3. **(Optional) Click the person icon in the bottom gray bar of the Publisher to add tags to your post.**

   Tags are ways of marking people you are with when you're writing a status update in a way that links back to their timeline and notifies them of your update. When you tag someone, an additional bit of text is added to the status, so it looks like this: "Off to play board games — with <Eric>." Eric then receives a notification that you tagged him.

   If you want to tag someone as part of a sentence as opposed to just noting that they are with you, add an @ symbol and begin typing the person's name. Facebook auto-completes as you type, and the tag appears as part of your status update; for example, "<Eric> kicked my butt at Settlers of Catan."

4. **(Optional) Click the location pin icon to add a location.**

   Facebook Places is a feature I cover in Chapter 15. You can click this pin and begin typing a city or place name, and Facebook tries to auto-complete the place where you are. Letting friends know where you are (also called *checking in*) is a great way to increase the chances of serendipitous encounters. I've often had a friend text me when they see a status to ask if I'm still at the coffee shop, wanting to know if they can swing by to say hi.

5. **(Optional) Click the audience menu in the bottom-right corner to change who can see this particular post.**

   I cover timeline and publishing privacy in the next chapter, so even if this sounds confusing now, just make a mental note of where this menu lives.

6. **Click Post.**

Frequently, people use their status updates to bring attention to something else on the Internet. It may be an article they found interesting, or an Event, a photo album, or anything else they want to publicize. Usually, people add a comment to explain the link; other times, they use the link itself as their status, almost as though they're saying, "What I'm thinking about right now is this link."

Posts with links mean you can share something you like with a lot of friends without having to create an e-mail list, call up someone to talk about it, or stand behind someone and say, "Read this." At the same time, you're almost more likely to get someone to strike up a conversation about your content because it's going out to more people, and you're reaching a greater number of people who may be interested in it.

To post a link, simply follow the instructions for updating a status and copy and paste the link you want into the field where you normally type a status. This automatically expands a preview of what your post will look like, including a preview of the content. You can then choose a thumbnail to accompany the preview or edit the content of the preview by hovering over the thing you want to change and clicking it when it turns yellow. Add your own comment or explanation in the space where you'd enter a status.

Photo

Facebook is actually the Internet's number one photo-sharing website. In other words, people love to share photos, and they post a lot of them on Facebook. Consider this fact a teaser trailer for Chapter 12, where I go over the entire Photos application, including adding photos from the Publisher. Photo also gives you the ability to add videos, which I cover in Chapter 12.

Place

The third type of post that Facebook gives you a special tab for within the Share menu is a location check-in. Typically, check-ins are part of another post, like a status, but if all you want to do is note where you are, click Place and start typing the name of your location. You can also add tags or a comment to your check-in. Click Post when you're done.

Sharing past events

Although it's not required, you may feel an urge to fill out the gaps in your timeline. If you're new to Facebook, you may want to expand your timeline back past the day you joined. Facebook offers several ways for you to mark different points in time when something happened.

First of all, when you're posting a status, photo, or check-in, you can click the clock icon to select a date for that post other than right now. Clicking this icon expands a date selector, starting with a year. You can then post your update to the right date.

Second, across the top of the share menu are several categories of "life events" that you might want to include on your timeline. These include Work and Education, Family and Relationships, Living, Health and Wellness, and Milestones and Experiencing. Clicking any of these reveals a menu of specific options:

- ✔ **Work and Education:** Specific milestones include Add a Job, Retired, Studied Abroad, Graduated, Volunteer Work, Military Service, Other.

- ✔ **Family and Relationships:** Add a Relationship, Got Engaged, Got Married, Add a Child, Add a Pet, Ended Relationship, Lost a Loved One, Other Life Event.

- ✔ **Living:** Moved, Bought a Home, Home Improvement, Add a Roommate, Add a Vehicle, Other Life Event.

- ✔ **Health and Wellness:** Changed Eating Habits, Lost Weight, Got Glasses or Contacts, Broke a Bone, Had Surgery, Diagnosed with an Illness, Overcame an Illness, Other Life Event.

- ✔ **Milestones and Experiences:** Add a Hobby, Learned an Instrument, Learned a Language, Got a Piercing or Tattoo, Got a License, Traveled, Achievement or Award, First Word, Kiss, or Other, Add a Sport, Other Life Event.

All of these events can be added to any point on your timeline; when you select it you'll be asked to provide more details. For example, if you choose to add that you moved, a pop-up window appears, asking you for more information, as shown in Figure 4-8. You can include details about when and where you moved, who you moved with, and even include a photo of the move. Click Save when you are done and you will be taken to the post in your timeline.

Figure 4-8:
Add a life
event from
the recent
or distant
past.

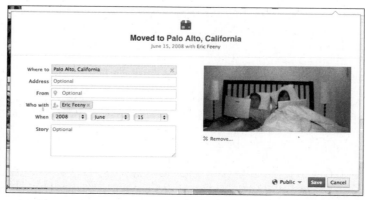

As you scroll down through your history, you may realize that you want to add an event or milestone. Don't worry about scrolling back up to the top of the page. A white bar should be following you as you scroll down, showing your name and the year you're looking at. Click the + button on the right side of this bar to reveal all of the usual share menu options. You can also hover your mouse over the thin blue line and click to add a milestone or post there.

Recent activity

Aside from all the posts you've added, you'll also notice little blocks of one-line statements about you (shown in Figure 4-9). These Recent Activity blocks detail what sort of activities you've been doing around the site. It basically encapsulates anything you do outside the Publisher, which are things like "Carolyn became friends with John Wayne" or "Carolyn is attending the rodeo," and so on. These activities are considered less important to telling the story of you because they offer less insight than a post does. They round out the story, but they aren't the meat of it.

Figure 4-9:
Recent activity shows what you've been up to.

Application activity

Applications are websites, games, and other programs that allow you to integrate some aspect of Facebook into using them. For example, Spotify is a music-streaming program that you can add to your computer. You can also integrate Facebook into Spotify so your friends can see what you are listening to. Many applications may have some aspect of automatic sharing, so that once you've signed up, every time you take a certain action — reading articles on the Washington Post, watching a TV show on Hulu — that activity will be added to your timeline. This sort of activity gets its own box with info about the application you used, as shown in Figure 4-10.

Figure 4-10:
Application activity on your timeline.

If you don't want activity published to your timeline from a particular application, you can always remove that app. Hover over the recent activity box from that app, and then click the pencil icon that appears in the upper-right corner. You can then remove the app or mark its posts as spam.

Timeline Curation

If you've been on Facebook for a while and start scrolling backward through time, you may notice that you're not actually seeing everything. You see everything that you've done in the last week, sure. And most things from the last month. But as you scroll back you see more and more "compiled" events. For example, a post summarizing the number of friends you added in the month of October. If you scroll back a year, you'll see a summary of all the friends you added last year. You might not see every photo you added, but maybe one photo from a big event that a lot of people commented on.

I like to call this *curation*. In other words, Facebook knows that not all posts are created equal, so it attempts to curate a selection of the best posts to represent your history. It compiles some things, features others, and ignores some things entirely. Facebook does this based on algorithms that look at things like how many likes or comments a certain post got. It favors things like photos. But Facebook doesn't always get it right, so you can always go back and curate your own timeline.

Hover over any post in your timeline to reveal two buttons in the upper-right corner of that post (you can see these in Figure 4-11). The star button allows you to Feature a post. Featuring a post makes it bigger: Instead of taking up a box on one-half of the screen, it gets a box across the entire screen.

Figure 4-11: Feature, Edit, or Remove a post.

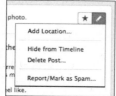

Clicking the pencil button allows you to edit the post. Editing it includes four options: Add Location, Hide from Timeline, Delete Post, or Report/Mark as Spam.

Hiding a post is different from deleting it. When you hide a post, you keep that post from appearing on your timeline, but the post still exists. So if, for example, you hide a particularly bad photo from your timeline, the photo album still exists. Anyone with permission to see it could navigate to your Photos section and check it out. But it's not going to get called out on your timeline. If you delete a post, it's gone forever; even you won't be able to find it on Facebook.

Keep this in mind if you're looking to remove things like photos or videos that only exist on Facebook (trust me, one hard drive crash and your photos are Facebook-only). It might be more practical to change the audience that can see the photo album than to delete it entirely.

Also, for your own reference, Facebook provides an Activity Log of your timeline that only you can see. From the At-a-Glance box, click the View Activity button. This takes you to your Activity Log. This is a condensed version of your Profile (in other words, it's not as pretty). Scan through the items in this log. Click the down arrow to the right of any item to reveal a menu for it. Use this menu to hide or feature things from your timeline, change who can see something, or permanently delete it from Facebook.

Your Friends and Your Timeline

Your timeline is what your friends look at to get a sense of your life, and it's also where they leave public messages for you. In this way, your friends' posts become part of your history (just like in real life). Think about all the things you learn about a friend the first time you meet his parents, or all the funny stories you hear when your friend's significant other recounts the story of how they met. These are the types of insights that your friends may casually leave on your Wall, making all of your friends know you a little better.

When friends visit your timeline, they'll also see a version of the Share menu that you see. They can't add life markers, but they can post a check-in (Place), a photo, or a text message called a *Wall Post* (or just *post*). Check out the Wall posts on your friends' timelines. Chances are you'll see a few "Hey, how are you, let's catch up" messages; a few "That was an awesome trip/dinner/drink" messages; and maybe a few statements that make so little sense, you're sure they must be inside jokes.

If you're on a friend's timeline around his birthday, you are sure to see many "Happy Birthday" posts. There aren't many rules for using Facebook, but one tradition that has arisen over time is the "Happy Birthday" Wall post. Because most people see notifications of their friends' birthdays on their Home pages, the quickest way to say, "I'm thinking of you" on their special day is to write on their timeline.

Honesty's the best policy

There's a lot of talk in this chapter about sharing and representation and showing yourself to the Facebook world. Metaphors about autobiographies aside, all people care about on Facebook is getting to know you. Facebook is a great way to build closer relationships with people, and lying on your timeline does not accomplish this. In fact, lying just makes other people think that they should lie, too. The utility of Facebook is destroyed by people giving fake names, fake birthdays, fake work histories, and so on. Facebook is a great place to get *real* information. If you are uncomfortable with certain pieces of information being shared, there are two solutions for you:

✔ **Don't share anything that makes you uncomfortable.** If having your phone number listed is just too creepy for you, so be it.

✔ **Become well acquainted with Facebook's privacy options.** Using the privacy options enables you to limit certain people or certain groups of people from accessing your information. This is certainly a better choice than lying for enhancing your Facebook experience.

While I think that the back and forth between friends is one of the delights of the timeline, some people find it a little hard to let go. If you are someone who doesn't like the idea of a friend being able to write something personal on your Wall, you can prevent friends from being able to post on it within your Privacy Settings page. You can also limit who can see the posts your friends leave. From the Privacy Settings page, click Edit Settings in the How You Connect section and look for the settings related to who can post and see your Wall.

The best way to get used to the timeline is to start using it. Write on your friends' timelines, post a status update or a link on your own, and see what sort of response you get from your friends. After all, that's what the timeline is all about — sharing with your friends.

Chapter 5

Privacy and Safety on Facebook

In This Chapter

▶ Navigating the many privacy options on Facebook

▶ Protecting yourself online and on Facebook

▶ Deciding what to share and when

*U*nfortunately, you hear a lot of horror stories about the Internet, especially about social networking sites. Many of them involve teenagers and predators, some of them involve identity theft, and others involve far less salacious (but no less real) problems, such as spamming and computer viruses. The bad news is that these things are out there. The good news is that Facebook has some of the most granular privacy controls on the Internet, enabling you to share real information comfortably on Facebook.

Facebook has created a trusted environment that provides some major assets:

✔ **In general, people create real accounts for themselves, and people are who they say they are on Facebook.** This means that the community enforces a standard of reality. When people ask you to view their webcasts or click some mysterious link, those actions are reported by the community, and the offenders are removed from Facebook. This also means that it's usually easy to tell a real person from a fake one, and you can make informed choices about whom you interact with online.

✔ **In general, people on Facebook interact with the same people they interact with in real life.** This allows you to have the same sense of familiarity that you have walking down the streets of your own neighborhood. Although you still lock your doors at night, it's pretty easy to spot people who don't belong or are looking to do some damage.

✔ **Facebook provides granular privacy controls that are built in to every piece of information you create on the site.** In fact, the bulk of this chapter is dedicated to explaining these options.

✔ **Facebook makes it easy for you to see your own timeline as other specific people see it.** This means you can easily verify that you're sharing the information you want to share with the right set of people.

What's a network?

Once upon a time (like, 2004), Facebook was only available to college students. Rather than limiting privacy by who your friends and their friends were, Facebook limited privacy by creating *networks*. Each network represented a college, and in order to join Facebook at all, you had to have a college-specific e-mail address that ended with the .edu suffix. When you joined with that e-mail, Facebook automatically placed you in your school's network. Your information was automatically visible to the other people in that network and not to anyone else. Networks eventually were used to represent colleges, high schools, and workplaces.

People who join with school- or job-specific e-mails still have the opportunity to use their networks to control their privacy. So if you are a student and have joined Facebook with your .edu e-mail address, you may notice that you have a few additional privacy options that include the word *Networks*, such as the ability to share a piece of content with all the members of a network, regardless of friendship status.

Know Your Audience

Before getting into specifics about all of the privacy controls, you should understand some basic parts of the Facebook vocabulary. These terms are related to how Facebook thinks about the people you may or may not want to share with. For most pieces of information, you have five options for the audience to which you want to make a piece of content visible:

✔ **Public or Everyone:** By setting the visibility of something you post or list to Public, you're saying that you don't care who, on the entire Internet, knows this information about you. Many people list their favorite bands, and, just as they'd shout this information from the treetops, they set the visibility to Public. This is a totally reasonable setting for innocuous pieces of information. In fact, some information is always available as Public Information that everyone can see. This includes your name, current timeline picture, gender, any networks you belong to, your username, and your cover image.

Now, just because everyone *can* see something doesn't mean everyone *does* see everything. Your posts, information, friendships, and so on populate your friends' News Feeds (assuming your friends can see this information), but never the News Feeds of people you're not friends with (unless you allow subscribers to see your public posts). When I think about who will see the information I share as Public, I imagine someone like you searching for me by name and coming to my timeline. Although (hopefully) that might be a lot of people, it isn't anywhere close to the number of people who use Facebook. By default, much of your timeline and all of your posts are publicly visible. This chapter covers how to change these settings if you would like.

✔ **Friends:** Any information for which you set visibility to Friends will be accessible only by your confirmed Facebook friends. If you trust your friends, this is a reasonably safe setting for most of your information. If you feel uncomfortable sharing your information with your friends, you can use custom privacy, or you can rethink the people you allowed to be your friends.

✔ **Custom:** If you have very specific needs, customized privacy settings may help you feel more comfortable sharing on Facebook. The Custom privacy option allows you to choose specific people (or lists of people) who can see something, or choose specific people (or lists of people) who can't see something.

✔ **Friends of Friends:** One commonly used custom setting that allows you to share with a few more people is the Friends of Friends option. By setting the visibility of some information to Friends of Friends, you're saying that the only people who can see that information are your friends and their friends. This setting is really useful for sharing things that involve your friends. For example, if you post a photo album that has pictures of your friend, she may want her friends to see those photos as well. Although Facebook strives to maintain the real-world strength of having a friend in common, this setting can still allow your content to be visible to many people.

Privacy on the Go

Privacy on Facebook isn't a one-time thing. Because you are constantly adding new statuses, photos, and content to Facebook, constantly interacting with friends and reaching out to people, privacy is actually an ongoing affair. To that end, one of the most common places you should know your privacy options is in the Share menu.

We covered the Share menu first in Chapter 4. It's the blank text box that sits under the About section of your timeline and at the top of your Home page. It's where you go to add status updates, photos, Questions, and more to Facebook. The part of the Share menu that's important for this chapter is the privacy control, known as the Audience Selector, right next to the Post button, shown in Figure 5-1.

Whenever you are posting a status or other content, the *audience,* or group of people you've given permission to see it, is displayed next to the blue Post button. The audience you see displayed is always the audience you last shared something with. In other words, if you shared something with the Public last time you posted a status, it displays Public the next time you go to post a status.

Figure 5-1:
Use the
Audience
Selector
to adjust
privacy for
an individual
post.

Hovering your mouse pointer over this word turns it into a button. Click that button to reveal the Audience Selector. It shows a few options: Public, Friends, and a sample of your frequently used Friend Lists. If you've added people to your Acquaintances list, you'll also see an option for Friends except Acquaintances (check out Chapter 6 for more about Friend lists). Click the setting you want before you post your status, link, or photo. Most of the time, I share my posts with Friends. As a result, I don't actually change this setting that often. But if you do share something publicly, remember to adjust the audience the next time you post something.

Sometimes, you may find that you want to share something with only a portion of your friends. To do that, choose Custom from the Privacy menu. This reveals the Custom Privacy box shown in Figure 5-2.

Figure 5-2:
Customize
your privacy
down to the
person.

Custom Privacy here applies to the post you're creating, but this dialog box will appear any time you choose Custom as a privacy setting for any type of information. Customized privacy has two parts: those who *can* see something and who *can't.* The top portion controls the former. The These People or Lists menu has four options:

- ✔ **Friends of Friends:** This means your friends and their friends can see whatever you post.

- ✔ **Friends:** This option allows only your friends to see what you post. Keep in mind that when you tag people in posts, their friends will be able to see that post, even if they aren't your friends.

- ✔ **Specific People or Lists:** Choosing this option opens a blank text box. You can start typing a name or the name of a list of friends here. After you save these settings, only the people you've entered can see your post.

- ✔ **Only Me:** This option isn't one you'd typically use for a post, but you might use it later on if there's any information you want to store on your timeline but you don't want to share with others.

The lower section controls who can't see something. Similar to the Specific People or Lists setting, the Hide This From section has a blank text box where you can type the name of people or lists of people. When you've added their name to this box, they won't be able to see the content you post.

Whatever customized audience you create for one post will be the audience next time you go to post something. Make sure you check the audience next time you post!

A post's privacy icon (Public, Friends of Friends, Friends or Custom) is visible to anyone who can view that post. Friend Lists appear as Custom privacy unless the viewer is a member of a list you shared the post with. Members of a default (Close Friends, Acquaintances) or custom Friend List can see other people included on the list, but are unable to see the name of the list. Members of a smart list (Family, Coworkers, School) can see the name of the list, but are unable to see other members.

Changing Privacy

After you post something, you can always change the privacy on it. From your timeline, follow these steps:

1. **Hover your mouse over the privacy icon at the top of the post whose audience you want to change.**

   Every post displays the icon for Public, Friends, Friends except Acquaintances, or Custom.

2. **Click the button to reveal the Audience Selector.**

   You'll see the usual options: Public, Friends, Friends except Acquaintances, Custom, or specific Friend Lists.

3. **Click the audience you want.**

   A change to Public, Friends, Friends except Acquaintances, or a specific Friend list is automatically saved. Changing to Custom requires you to make selections within the Custom Privacy pop-up again.

The Privacy Pages

Anytime you want to change or check your general privacy settings, you need to go to the Privacy pages. These can be found by clicking the Account menu, the white downward-facing arrow, in the big blue bar on top, and then clicking Privacy Settings. This brings you to the Privacy page, shown in Figure 5-3.

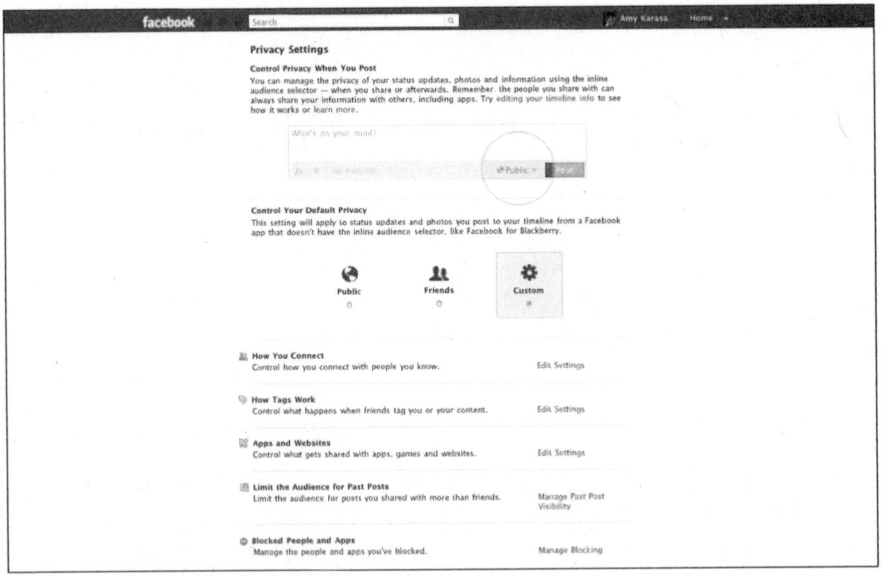

Figure 5-3: Start here to set privacy options.

There are seven separate sections on this page. I go through each section here, from top to bottom, before moving on to privacy settings that you'll find elsewhere on Facebook.

Control Privacy When You Post

This section is a reminder that you can actually set privacy anytime you share anything using the Share menu on your timeline. I covered this in more detail in the "Privacy on the Go" section earlier in this chapter.

Control Your Default Privacy

Default Privacy applies to the things you post when you aren't using the Share menu. For the most part, this applies to posting via Facebook's app for mobile phones. Figure 5-3 displays the three options you can select for this default: Public, Friends, or Custom. Simply click the setting you would like. Personally, I recommend keeping your Default Privacy to Friends.

How You Connect

The How You Connect section is where you control the ways people can find you and interact with you on Facebook. For the most part, these settings have to do with what people can see and do on your timeline before you are friends. Click Edit Settings on the right of the How You Connect to open the How You Connect settings box, shown in Figure 5-4.

Figure 5-4: Edit how you connect to others here.

There are five settings in this section, each phrased in the form of a question. Click the drop-down menu to the right of each setting to change it. Click the Done button to close the box.

- ✔ **Who can look up your timeline by name or contact info?** In other words, this setting controls who can find you in search. You can allow Everyone, Friends of Friends, or only Friends to find you if they enter your name or other contact info (like your e-mail address) into the Search box. Often people who are shy and like the sense of feeling hidden set this to Friends, but I recommend leaving it open to Everyone. This allows your friends to actually find you and become your Facebook friends. If you don't allow people to find you, you'll likely be responsible for finding and connecting with people yourself.

- ✔ **Who can send you friend requests?** This setting determines who can request your friendship through the site. The default setting here is Everyone. This makes sense for most people because especially as you're getting started, many people you know may come across your timeline and send you a request. As you build up a lot of friends, you may consider changing the setting to Friends of Friends so that total strangers don't ask you to be a friend. The lowest possible setting here is Friends of Friends.

  People you subscribe to can send you a friend request regardless of your friend request settings.

- ✔ **Who can send you Facebook Messages?** This setting determines who can send you a message through Facebook. I like leaving this set to Everyone because you never know what sort of opportunities or long-lost friends might show up and send you a message. Messages from non-friends are already kept separate in your Inbox, so you don't have to worry about non-friends taking up too much space. Remember, friends can always send you messages on Facebook.

- ✔ **Who can post on your timeline?** Your timeline, which I talked about in Chapter 4 and expanded on in Chapter 7, is where you can post all your status updates, photos, and other content. It's also a place where your friends can leave you messages or posts. If you don't want your friends leaving these sorts of public messages for you (a common need if you're using Facebook as a professional or for networking), you can set this to Only Me. Remember, people who are not your friends can never post on your timeline.

- ✔ **Who can see posts by others on your timeline:** Another way to control the aforementioned "embarrassing friend on your timeline" problem is to limit who can see the timeline posts your friends have left. This option opens the Audience Selector.

How tags work

Tags on Facebook are a way of labeling people in your content. For example, when uploading a photo, you can tag a specific friend in it. That tag becomes information that others can see as well as a link back to your friend's time-line. In addition, from your friend's timeline, people can get to that photo to see her smiling face. You can tag people and Pages in status updates, photos, notes, check-ins at various places, and really any other type of post. And just like you can tag friends, friends can tag you in their photos and posts. This section allows you to control settings around who may tag you and who can see those tags. Click Edit Settings to the right of this section to open the How Tags Work dialog box, shown in Figure 5-5.

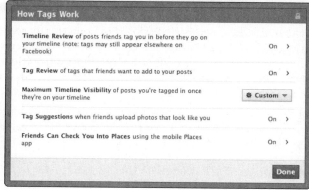

How Tags Work

Timeline Review of posts friends tag you in before they go on your timeline (note: tags may still appear elsewhere on Facebook) — On ›

Tag Review of tags that friends want to add to your posts — On ›

Maximum Timeline Visibility of posts you're tagged in once they're on your timeline — ⚙ Custom ▾

Tag Suggestions when friends upload photos that look like you — On ›

Friends Can Check You Into Places using the mobile Places app — On ›

Done

Figure 5-5:
Edit your settings for tags.

There are five settings here. To edit any of them, click On/Off or drop-down menu to the right of the setting:

- ✔ **Timeline Review:** Timeline Review allows you to review the tags people have added of you before it gets displayed on your timeline. By default, tags of you are automatically approved, so if you would like to manually approve each one, you have to turn Timeline Review on. Click the text in this section to open the Timeline Review pop-up box. Use the drop-down menu to select Enabled or Disabled. Click the Back button to return to the How Tags Work box.

    Tags that need to be reviewed can be found in the Pending Posts section of your Activity Log on your timeline.

- ✔ **Tag Review:** This setting lets you control whether you review tags your friends want to add to content you've uploaded. Click the text or On/Off to go to the Turn on Tag Review box. Use the drop-down menu to select Enabled or Disabled. Click the Back button to return to the How Tags Work box. If you don't turn this on, you will still be notified of tags your friends add, and you can always remove tags after the fact if you don't like them.

    You always need to approve tags from non-friends before they can be added to your timeline.

✔ **Maximum Timeline Visibility:** After you've approved tags (or if you leave Timeline Review off), you can still decide who can see the content in which you're tagged on your timeline. In other words, if your friend tags you in a photo, you can control who sees that photo on *your* timeline. Clicking the drop-down menu opens the Audience Selector. I recommend keeping this to Friends of Friends or Friends (a Custom setting).

✔ **Tag Suggestions:** Facebook employs some facial recognition software to help people tag photos. So if a friend is uploading 50 photos and you appear in 30 of them, Facebook might recognize your face and suggest to your friend that you be tagged in those 30 photos to save your friend time while he's adding photos. You can choose not to appear in the suggestions Facebook gives your friends by disabling this setting. Click in this section to open the Tag Suggestions box. Use the drop-down menu to select Enabled or Disabled. Click the Okay button to return to the How Tags Work box.

✔ **Friends Can Check You into Places:** Places is a Facebook feature that allows people to *check in* or mark where they are using their phones' GPS systems (for more about Places and Facebook Mobile, head to Chapter 15). Because information about where you are at any given time is very sensitive, you can block friends from tagging you when they check in somewhere. Click the text in this section to go to the Friends Can Check You into Places box. Use the drop-down menu to enable or disable the ability of friends to tag you in check-ins. Click Okay to go back to the How Tags Work box.

Apps and Websites

This section is where you go to edit how apps, games, and websites interact with your timeline. Click the Edit Setting link to the right of this section to go to the Apps, Games, and Websites privacy page, shown in Figure 5-6.

An *application* is a blanket term used to describe pieces of software that use Facebook data, even when those applications weren't built by Facebook. Developers all over the world build games, websites, and useful tools around the data you already share on Facebook. To make it easier to get people using these applications, they import the data from Facebook. This page lets you control which applications get what data:

✔ **Apps You Use:** This is a list of all the applications you use, in order of what you've used most recently. Apps you use require direct permission from you to begin accessing your data and posting to your timeline. The Edit Settings button takes you the App Settings page, which is discussed in Chapter 14, when all things app are covered.

✓ **How People Bring Your Info to the Apps They Use:** Even if you don't use applications, your friends may. Similar to the way that you may not add photos to Facebook, but your friends may add and tag photos of you, your friends may also pass on information about you to applications. You can restrict what applications can see using the check boxes pictured in Figure 5-7.

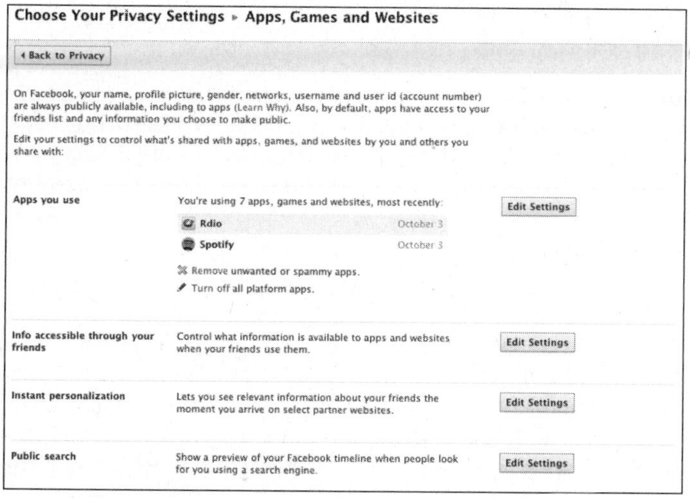

Choose Your Privacy Settings ▸ Apps, Games and Websites

◂ Back to Privacy

On Facebook, your name, profile picture, gender, networks, username and user id (account number) are always publicly available, including to apps (Learn Why). Also, by default, apps have access to your friends list and any information you choose to make public.

Edit your settings to control what's shared with apps, games, and websites by you and others you share with:

Apps you use	You're using 7 apps, games and websites, most recently:	Edit Settings
	☑ Rdio October 3	
	◯ Spotify October 3	
	✗ Remove unwanted or spammy apps.	
	✎ Turn off all platform apps.	
Info accessible through your friends	Control what information is available to apps and websites when your friends use them.	Edit Settings
Instant personalization	Lets you see relevant information about your friends the moment you arrive on select partner websites.	Edit Settings
Public search	Show a preview of your Facebook timeline when people look for you using a search engine.	Edit Settings

Figure 5-6:
My Apps, Games, and Websites Privacy page.

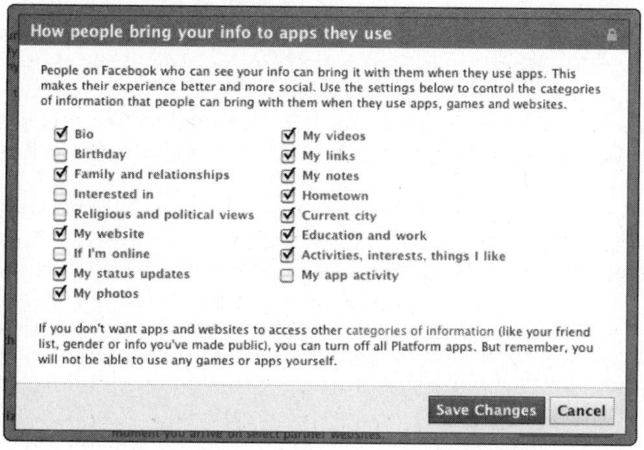

How people bring your info to apps they use

People on Facebook who can see your info can bring it with them when they use apps. This makes their experience better and more social. Use the settings below to control the categories of information that people can bring with them when they use apps, games and websites.

☑ Bio
☐ Birthday
☑ Family and relationships
☐ Interested in
☐ Religious and political views
☑ My website
☐ If I'm online
☑ My status updates
☑ My photos

☑ My videos
☑ My links
☑ My notes
☑ Hometown
☑ Current city
☑ Education and work
☑ Activities, interests, things I like
☐ My app activity

If you don't want apps and websites to access other categories of information (like your friend list, gender or info you've made public), you can turn off all Platform apps. But remember, you will not be able to use any games or apps yourself.

Save Changes Cancel

Figure 5-7:
What can your friends share with apps and games?

✔ **Instant Personalization:** Instant personalization is a Facebook feature that basically lets certain Facebook partners access your public Facebook information using browser information, as opposed to using the permission dialog boxes that most apps use before they get access to any information. These partners are websites like Bing, Yelp, and Pandora. You can turn off Instant Personalization by clicking Edit Settings and disabling it on the Instant Personalization privacy page. You may be presented with a pop-up window with a video first. You can watch the video or just close the window to continue onto the Instant Personalization page.

✔ **Public Search:** Public Search enables people who are searching your name in a search engine like Google or Bing to find your Facebook timeline in the results. You can prevent this from happening by clicking Edit Settings and disabling it on the ensuing page. If you leave Public Search enabled, click the See Preview link to view how your listing appears to others.

Limit the Audience for Past Posts

This section is less a setting than a reset button. Your privacy needs may change over time. You might be about to start a job hunt or another life change, and you may want content that was previously public to be more private. Click Manage Past Post Visibility to open the Limit the Audience box. Click Limit Old Posts, which opens another confirmation box. Click Confirm. After you have done this, any posts that were visible to more than just friends will become visible only to friends. Keep in mind that people who are tagged in your photos or posts and their friends will still be able to see that content.

If you don't want to change everything, but just one or two posts, you can always edit the visibility from those posts individually on your timeline.

Blocked People and Apps

Most of your privacy settings are preventative measures for making yourself comfortable on Facebook. Block lists are usually more reactive. If someone does something on Facebook that bothers you, you may choose to block them.

To get to your block lists, click Manage Blocking to the right of the Blocked People and Apps section. This takes you to the Manage Blocking privacy page, shown in Figure 5-8.

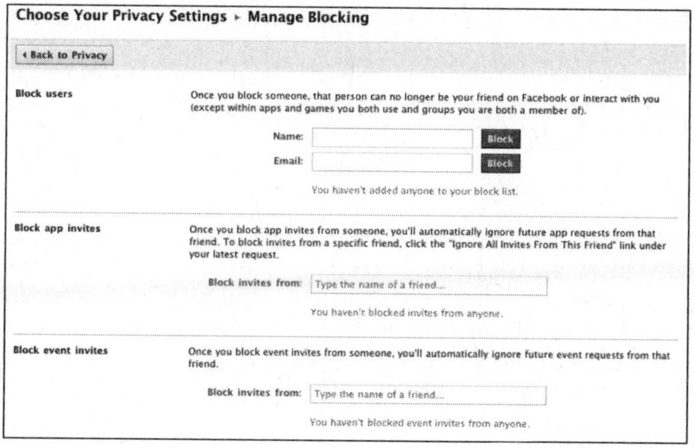

Choose Your Privacy Settings ▸ Manage Blocking

‹ Back to Privacy

Block users   Once you block someone, that person can no longer be your friend on Facebook or interact with you (except within apps and games you both use and groups you are both a member of).

Name: [　　　　　　] [Block]
Email: [　　　　　　] [Block]

You haven't added anyone to your block list.

Block app invites   Once you block app invites from someone, you'll automatically ignore future app requests from that friend. To block invites from a specific friend, click the "Ignore All Invites From This Friend" link under your latest request.

Block invites from: [Type the name of a friend...]

You haven't blocked invites from anyone.

Block event invites   Once you block event invites from someone, you'll automatically ignore future event requests from that friend.

Block invites from: [Type the name of a friend...]

You haven't blocked event invites from anyone.

Figure 5-8:
Edit your
Block lists
here.

Block Users

Blocking someone on Facebook is the strongest way to distance yourself from someone else on Facebook. For the most part, if you add someone to your Block list, he can't see any traces of you on Facebook. You won't show up in his News Feed; if he looks at a photo in which you're tagged, he may see you in the photo (that's unavoidable), but he won't see that your name has been tagged. When you write on other people's timelines, your posts are hidden from him. A few key things to remember about blocking:

- ✔ It's almost entirely reciprocal. If you block someone, he is just as invisible to you as you are to him. So you can't access his timeline, nor can you see anything about him anywhere on the site. The only difference is that if you blocked the relationship, you're the only one who can unblock it.

- ✔ People who you block are not notified that you blocked them. Nor are they notified if you unblock them. If they are savvy Facebook users, they may notice your suspicious absence, but Facebook never tells them that they have been blocked by you.

- ✔ From someone's timeline, click the gear button at the top of their About section to open a drop-down menu with the Report/Block option. When you block someone who is a friend, you are prompted to unfriend them in addition to reporting or blocking them. If you block from the privacy page, you can enter the name or e-mail address of anyone, and you automatically unfriend (if you were friends) and block that person.

Blocking on Facebook doesn't necessarily extend to Apps and Games you use on Facebook and around the Internet. Contact the Developers of the apps you use to learn how to block people within games and apps.

To add people to your Block list, simply enter their name or e-mail address into the boxes provided. Then click the Block button. Their name then appears in a list here. Click the Unblock link next to their names if you wish to remove the block.

Block App Invites

As you get going on the site, you may find out you know people who *love* to send a ton of application invites — "Play this game! And this game! Try this! Check out this!" You might even become that person. But say that you aren't a big fan of using applications. Rather than block the overly friendly person who's sending you all those invitations, you can simply block invitations. This option still allows you to interact with your friend in every other way, but you won't receive application invites.

Block Event Invites

Similar to App Invites, you may have friends who are big planners and love to invite all of their friends to their events. These may be events that you have no chance of attending because they are taking place across the country, and your friend has chosen to invite all of his friends without any regard for location. Again, your friend is cool; his endless unnecessary invitations are not. Instead of getting rid of your friend, you can get rid of the invitations by entering his name here.

Blocked Apps

The Blocked Apps section lists the apps you have blocked from that app's Page. Blocked apps cannot contact you or use your information in the app. Apps can be unblocked by clicking the Unblock link next to the app's name.

Timeline Privacy

Lots of information lives on the About section at the top of your timeline. This is information that's different from the dynamic content that lives on your timeline. This information, such as where you went to school or your relationship status, changes infrequently, if ever. You can edit the privacy for this content in the same place you edit the information itself. To get there, go to your timeline and then click the Update Info button at the top of the About section.

The About page has several boxes, each representing a different information category. You can augment your Work and Education information by typing the name of your employer or school in the available text boxes. Click the Edit button in the upper-right corner of a box to access additional editing options for that category. Next to each piece of information, an icon appears signifying who can see that piece of information. By default, most of this information is set to Public and visible to Everyone, although contact information is only visible to Friends by default.

Figure 5-9 shows me editing the privacy for a piece of information — in this case, my current city. Clicking the privacy icon to the right of the field displays the Audience Selector. When you've finished changing your settings for any particular category, remember to click Save wherever it appears.

Figure 5-9:
Edit privacy
for every
piece of
information
on your
timeline.

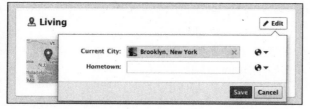

Timeline information is one of the places where the Only Me setting might come in handy. For example, lots of people don't like sharing their birthdays on Facebook, but Facebook requires you to enter a birthday when you sign up. By making it visible only to you, it effectively hides your birthday from everyone.

Click Save Changes when you are done editing privacy settings. Otherwise, the new settings won't stick.

Previewing Privacy

The View As setting allows you to explore how your timeline looks to other people, and also appears to you when you are looking at your own timeline. Click the gear button in the About section of your timeline to open a drop-down menu containing View As. Choosing this option takes you to a preview of your timeline as most people on Facebook see it. In other words, it shows you all the parts of your timeline that are set to Public.

You can also preview how your timeline looks to specific people by entering a name into the text field within the light blue box on top of the preview. For example, if you've purposely hidden some content from specific people, you can enter those people's names just to double-check that you did it correctly and that they only see what you want them to see.

Taking Personal Responsibility for Safety

No one wants anything bad to happen to you as a result of something you do on Facebook. Facebook doesn't want that. You don't want that. I definitely don't want that. I hope that these explanations help to prevent anything bad from happening to you on Facebook. But no matter what, *you* need to take part in keeping yourself safe. In order to ensure your own safety on Facebook, you have to make an effort to be smart and safe online.

So what *is* your part? Your part is to be aware of what you're putting online and on Facebook by asking yourself a few questions:

Is what I'm putting on Facebook legal or illegal?

Would I be embarrassed by someone in particular finding this information?

Will the audience with whom I'm sharing this information use it in a way I trust?

You need to be the one to choose whether displaying any given piece of information on Facebook is risky. If it's risky, you need to be the one to figure out the correct privacy settings for showing this information to the people you choose to see it — and not to the people you don't.

Your part is equivalent to the part you play in your everyday life to keep yourself safe: You know which alleys not to walk down at night, when to buckle your seatbelt, when to lock the front door, and when to toss the moldy bread before making a sandwich. Add these to your list:

I use my Facebook privacy settings wisely.

I am careful about what information I expose to lots of people.

Remembering That It Takes a Village to Raise a Facebook

Another way in which you (and every member of Facebook) contribute to keeping Facebook a safe, clean place is in the reports that you submit about spam, harassment, inappropriate content, and fake timelines. Facebook assumes that your friends aren't putting up bad stuff, but when you're looking at content of people you're not directly connected to, you should see a little Report link beneath it. This is true for Photos, Timelines, Groups, Links, Applications, Pages — and more. When you click one of these links, you see the Report page. Figure 5-10 shows an example of someone reporting an inappropriate photo. (Photo not pictured, for obvious reasons — sorry.)

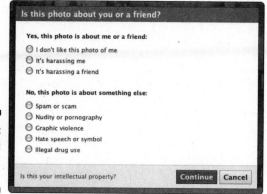

Figure 5-10:
Reporting inappropriate content.

The various Report options that you see may vary, depending on what you're reporting (a message as opposed to a photo, for example). These reports are submitted to the Facebook User Operations team. The team then investigates, taking down inappropriate photos; disabling fake accounts; and generally striving to keep Facebook clean, safe, and inoffensive.

When you see content that you don't like — for example, an offensive group name or a vulgar timeline — don't hesitate to report it. With the entire Facebook population working to keep Facebook free of badness, you wind up with a pretty awesome community.

After you report something, Facebook's User Operations team evaluates it in terms of violating Facebook's Statement of Rights and Responsibilities. This means that pornography gets taken down, fake timelines are disabled, and people who send spam may receive a warning or even have their account disabled. However, sometimes something that you report may be offensive to you but doesn't violate the Statement of Rights and Responsibilities and, therefore, will remain on Facebook. Due to privacy restrictions, User Operations may not always notify you about actions taken as a result of your support, but rest assured that the team handles every report.

Peeking Behind the Scenes

Facebook's part in keeping everyone safe requires a lot of manpower and technology power. The manpower involves responding to the reports that you and the rest of Facebook submit, as well as proactively going into Facebook and getting rid of content that violates the Statement of Rights and Responsibilities.

The technology power that we talk about is kept vague on purpose. We hope that you never think twice about the things that are happening behind the scenes to protect you from harassment, spam, and pornography. Moreover, we hope that you're never harassed or spammed, or *porned* — the unofficial verb form meaning "being assaulted by accidentally seeing unwanted porn." But just so you know that Facebook is actively thinking about user safety and privacy, I talk about a few of the general areas where Facebook does a lot of preventive work.

Protecting minors

Again, we keep this section purposefully vague to avoid becoming *Gaming Facebook's Systems For Dummies*. In general, we want you to note that people under the age of 18 have special visibility and privacy rules applied to them. For example, users under the age of 18 don't have Public Search Listings created for them. Public Search Listings enable people to be found in outside search engines, such as Google. Facebook decided never to expose minors in this way. Would anything bad have happened if Facebook had decided otherwise? Probably not, but better to be safe than sorry.

Other proprietary systems are in place that are alerted if a person is interacting with the timelines of minors in ways they shouldn't, as well as systems that get alerted when someone targets an ad to minors. Again, with reference to the personal responsibility part, as a teenager (or as the parent of a teenager), you are responsible for understanding privacy and safe behavior on Facebook. Facebook tries to prevent whatever it can, but at the end of the day, you have to be a partner in that prevention.

You must be at least 13 years old to join Facebook. No one younger than that can have an account without violating the Statement of Rights and Responsibilities.

Preventing spam and viruses

Ah, spam, that delicious little can of . . . something once meat-like? Male-enhancement medications? Prescription drugs delivered to your door? "Please sir, send me $, and I promise to return $$$." Everyone can agree that spam is the bane of the Internet, all too often sliming its way through the cracks into e-mail and websites — and always trying to slime its way into Facebook as well, sometimes in the form of messages to you, or timeline posts, or groups of events masking as something it's not to capture your precious attention.

The spam reports that you provide are incredibly helpful. Facebook also has a bunch of systems that keep track of the sort of behavior that spammers tend to do. If you haven't read this yet, hop to Chapter 2 for the scoop on CAPTCHAs, the first line of defense against spammers creating multiple dummy accounts (the bad kind of dummy) that can be used to harass people with unwanted ads. The spam systems also keep track of those who message people too quickly, friend too many people, post a similar link in too many places, and do other such behaviors that tend to reek of spam. If you end up really taking to this Facebook thing, at some point you may get hit with a warning to slow down your poking or your messaging. Don't take it too personally, and just follow the instructions in the warning — this is the spam system at work.

Preventing phishing

Phishing is a term that refers to malicious websites attempting to gain sensitive information (like usernames and passwords to online accounts) by masquerading as the sites you use and trust. Phishing is usually part of spamming: A malicious site acquires someone's Facebook credentials and then messages all that user's friends with a link to a phishing site that looks like Facebook and asks them to log in. They do so, and now the bad guys have a bunch of new Facebook logins and passwords. It's a bad cycle. The worst part is that many of these Facebook users get locked out of their own accounts and are unable to stop the spam.

Just like spam and virus prevention, Facebook has a series of proprietary systems in place to try to break this cycle. If you do have the misfortune to get phished (and it can happen to the best of us), you may run into one of the systems that Facebook uses to help people take back their timelines and protect themselves from phishing in the future.

The best way to protect yourself from phishing is to get used to the times and places Facebook asks for your password. If you just clicked a link within Facebook and suddenly there's a blue screen asking for your information, be suspicious! Similarly, remember that Facebook will never ask you to e-mail them your password. If you receive an e-mail asking for something like that, report it as spam immediately.

If you want to stay up-to-date with the latest scams on Facebook, or want more information about protecting yourself, you can Like Facebook's Security Page at www.facebook.com/security. This provides you with ongoing information about safety and security on Facebook.

Part II
Connecting with Friends on Facebook

"These are the parts of our life that aren't on Facebook."

In this part . . .

If the last part was all about you, this part is all about your friends. Without friends, trust me, Facebook can be a dull place. You'll want them interacting with you on Facebook just like you want them interacting with you from day to day, in your life outside of a screen.

First, this part covers what a friend is and how you can find and add them. After that, I cover the various ways Facebook makes it easy to stay in touch and communicate with friends near and far.

Chapter 6

Finding Facebook Friends

. . . .

. . . .

*H*undreds of sayings abound about friendship and friends, and most of them can be boiled down into one catch-all adage: friends, good; no friends, bad. This is true in life and it's also true on Facebook. Without your friends on Facebook, you find yourself at some point looking at a blank screen and asking, "Okay, now what?" With friends, you find yourself at some point looking at photos of a high school reunion and asking, "Oh, dear. How did that last hour go by so quickly?"

Most of Facebook's functionality is built around the premise that you have a certain amount of information that you want your friends to see (and maybe some information that you don't want *all* your friends to see, but that's what privacy settings are for). So, if you don't have friends who are seeing your timeline, what's the point in creating one? Messages aren't that useful unless you send them to someone. Photos are made to be viewed, but if the access is limited to friends, well, you need to find some friends.

On Facebook, friendships are *reciprocal,* which means if you add someone as a friend, they have to confirm the friendship before it appears on both timelines. If someone adds you as a friend, you can choose between Confirm and Not Now. If you confirm the friend, congrats: You have a new friend! And if you ignore the friend, the other person won't be informed.

If you're low on friends at the moment, don't feel as though you're the last kid picked for the team in middle-school dodge ball. There are many ways to find your friends on Facebook. If your friends haven't joined Facebook, invite them to join and get them to be your friends on Facebook as well as in real life.

What Is a Facebook Friend?

Good question. In many ways, a *Facebook friend* is the same as a real-life friend (although, to quote many people we know, "You're not real friends unless you're Facebook friends"). These are the people you hang out with, keep in touch with, care about, and want to publicly acknowledge as a friend. These aren't people you met on Facebook; rather they're the people you call on the phone; stop and catch up with if you cross paths at the grocery; or invite over for parties, dinners, and general social gatherings.

In real life, there are lots of shades of friendship — think of the differences between acquaintances, a friend from work, an activity buddy, and best friends. Facebook gives you a few tools for negotiating these levels of friendship, which I cover in this chapter, but by default, most friendships are lumped into a blanket category of "friend."

So here's what happens, by default, in a Facebook friendship.

✔ **They can see your posts and other information on your timeline.**

Remember, this is what happens by default. You can actually control which friends can see which posts more specifically by learning about your privacy options (which you can do in Chapter 5), and about Friend Lists, which I go over later in this chapter.

✔ **They also see new posts in their News Feeds and Tickers on their Home page.**

Again, the information your friends see in their News Feeds and Tickers depends on the audience you've chosen to share each post with Friends (or subscribers) can only see posts you've published to that audience.

✔ **You can see their posts and other information on their timeline.**

This, of course, depends on their own privacy settings, but in general, you'll be able to see more as a friend than you did before you became friends.

✔ **You also see new posts from them in your News Feed and Ticker on your Home page.**

This depends on your friend's sharing settings, but more importantly, you can control whose posts you see in your News Feed and Ticker through managing your *subscriptions*. Subscribing to someone's posts is similar to subscribing to a daily newspaper: their posts show up every day on your front stoop . . . er, Home page. Like a very advanced newspaper subscription, you can control how much you see about any one person, and even choose certain types of posts you want to see. You can also fully unsubscribe from someone's posts while still remaining friends with them.

✔ **You'll be listed as friends on one another's timeline.**

This is a small detail, but it's important in understanding the difference between becoming friends with someone and simply subscribing to someone's posts. Lots of people, especially public figures or people who have a business of some sort, allow you to subscribe to their posts without becoming friends. In these cases, you see their posts on your Home page, but they won't see your posts unless they choose to subscribe to you.

Adding Friends

Facebook has some unique language that it has created over time. One of the most important Facebook verbs is to *friend*. Friending is the act of adding someone as a friend. You may overhear people use this casually in conversation: "Oh, you won't believe who finally friended me!" And now, you too, will be friending people.

Sending Friend Requests

Now that you know what a friend is, it's time to send some requests, and maybe even accept some pending ones. For the purposes of this example, I searched for the name "Steve Hayes" (he's on Team Dummy, so he won't mind being made an example of) using the search box in the blue bar on top. I cover Search in detail later in this chapter, so for now just remember that you have two ways to view the result. The first, shown in Figure 6-1, is a list of search results of all people named Steve Hayes. To the right of each name, you may notice a big button that says Add as Friend.

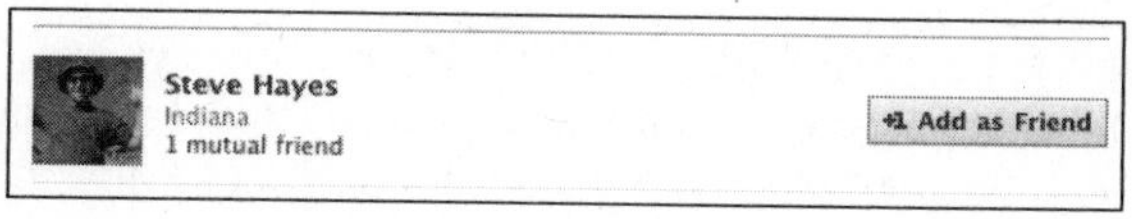

Figure 6-1:
The Search results for Steve Hayes.

Steve Hayes
Indiana
1 mutual friend

+1 Add as Friend

Alternately, I could use Search to go straight to Steve's timeline. As shown in Figure 6-2, right below the cover photo are two buttons: Add Friend and Subscribe.

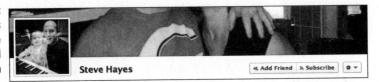

To add a friend, just follow these steps:

1. **Click the Add Friend button.**

   This opens a menu asking you if you want to add Steve to any of your Friend Lists. It also changes the Subscribe button to a Subscribed button, indicating that you want to see Steve's posts in your News Feed and Ticker.

2. **(Optional) Add Steve to any of the lists you've created or to any of the smart lists Facebook has created for you.**

   Friend Lists and Smart Lists are covered in the Friend List management section of this chapter.

3. **(Optional) Change your subscription settings by clicking the Subscribed button.**

   This opens a menu of subscription options. You can choose to see All, Most, or Only Important Posts from Steve. By default, you'll be subscribed to most updates and all update types. You can choose to see certain types of posts or not see them by checking and unchecking the options Facebook offers. For example, if you want to see Statuses but not Photos, leave Status Updates checked and uncheck Photos in the subscription menu.

You won't be friends with someone until they confirm your Friend Request. You'll be notified after they do by a red bubble appearing above the notifications icon in the blue bar on top.

So what does Steve see after I send a request? That is a brilliant bridge into our next topic, accepting Friend Requests.

Accepting Friend Requests

You may see your incoming Friend Requests in any of several places, including your e-mail account, your Friends page, and your Home page. When you receive a new request, you'll also notice a little red flag appear on the friends icon to the right of the word *Facebook* in the big blue bar on top. Figure 6-3 shows an example.

Figure 6-3:
Someone
wants to be
your friend!

Clicking this icon opens the Friend Requests menu, shown in Figure 6-4.

Figure 6-4:
Click
Confirm or
Not Now.

To accept the Friend Request, click the Confirm button. You now have a friend. To reject the request, click Not Now. Clicking Not Now rejects the Friend Request, but technically this request is hidden by Facebook indefinitely. In other words, if you later change your mind, you can go back to the request and accept it at a later time, or you can fully delete the request.

To get back to hidden Friend Requests, go to the Friends page from the left-side menu and click the Manage Friends button. This takes you to the Manage Friends page. From here, click the Requests item on the left. This shows you a list of outstanding requests as well as a See Hidden Requests link. Clicking this link reveals the requests, which you can then accept or delete.

You can also access hidden requests by going to the timeline of the person who sent the request. There, the Add Friend button is replaced with a link to accept the Friend Request. Click the button to become official Facebook friends.

Some people worry about clicking that Ignore or Not Now button. If you're not sure what you want to do, you can always leave the request untouched. But never hesitate to click Not Now or Ignore for someone you really just don't want to be friends with. Facebook won't notify them that you ignored their request.

Choose your friends wisely

Generally, you send Friend Requests to and confirm Friend Requests from only people you actually know. If you don't know them — *random Friend Requests* — click Not Now. For all the reasons enumerated in the preceding section — your privacy, News Feed, and reflection of reality — don't declare friendship unless some kind of relationship actually exists. Remember the lecture you got about choosing good friends when you were in high school? It's every bit as true now. Accept a Friend Request that you shouldn't, and the next thing you know, you're fleeing for the border on the back of a motorcycle belonging to some guy who insists his name is Harley. Trust me: It will happen exactly like that.

If there are people you don't know personally, but find interesting (maybe someone you met at a conference, or a writer of brilliant *For Dummies* books who you think sounds interesting), you can always choose just to subscribe to their posts as opposed to adding them as a friend. This gets you the benefits of friendship without exposing your own profile to Harley and his ilk.

It's quality, not quantity

Another common misperception about Facebook is that it's all about the race to get the most friends. This is very, very wrong. Between the News Feed and privacy implications of friendship, aim to keep your Friend List to the people you actually care about. Now, the number of people you care about — including the people you care about the most and those you care about least — may be large or small. The average number of friends that a person has on Facebook is around 120. Does a person with 120 friends care about them all equally? Probably not. Does this mean that person is shallow? No. It means that this person is keeping up with and keeping track of all the friends who have come and gone through a lifetime. Changing jobs, schools, and locations also comes with new friends, but that doesn't displace the fact that you care about friends from your past.

Should you aim to have 120 friends? No. My mom has a great Facebook experience with fewer than 30 friends. With that number, she still can share her photos with her friends, play games with people she knows, and have a pretty active News Feed. Aim to have all the people you care about on your Friend List. Maybe that's a big number, or maybe it's a small number; the part that counts is that you want to see them in the list, smiling back at you.

Finding Your Friends on Facebook

How do you get to the people you want to be your friends? Facebook is big, and if you're looking for your friend John, you may need to provide some more detail. Facebook has a couple of tools that show you people you may know and want as your friend, as well as a normal search-by-name functionality for finding specific people.

If only real life had a Friend Finder

Friend Finder is a tool that matches e-mail addresses from your e-mail address book to people's timelines on Facebook. Because each e-mail address can be associated with only one Facebook account, you can count on your matches finding the right people whom you already know through e-mail.

With your permission, Friend Finder also invites those people who don't have a Facebook account that matches the e-mail in your address book to join Facebook. Sending invites this way causes a Friend Request to automatically be sent to that person. If they join based on an invite you send, they find a Friend Request from you waiting when they join.

To use Friend Finder, you need to give Facebook your e-mail address and e-mail password. Facebook doesn't store this information: It just uses it to retrieve your contacts list that one time.

Chances are that you came across Friend Finder when you first set up your account. The following steps make several assumptions, namely, that you use web-based e-mail (Hotmail, Gmail, Yahoo! Mail, and so on), that you haven't used Friend Finder recently, and that the address book for the e-mail has a bunch of your friends in it. We cover other options, such as a client-based address book or using an Instant Messenger Buddy List later in this chapter. Here's how to use Friend Finder:

1. **Click the Friends icon next to the word *Facebook* on the big blue bar on top.**

   This opens the Friend Request menu.

2. **At the top-right corner of the menu, click the Find Friends link.**

   Figure 6-5 shows the Friend Finder. Below it, you may also see People You May Know, which we cover later in this chapter.

3. **Select the e-mail or instant message service you use.**

   This may be Windows Live Hotmail, AOL, or any number of other e-mail services.

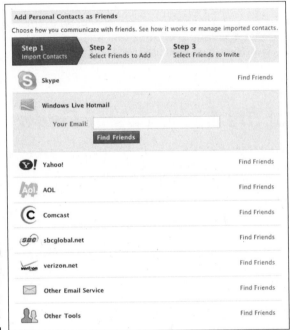

Figure 6-5:
An unfilled
Friend
Finder.

4. **Enter your e-mail address into the Your Email field.**

5. **Enter your e-mail password (not your Facebook password) into the Email Password box and then click Find Friends.**

   These instructions are meant for first-time users of the Friend Finder. If you've used it before, or if you're currently logged into your webmail client, you may see some fields prefilled or additional pop-up prompts asking you for your permission to send information to Facebook. Don't worry if it doesn't match the figures here at the beginning.

   If Facebook finds any matches with the e-mails in your address book, you see a page that looks similar to Figure 6-6. (If it doesn't find any friends, go to Step 6.) These people are the ones Facebook thinks you may know. Anyone you select is sent a Friend Request from you, and by default everyone is selected. If you want to send only a few people Friend Requests, click the Select All box at the top to deselect everyone. Then you can just select the boxes next to the people you do want to add.

Figure 6-6:
The Friend
Selector
portion
of Friend
Finder.

6. **Decide whether to**

   - *Add everyone as a friend.* Click Add as Friends.

   - *Not friend anyone.* Click Skip.

   - *Add many people as a friend.* Click the faces or check boxes to the left of the specific names that you don't want to be friends with. After you deselect all the people you don't want, click Add as Friends.

   - *Add a few people as friends.* Uncheck the Select All box at the top of the screen. Then, check the box to the left of the name or click the face of anyone you want to add as a friend. When you've selected everyone you'd like to invite, click Add as Friends.

After you click either Add as Friends or Skip, you land on the Invite portion of Friend Finder. It should look something like Figure 6-7. These e-mails are those that have no matches on Facebook.

Figure 6-7:
The Invite
portion
of Friend
Finder.

7. **(Optional) Invite people to join Facebook and become your friend.**

   Similar to adding friends, you can

   - *Invite all these contacts.* Click Invite to Join.

   - *Invite none of these contacts.* Click Skip.

   - *Invite some of these contacts.* Select the Invite Some Friends option and then use the check boxes to the left of their e-mail addresses to choose which ones you want to Invite to join Facebook.

   When you've made your selections, click Send Invites or Invite to Join. If you don't want to send any invitations, click Skip.

After taking all these steps, I hope you manage to send a few Friend Requests. Your friends need to confirm your requests before you officially become friends on Facebook, so you may not be able to see your friends' timelines until that confirmation happens.

If the whole experience yielded nothing — no friends you wanted to add, no contacts you wanted to invite — you have a few options. You can go through these steps again with a different e-mail address. You should probably use the one that you use for personal e-mail (from where you e-mail your friends and family). If that's not the problem, you have more ways to use Friend Finder.

Import an address book

If you're someone who uses a *desktop e-mail client* — a program on your local computer that manages your e-mail (like Microsoft Outlook or Entourage) — create a file of your contacts and import it so that Facebook can check it for friend matches. The way to create your contact file depends on which e-mail client you use. Here's how to get the right instructions:

1. **From the Friend Finder, select the Other Tools option at the bottom of the screen.**

2. **Click Upload Contact File, the first blue link.**

   A button appears asking you to choose your contact file. If you don't know where to find your contact file, click the How to Create a Contact File link just above the upload field. This expands a window with instructions for most desktop e-mail programs, as well as a few websites such as LinkedIn.

3. **After you have created and saved a contact file, click Choose File.**

   This opens a window that lets you select your file from your computer's hard drive.

4. **After you have selected a file, click Upload Contacts.**

   This takes you through Steps 6 and 7 in the previous section.

People you may know

After you have a friend or two, Facebook can start making pretty good guesses about others who may be your friends. Facebook primarily does this by looking at people with whom you have friends or networks in common. In the People You May Know box, shown in Figure 6-8, you see a list of people Facebook thinks you may know and, therefore, may want as friends. In this list, if you see the name of someone you know, simply add her as a friend by clicking the aptly named Add as Friend link beneath the person's name. If you're not sure, you can click a name or timeline picture to gather more evidence from the timeline about whether and how you know that person. Then you can decide whether to add that person as a friend.

Figure 6-8: Facebook suggests friends.

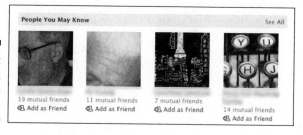

If you're sure you don't know someone, or if you do know someone but are sure you don't want that person as your Facebook friend, mouse over the person's picture and click the X that appears. After you do that, she stops appearing in your People You May Know list. As you add or remove people from suggestions, more pop up to take their place. This fun can last for hours, so make sure you have time and a comfortable chair before you decide to start going suggestions-crazy.

You'll also see a smattering of suggestions on your Home page every day when you log in. Finding friends is an ongoing thing, so don't feel like you must go through every single Friend Finder option in one day. Pay attention to the right side of your Home page, and your Friend List will expand pretty quickly.

Find classmates and co-workers

Friend Finder works by looking for large groups of people you might want to become friends with. A common assumption is that you'll want to become friends with people you've gone to school with and worked with over the years. To find these people, follow these steps:

1. **Click the Friends icon next to the word *Facebook* on the big blue bar on top.**

   This opens a little menu.

2. **At the top of the menu, click the Find Friends link.**

   This brings you to the Friend Finder page.

3. **Click Other Tools (usually the bottom option).**

   This expands a menu of possibilities based on information you have filled out on your timeline.

4. **Click any of the Find Coworkers From or Find Classmates From links.**

   All these links go to the same place, which is a page for browsing people on Facebook shown in Figure 6-9.

5. **Use the check boxes on the left side of the page to look for people from your various jobs or schools.**

   Selecting a check box displays people from that school or company. You can also look for people from your hometown, current city, or workplace by entering a mutual friend's name.

When you check more than one box, it actually shows you *fewer* people because now Facebook is looking for people who both worked at Mom's Pizza *and* went to Hamilton High School. To find more people, check only one box at a time.

You can actually browse for people in cities, companies, and colleges other than the ones you've listed on your timeline. Look for the empty boxes that say Add Another and type in the school, city, or company where you think you know people.

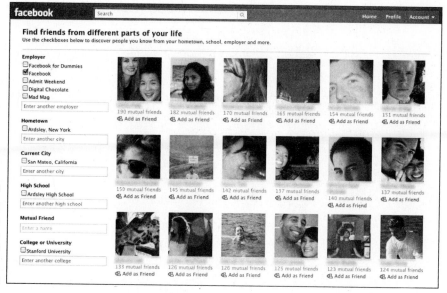

Figure 6-9:
Use the
check boxes
to find your
friends.

Find what you're looking for: Search

Friend Finder is a great way to build your Friend List quickly without a lot of work. After you build it a bit, though, what if you find other people who may want to be your friends? Facebook Search offers you the capability to seek out certain friends by name.

The search box in the blue bar on top lets you search a whole lot of things on Facebook: Pages, groups, events, even questions. But most of the time, you use it to search for people. It may be people you are already friends with and you just want to go to their timeline. Sometimes it will be people you aren't friends with yet that you want to reach out to.

Basic search can be a little confusing because Facebook auto-completes the names that you type and assumes you are trying to get to your friends' time-lines. If you're the type of person who is used to pressing the Enter key to begin a search, this can lead you landing on friends' timeline pages when you meant to search for someone *else* named James.

There are two basic ways you'll wind up using search. The first is if the person you're looking for (or at least, someone with their name) appears in the auto-complete menu. That sort of search can be accomplished following these steps:

1. **Begin typing their name into the search box.**

   Pay attention to the people who appear in the auto-complete menu. Facebook displays first your friends and then friends of friends. There's a good chance that you may find the person you're looking for in this menu that appears.

2. **If you see them in the auto-complete menu, use your mouse or arrow keys to highlight the person you are looking for.**

3. **Click their name or press Enter.**

   This brings you to their timeline, where you can verify that you know them and add them as a friend.

If you don't see the person you're looking for, don't despair; you can get more results:

1. **Type their full name into the search box.**

2. **Click the search icon (do not just press Enter) to begin the search.**

   This brings you to a full list of search results, as shown in Figure 6-10.

3. **Click the particular person you are looking for to get to their timeline and add them as a friend.**

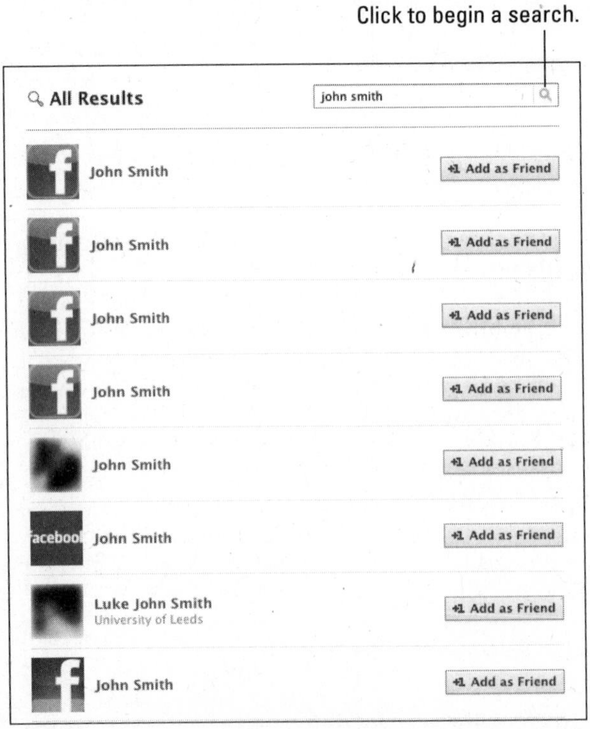

Click to begin a search.

Figure 6-10:
Looking for
John Smith?

Keeping Track: Friend List Management

After you do all this work finding and adding your friends, at some point, you may find that things are feeling a little out of control. Chances are you may be subscribed to a few people you find uninteresting; you might not be sure who, exactly, can see your own posts anymore. At this point, it's a good idea to get acquainted with the way that Facebook automatically helps you end the madness, as well as some of the more specific and manual things you can do.

Friend Lists

Friend Lists (capital L) are subsets of your giant list of friends (lowercase l). Confused yet? Friend Lists are a way of organizing your friends into lists to make your Facebook experience even easier and more personalized to you and your types of friends. Organizing your friends into Friend Lists allows you to

- **Share different types of information with different sets of friends.** For example, your best friends may get to see your party photos, and your family may get to see your wedding photos. I discuss using Friend Lists for privacy in Chapter 5.

- **Communicate with the same groups of people.** Friend Lists can be used in the Inbox. Say that you always invite the same group of people to go biking. Add them all to a Friend List, and then, each time you want to send an invitation, you can simply message the list rather than typing their names each time. To send a message to a Friend List, simply type the name of the list in the To line where you normally type a name.

- **Use Friend Lists in Chat.** You can show yourself as online or offline to different groups of people, or easily scan for certain types of friends currently online, such as social friends if you're looking for a dinner date, or carpool friends if you need a ride. I tell you more about this in Chapter 8.

The options for how you create Friend Lists are virtually limitless. You can have 1,500 friends on each list, each friend can be on more than one list, and you can make up to 100 Friend Lists. Your lists can be for silly things (Girls' Night Out Girls), real-world needs (Family), or general bucketing (co-workers).

Smart Lists

Smart Lists are the lists that Facebook makes on your behalf. These lists are created automatically based on your interactions with your friends, and shared characteristics of your friends. Some common Smart Lists are

- **Close Friends:** Facebook creates this list based on things like people you interact with a lot on Facebook, people you appear in a lot of photos with, and so on.

- **Acquaintances:** The opposite of the Close Friends list. This list is meant to be a place where you can cordon off the people you don't know as well. They might be perfectly nice people, but they aren't necessarily the people you want to share everything with. In fact, one of the default privacy options when you post something from the Share menu is Friends Except Acquaintances, which is Facebook's way of saying, "Only share this with my *real* friends."

- **Family:** Based on information you have entered about your family, they may show up on this Smart List.

- **<Your High School>:** If you've caught up with a lot of old friends on Facebook, a Smart List might be created so you can post photos from the reunion or share memories just with them.

- **<Your college/university/workplace>:** Similar to a high school list, depending on the information your friends have listed on their profiles, additional Smart Lists may be created for these groups. For example, I have Smart Lists for Stanford (where I was an undergraduate), CCA (where I'm currently a graduate student), and Facebook (where I used to work).

Although Facebook is smart, it's not perfect. Although these lists will be mostly accurate, you may find that you have to do some editing to them. It may also depend on how you want to use your lists. For example, you may want your Family list to make it easy to share with just your immediate family, and therefore need to remove the more distant members. Or, you want it to be a giant family reunion all the time, in which case you need to add some of the third and fourth cousins once removed to the mix.

To edit a Smart List, follow these steps:

1. **Navigate to the list you want to edit by clicking it on the left side of your Home page in the Lists section).**

   If you're not seeing the list you're looking for there, hover over the Lists header and click the More link. This takes you to a list of all your Lists. Click the one you want to edit.

This takes you to a News Feed full of posts from the people on that list. On the right side of the page is an On This List section, where you can check out the current members of the list.

2. **To add people to a list, type their names into the text box in the On This List section.**

   Facebook auto-completes as you type. Select your friend's name when you see it.

3. **To remove people from a list, click See All in the On This List section.**

   A pop-up window displays the names and pictures of all members of the list.

4. **Hover over the person you want to remove.**

   A small X should appear in the upper-right corner of their picture.

5. **Click the X.**

Creating your own Friend Lists

For most people, Smart Lists can usually help you figure out both who you want to see in your News Feed and who you want to share your own posts with. But sometimes you might want a specific list that Facebook can't figure out. This might be a sub-sub-group, like all the people you played Frisbee with in college. In these cases, you can create your own list.

To create a Friend List, follow these steps:

1. **Hover over the Lists section of the left-hand menu on the Home page and click the More link that appears.**

   This brings you to a list of all your lists.

2. **Click the Create a List button in the upper-right corner.**

   This pops up the Create a List window.

3. **In the window that opens, type the name of your list.**

   Maybe something like *Dummies* for the Dummies Team (see Figure 6-11).

Figure 6-11:
Creating a
Friend List.

4. **Select friends who belong on this list by clicking their names or faces.**

   There is a small search box that says Enter a Name. If you begin typing there, you can simply click the person's face as soon as you see it.

5. **Click Create List.**

   Now, wherever Friend Lists appear on Facebook, including where you set privacy, Chat, the Inbox, and the Friends page, you have access to the new list you just created. It also appears on the left side of the Edit Friends page.

You can always edit the name or membership of a list later by selecting the list name from the tab on the left of the Friends page. From there, you can change the name, or delete or add members. Also, whenever viewing friends on the Manage Friends page, you can add them to lists by selecting the Add to List drop-down menu to the right of their names (this appears when you hover your mouse over their name) and checking the list to which you'd like to add them.

Friend Lists are private, so even if the list you're messaging is known in your mind as *Annoying Co-Workers*, all that your annoying co-workers see is a list of names.

Groups

Groups are, in many ways, a more public version of Friend Lists. Instead of your friends not knowing which list they are on, friends are always notified when they are added to a group. In turn, they can add their friends to the group if they think the information shared there is relevant to them. Groups are extremely useful for sharing information that only a specific group of people might care about. For example, a funny video from a family gathering that perhaps only members of your crazy family will understand, is a good candidate to be shared via a family group. Groups are covered in great detail in Chapter 9.

Unfriending

It happens to everyone: After a while, you start to feel like a few people are cluttering up Facebook for you. Maybe you just feel like you have too many friends, or maybe you and a friend have legitimately drifted apart. Maybe you had a big falling out and just need a break. Don't worry; Facebook friendships are not set in stone. You can *unfriend* just like you friend people.

To unfriend someone:

1. **Go to their timeline.**

2. **Click the Friends button.**

   This opens a menu for assigning people to Friend Lists. The bottom item in this list is Unfriend.

3. **Click the Unfriend link.**

   A pop-up appears asking if you are sure you want to remove this friend.

4. **Click the Remove from Friends button.**

   Take a moment of silence. Okay, that was long enough.

People aren't notified when you unfriend them, but people who care about you (that is, family, close friends) have a tendency to notice on their own that, hey, you're not in their Friend List anymore. This can sometimes lead to awkwardness, so it might be worth using Lists or Privacy to further limit these people's knowledge of your life.

Lots of people go through periodic friend-cleaning. For example, after changing jobs or moving, you may notice that although you want to keep in touch with some co-workers, others, you just don't.

Chapter 7

Keep in Touch: News Feed, the Ticker, and the Timeline

. . . .

In This Chapter

▶ Finding out what your friends are up to by reading News Feed and ticker

▶ Checking out what an individual friend is doing on their timeline

▶ Taking a trip down memory lane with Friendship Pages

. . . .

Reaching out to all the friends you care about to find out what's going on in their lives is a lot of work. That's one of the reasons why, in a pre-Facebook world (talk to a 14-year-old — they won't believe such a thing existed) people frequently lost touch with friends as they moved through their lives. Calling each friend once a week, or even once a month, was time-consuming. In this happy, shiny, post-Facebook world, however, keeping in touch with friends is much easier.

There are three main parts of keeping in touch, discussed at length in this chapter: your News Feed, the ticker, and your friends' timelines. You've been hearing references to all of these things in many previous chapters and now it's time to learn what they are, how they work, and how you can get the most out of them. Additionally, if you're ever feeling a bit nostalgic, Friendship Pages are a virtual scrapbook that may just bring tears to your eyes.

Your Daily News . . . Feed

News Feed is the centerpiece of your Home page. When you log in to Facebook, you see the familiar blue bar and left menu, but mostly you see News Feed.

So what is News Feed? It's primarily a collection of stories by and about your friends. Each of the words in this previous sentence could actually have a little star next to it for a precise definition:

- ✔ **Collection:** Depending on the number of friends you have and how often you (and they) use Facebook, the little robots at work creating News Feed may show you different things. You may see everything your friends have done or shared, or you may see only a fraction of your friends, and only a fraction of the things they do and share. Luckily, the robots are open to suggestions. Much of what you see will be based on tweaks *you* make to your News Feed settings.

- ✔ **Stories by your friends:** Most of your News Feed will probably be things like people updating their status and posting photos, links, and videos. These are things your friends actively want to share with you, so Facebook puts them right on your Home page. Condensed versions of the same stories may appear in ticker, a scrolling stream of updates on the right side of your Home page. The difference between News Feed and ticker is explained later in this chapter.

- ✔ **Stories about your friends:** Lots of this book is dedicated to all the things you can *do* on Facebook. You can add friends, Like Pages, RSVP to events. These sorts of actions that your friends may take also appear as stories in News Feed.

You may wander out to the front step in your robe and slippers every morning, searching for the paper to let you know what's happened in the world. Many people log in to Facebook first thing in the morning to find out what their friends have been up to since they last checked. News Feed is like a newspaper centered around you and your friends.

Your News Feed may also include Public posts from people you subscribe to or Pages you Like. We explore both types of posts later in this chapter.

Anatomy of a News Feed story

Figure 7-1 shows a sample News Feed story. In this case, it's a status post from a friend.

Figure 7-1:
Just your
average
status
update.

Steve Hayes
I wonder what percentage of my time these days is dedicated to waiting for a computer to do something.
Unlike · Comment · Tuesday at 10:25am · 🕮

👍 You like this.
💬 View all 5 comments

Even in this tiny example, there are six significant parts of the story:

- ✔ **Name and timeline picture:** The first part of any story is who it's about or who wrote it. The name is in blue. This means the person's name is an active link. If you click it, you'll go to their timeline.

- ✔ **Content:** In Figure 7-1, it's the actual status, but depending on the content, this might be a preview of an article, or a video, or a photo album. It could also be a location where someone has *checked in*, or marked their location via GPS, using their phone. The content is the part of the story that is the most important.

- ✔ **Like and Comment:** These links allow you to interact with your friends about the content they've posted. We cover a whole lot more about liking and commenting later in this chapter. In addition, you can see how many people have already Liked this post, and you can click the link or the word bubble icon to see what people have said about it.

- ✔ **Timestamp:** The little gray text to the right of Like and Comment tells you how long ago this post was added.

  Privacy Info: The gray icon next to the timestamp represents whether your friend has shared this post with everyone (Public), just friends (Friends), or some other group of people (Custom). Hover over the icon to see who else can see it.

- ✔ **Other Links (not shown):** In addition to Like and Comment, many stories have specific links. For example, posts with articles in them will have links enabling you to Share them. Stories about one friend writing on another friend's timeline give you a link to see the Friendship Page about those two people.

The ticker: News Feed lite

To expand on the newspaper analogy, if News Feed is like a newspaper centered around you and your friends, ticker stories are similar to headlines — brief, impactful text that conveys a story's subject matter and entices you to read further (or skip to the funnies). Together, News Feed and ticker posts provide you with a complete picture of what's going on in your friends' lives.

Ticker updates about your friends' activities are posted in real-time, allowing for more shared experiences between you and your friends. Social apps from companies, such as the video service Hulu or newspaper *The Wall Street Journal*, make the ticker your destination for learning which films, TV shows, albums, and articles your friends are watching, listening to, and reading at this very moment. Join in on the activities that interest you by clicking a post to see its full version containing the familiar Comment and Like options. Figure 7-2 shows a sample ticker story.

I haven't even told you the best part. Clicking an active link for a song, video, or article opens that piece of content within Facebook, eliminating the extra time it takes for another site to load in your browser.

If your computer has a wide screen, you can drag your browser window to its maximum width, which should move the ticker and chat sidebar to the far right of the page. (It will remain in place while you visit other areas of the site, such as Groups or Events.) Once it's in the proper location, grab the gray bar between the ticker and chat sidebar and drag it up or down to adjust the number of ticket stories you see at one time.

Common story types

News Feed is made up of all sorts of stories. Although the basic anatomy is the same, here are some of the common story types you might encounter:

✔ **Status Updates:** The Status Update post appears in Figure 7-1. Status updates are the short little posts that your friends make about what's going on in their lives.

✔ **Links:** Figure 7-3 shows a post sharing a link. This is one of the chief ways I get my news: Friends share links to articles, and the previews are so interesting to me I have to read the whole article. Click the links (or the article's title) to go to the articles.

Figure 7-3:
Use your
status to
share links
to articles.

✔ **Photos:** Figure 7-4 shows a post about photos. When people add photos or are tagged in photos, it creates this type of post, with information about who was tagged and a sample of the photos that were added. Click the photos to see bigger versions and browse the entire album.

Figure 7-4:
Photo
stories.

✔ **Videos:** Figure 7-5 shows a video story. Clicking the Play button on the preview expands the story to show a playing card–sized version of the video. Clicking the title of the video will take you to the video's page, which may be on Facebook (if your friend used Facebook to add the video) or another video site like YouTube (if your friend used another video site and posted the link to Facebook).

Figure 7-5:
Video
stories.

> ✔ **Timeline Posts:** Figure 7-6 shows a timeline post story between two friends. The first person wrote the message on the second person's timeline.

Figure 7-6:
A time-
line post
between
friends.

You only see timeline post stories when you are friends with both of the people involved. You won't see stories about a friend posting on a non-friend's timeline.

> ✔ **Check-ins/Check-in tags:** A check-in is something that you can do from either your mobile phone or the share menu on News Feed or timeline. It allows you (or your friends) to use GPS to mark, on Facebook, where you are. Check-ins are often accompanied by mobile photo uploads or status updates. For more about check-ins, see Chapter 15.

> ✔ **Likes:** Like stories are usually just quick little stories that let you know what Pages your friends have Liked recently. The Pages are linked so you can click right through to check them out yourself.

> ✔ **Read/Watch/Listen:** Certain services and websites, such as the music site Spotify, may prompt you to grant blanket permission to automatically post specific actions you take on their site to Facebook. See Chapter 14 for more information about how these applications work. Figure 7-7 shows an automated News Feed post from Spotify.

Figure 7-7:
Which songs do you rock out to?

- ✔ **Friendships:** Friendship stories might be about just two people becoming friends or about one person becoming friends with lots of different people.

- ✔ **Changed Timeline Pictures:** Timeline picture stories are simply about your friends' new timeline pictures. Click through to look at the full-sized ones; the preview can be tiny!

- ✔ **Events:** Stories about events (usually letting you know which friends have RSVPed *yes* to an event) include a link to the event, so if you're looking for someplace to go, you can say *yes*, too. Only public events show up here, so if you've added a private event don't worry about people who weren't invited seeing it in News Feed.

Top Stories versus Recent Stories

Just below the Share menu on your Home page is the News Feed column, divided into two sections, which can be seen in Figure 7-8: Top Stories and Recent Stories.

Figure 7-8:
Welcome to News Feed.

TOP STORIES SINCE YOUR LAST VISIT (14)　　　　　　　　 ✦ 82 MORE RECENT STORIES

Top Stories and Recent Stories are two different sides of the same News Feed coin. Think about Top Stories as the front page of your newspaper: It's the most important stuff (well, what Facebook thinks you'll find most important).

Top Stories is sorted by a whole bunch of different factors. One of them is your relationship with a particular friend. A story from your mom might be considered more important than a story from that guy you met that one time at that place. Top Stories are easily recognizable by their upper-left corner, which is blue. Clicking this blue corner removes Top Story status. Inversely, you can assign Top Story status by hovering over the upper left of a Recent Story and clicking the blue corner when it appears. Changing the status of a News Feed story tells Facebook which story types you want to see more or less of in the future.

Recent Stories shows you stories based entirely on what has happened most recently. The newest stories are at the top and, as you scroll down, you'll see older and older stories. Most Recent doesn't usually show you all the stories from everyone, but it does show you more than Top Stories.

Depending on how long it's been since you've last logged in, Facebook may default you to Recent Stories instead of Top Stories. If you've been gone for a day, chances are you'll see Top Stories when you first log in. You'll never have to worry about missing important news again.

Making News Feed Better

As much fun as the blue corner can be, bestowing and revoking Top Story status isn't the only effective way to enhance your News Feed.

Caring about the caron

The easiest way to influence News Feed is to let it know when you don't Like a post. Whenever you hover over a particular story, a small icon resembling a lowercase letter *v*, called a *caron*, appears in its upper-right corner. Clicking the caron reveals a menu, as shown in Figure 7-9.

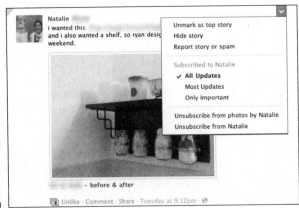

Figure 7-9:
Don't fear
the caron.

You have several options when it comes to posts:

- ✔ **Unmark as Top Story (Top Stories Only):** This is an alternative to un-clicking the blue corner on News Feed stories, as described in the previous section.

- ✔ **Hide Story:** This option simply hides an offensive, annoying, or boring post from appearing in your News Feed. Sometimes people post something without realizing that all their friends can see it. This option lets you not see it without hiding that person permanently.

- ✔ **Report Story or Spam:** This is one that you (hopefully) won't need to use very much. Although your friends might sometimes post less-than-interesting statuses, they probably aren't spamming you. Unfortunately, the applications they use might sometimes do that. If you see an application posting something that seems way too promotional or that is selling something fishy (like an iPad for 50 bucks), mark it as spam. Facebook uses these reports to determine whether applications need to be shut down.

- ✔ **Subscribe Status:** Use these settings to fine-tune the level of content you see from a friend in your News Feed.

- ✔ **All Updates:** You'll see every post from that friend in your News Feed.

- ✔ **Most Updates:** No change to the amount of posts that currently appear from that friend in your News Feed.

- ✔ **Only Important:** Limit News Feed posts from that friend to major life events, such as an engagement or graduation.

- ✔ **Unsubscribe from (story type) by Friend:** Perhaps you have a friend who's a top-notch photographer. You love flipping through her gorgeous portraits, but wish they weren't sandwiched between mundane status updates about the ins and outs of her profession. This handy option lets you unsubscribe from a particular story type, such as photos, status updates, or comments and Likes.

- ✔ **Unsubscribe from Friend:** If you choose to unsubscribe from a person, you won't see their posts in your News Feed anymore, but you remain Facebook friends.

When you use these settings, your friends never find out that you hid a post or hid them entirely from your News Feed. So use the caron and you'll start seeing fewer of the things you don't care about.

If you find your News Feed filled with stories that are less than compelling, you can use your custom Friend Lists or Facebook-provided smart lists to ensure you see content from those friends you care about most. To view the posts and photos from members of a specific list, navigate to the Lists section from the left menu of your Home page and click the list name. Head over to Chapter 6 for the full scoop on Friend Lists.

Edit options

If the caron doesn't quite do the trick, you can always edit the options to further control what you see in News Feed. To get to the Edit Your News Feed Settings dialog box, follow these steps:

1. **Scroll to the bottom of your News Feed.**

   This might take a few tries; Facebook has a tendency to simply add on more stories to the bottom of the page when you scroll down.

2. **Click Edit Options.**

   This opens the Edit News Feed Settings pop-up box, shown in Figure 7-10.

Figure 7-10:
Edit your
News Feed
here.

This is a list of the Friends, apps, and Pages you have hidden from your News Feed. Anytime you've hidden someone, as described in the previous section, they are added into this list, where you can remove them at any time. If you find yourself missing important news from a particular friend, make sure you haven't hidden them by checking this list. If you have, click the X next to their name to add them back into News Feed.

Don't forget to click Save when you're done editing these options. Otherwise, your preferences won't be applied to News Feed.

To Subscribe or Not Subscribe

That is the question. The recent addition of Subscriptions means you can receive public posts from your favorite blogger or pundit in your News Feed without the hassle of mutual friendship or Liking their Page.

Getting started with subscriptions is simple. Just navigate to a user's timeline and click the Subscribe button that appears in their info section (directly beneath the cover photo). Additionally, you may see recommendations from Facebook in the People to Subscribe To section on the right column of your Home page.

To save you from the potentially time-consuming task of subscribing to your friends one by one, you're automatically subscribed to Most Updates from all of your friends.

Edit subscriptions

To change your subscription settings for an individual friend or user, complete the following steps:

1. **Go to your friend's timeline.**
2. **Click the Subscribe button at the top right of the page.**
3. **From the menu that appears, control which updates you want to receive from this friend by clicking the relevant options.**

   A check mark to the left of that option means you are currently subscribed. Figure 7-11 shows the Subscribe menu in all its glory.

Figure 7-11:
The Subscribe menu offers granular controls.

To adjust more than one subscription at a time, head over to the Manage Subscriptions page. There are a few ways to access this page, but I suggest clicking the Subscriptions box from the Info section of your timeline. The Manage Subscriptions page lets you to view subscriptions by Friend

Subscriptions or Public Subscriptions. Click the Subscribe button to the right of the names in either list to open the Subscribe menu shown in Figure 7-11.

When choosing which of your friends to subscribe to along with the level of subscription, it's worth keeping in mind that the people you interact with, whether through messaging, commenting, or writing on each other's time-lines, are the people you tend to care about. The same status can feel very different coming from different people, so keeping Facebook about the people you actually want to hear from is pretty useful.

Allowing subscribers

You have the option of adding a Subscribe button to your own timeline to enable non-friends to receive your public updates in their News Feeds. Enable subscriptions by following these steps:

1. **Go to your timeline and click Subscriptions on the left menu, directly below your timeline picture.**

2. **A blue tab appears at the top of your timeline. Click Allow Subscribers.**

3. **From the Edit Subscriber Settings pop-up window, choose who can comment on your posts and how you're notified about new subscribers.**

4. **Click OK.**

You do not need to share anything you don't feel comfortable sharing. Allowing subscribers is completely optional. If you allow subscribers, only posts you set to Public appear in your subscribers' News Feeds.

Good Timelines Make Good Neighbors

Your News Feed pulls posts that your friends make into one place so you can read them all at once. But sometimes you want to read all about just one person. Fortunately, all of their posts have been collected on their timelines. Figure 7-12 shows a sample timeline, full of all different kinds of content.

The timeline is kind of like a News Feed all about one person. The links, videos, photos, and statuses they've posted all appear here, organized from newest to oldest by month and year, as well as posts their friends have left for them.

Figure 7-12:
My timeline,
a digital
scrapbook
of my
Facebook
activity.

People post on their own timelines with different intentions and frequencies (and subsequently, wind up appearing in your News Feed in varying amounts). Here are some of the types of information different kinds of people may tack up on the timeline:

- ✔ **Major life milestones:** Timelines come with specially allocated spaces for the big stuff: a recent move, a college graduation, a new job, or a wedding engagement. You can add past milestones at any time.

- ✔ **Detailed account:** On the other end of the extreme, you get people who tell the stories of their lives through the sum of all the little things. These are the friends who post to their timeline about their daily activities, thoughts, feelings, and plans. You know when they're relaxing at home, and when they're out to lunch; you know when they're about to leave work, and when they just left. You know when they have a piece of popcorn stuck between two teeth, and you'll be relieved to know when they get it out.

- ✔ **Something to share:** Some people reserve their timelines as a place to disseminate generally useful or enjoyable information to their friends. These people may post a link to an article they read or upload interesting mobile photos. They post news articles or write detailed accounts of things that just happened to them that others would find useful to know.

- ✔ **Meet up:** Some people use their timelines as a way to meet up with friends. They post when they're hanging out at a park or planning to visit a new city. If a friend is nearby and happens to read the post, they can have a serendipitous adventure together.

- ✔ **Go public:** You may see promotional posts on the timelines or Pages of celebrities or brands. Bands may remind their fans about an upcoming tour or album release. A company may let people know about an upcoming contest in which fans may want to participate.

Timelines wind up being one of the places you are most likely to reach out to a friend. Usually leaving a timeline post or a message that is visible on a timeline is a way of tapping a friend on the shoulder to remind him you're there. Sometimes people have entire conversations on each other's timelines.

To post on your friend's timeline, follow these steps:

1. **Go to his timeline.**

   Unless he has changed his privacy settings, he has a Share menu (previously known as the Publisher) at the top of his timeline, just like you have in yours.

2. **Click the type of post you want to leave.**

   You can post just text by clicking into the text box that says What's on Your Mind? You can click Photo to post a photo or video. Clicking the relevant icon opens up the same posting options that I cover in Chapter 4.

3. **Type out your comment to your friend.**

4. **When you're done, click Post.**

Although there aren't any rules around when you can or can't post on someone's timeline, one convention that has evolved over time is the Happy Birthday timeline post. Because people get reminded of birthdays on Facebook, it's pretty easy to pop on over to your friend's timeline and write a quick "Happy Birthday!" in honor of their day. It makes for a pretty sweet day on the receiving end as well.

Unlike the posts you write for your own timeline, you don't have specific privacy controls on the timeline posts you leave for friends. They may be seen by mutual friends (in their News Feeds), or by someone visiting your friend's timeline. If you're worried about who's going to see what you're writing, you may be better off sending a private message.

Sharing Is Caring

You've probably noticed the word *share* being used a lot on Facebook. Practically every time you're posting something, you're clicking a Share button. In addition to the Share menu at the top of your News Feed and timeline, Facebook has a specific Share feature, designed to make it easy to post and send content that you find both on Facebook and on the web.

Perhaps you've already noticed the little Share links all over Facebook. They show up on albums, individual photos, notes, events, groups, News Feed stories, and more. They help you share content quickly without having to copy and paste.

If you're looking at content on Facebook that you want to show someone, simply click the Share link near it. This opens the Share box, shown in Figure 7-13.

Figure 7-13:
Share here.

The Share box gives you five options for sharing. You can share

- ✓ **On your own timeline:** This option posts the content to your timeline the same way you would post a link or a photo from your Share menu. This means it will go into your friends' News Feeds as well.

- ✓ **On a friend's timeline:** This option is the same as copying and pasting a link into a timeline post you leave on your friend's timeline (but it's much easier than all that copy/paste nonsense).

- ✓ **In a group:** This option allows you to post the content to a group you are a member of. You can learn more about sharing with groups in Chapter 9.

- ✓ **On your Page** (for Page owners only): Pages don't have timelines yet, but if you are the admin of a Page — a Profile for non-people — you can share things as a post from your Page.

- ✓ **In a private Message:** This accomplishes the same thing as copying and pasting a link into a message to a friend. In other words, only the friend you send it to will see the link, whereas sharing via the timeline means anyone viewing your friend's timeline can also see the link. Messages are talked about in Chapter 8.

If you are choosing to share on your own timeline, you can click the drop-down menu to set privacy on the post.

After you've chosen how you want to share the item, you can write something about what you're sharing. If you are sharing an article, you can edit the preview that appears in the post. The Share box shows you the preview, and you can hover over the headline and teaser text to highlight them. Click the highlighted text to begin editing the preview. You can also choose a thumbnail to accompany most shared links. Use the arrow keys next to the words Choose a Thumbnail to see your options. If you don't like any of them, check the No Thumbnail box.

If you click Share on a friend's post, the friend who originally shared it is given a credit. So if you reshare an article, the post that your friends see will say Via *<Friend's Name>* so that everyone knows where you found it.

Comments and Likes

In addition to leaving a timeline post, you can interact with your friends on Facebook by commenting or liking the things they post. Frequently, people post things that you want to respond to. You may read an article they posted and want to respond to the viewpoint with one of your own. Their photos may be so beautiful that you just have to tell them. Or, like this status (shown in Figure 7-14), you may just need to point out something they hadn't considered.

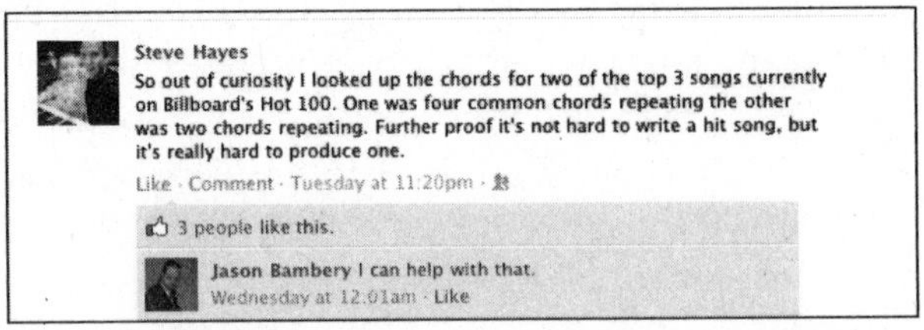

Figure 7-14:
Who doesn't
love a
good CGAF
progression?

> **Steve Hayes**
> So out of curiosity I looked up the chords for two of the top 3 songs currently on Billboard's Hot 100. One was four common chords repeating the other was two chords repeating. Further proof it's not hard to write a hit song, but it's really hard to produce one.
> Like · Comment · Tuesday at 11:20pm · 👥
>
> 👍 3 people like this.
>
> **Jason Bambery** I can help with that.
> Wednesday at 12:01am · Like

To comment on anything on Facebook, follow these steps:

1. **Click Comment.**

   This expands the comment box. Frequently, this box is already open, in which case you can simply . . .

2. **Click in the text box that appears.**

3. **Type what you want to say.**

4. **When you're finished, press Enter.**

Frequently, comment *threads,* or a series of comments, can become like an ongoing conversation. If you are responding to someone who commented above you, type the @ symbol (shift + 2) and start typing the name of the person you want to respond to. You'll be able to select their name from an auto-complete list that appears as you type.

After you comment on something, you'll be notified about subsequent comments so that you can keep up on the conversation. If you decide, on second thought, that maybe you didn't really want to say that thing, you can always delete your comment by hovering your mouse over it and clicking the X that appears. You can do the same when someone comments on something you've posted and you don't like what they have to say.

Liking

Sometimes, a status or photo or link is just good. You might not have a brilliant comment to make, or you might just feel a little lazy. A great example of this is news about someone's engagement. That's awesome, you might think. And then you look and notice about 50 comments saying simply, "Congrats!" Because, while the engagement is empirically good, there's not much to say beyond "Congratulations" or "I'm so happy for you" or "Mazel Tov!" That's where Liking comes in. Liking is just a fast way for you to let your friends know that you're paying attention and you like what you're seeing.

To Like something, simply click the word *Like* (it's a small blue link) below or next to the item. Your friend will be notified that you Like it. If you didn't mean it, really, click Unlike and your Like will be taken away.

Liking Pages

You can Like almost anything on Facebook. You can Like a photo or a status; you can even Like a comment on a photo or status. But there's a slight difference between Liking this sort of content and Liking Pages.

Pages are sort of official Profiles that companies, bands, and public figures make to represent themselves on Facebook. They mostly work like timelines (the key differences are covered in Chapter 13), except instead of friending or subscribing to Pages, you Like Pages.

This sort of liking has one big implication you should be aware of. It means you may start seeing posts and updates from the Page in your News Feed, alongside stories from your friends. These sorts of updates can be really interesting and cool if you're into the particular company or brand (for example, Old Spice Guy or *The New York Times*). If they start to bother you, you can always click the trusty ol' caron to adjust your settings, just like with people.

Commenting, Liking, and Sharing across the Internet

If you're a reader of blogs, you may notice that the comment and Like links and icons appear in lots of places. For example, at the top of blog posts on Jezebel, a Gawker Media blog, a little Like button counts the number of people who have Liked any particular post, as shown in Figure 7-15.

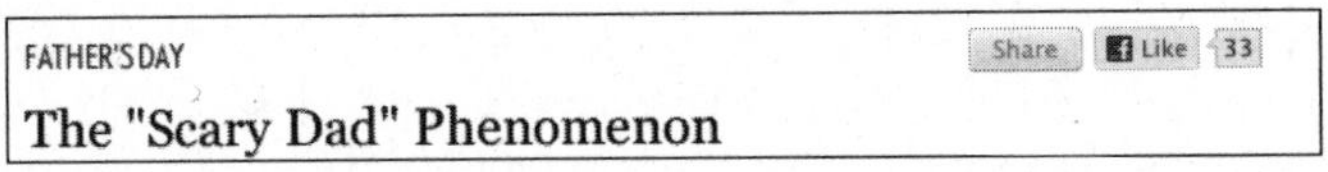

Figure 7-15:
Like this
post? Let
the blog
authors
know.

FATHER'S DAY	Share ◼ Like ⦁33
The "Scary Dad" Phenomenon	

You can Like posts on any website you're viewing, and those Likes will be recorded on your timeline and may appear in your friends' News Feeds or ticker. Through something called *Social Plug-ins*, Facebook allows other website developers to enable certain Facebook features like the Like button on their own websites. If you are currently logged in to Facebook, you may start noticing these buttons all over the Internet. This a really quick way to let your Facebook friends know about the most interesting content you've come across online.

Other websites have Share links that generate the same Facebook Share box that you find on Facebook itself. So from an entirely separate website, you can choose to post to a friend's timeline, your own timeline, to a group, or to a message thread.

Similarly, some blogs use Facebook comments as their primary commenting system. Figure 7-16 shows an example from TechCrunch, a blog about technology and Silicon Valley.

Figure 7-16:
Care to
comment?

The preview in Figure 7-16 should look familiar: it's you, your timeline picture, and a space for you to add a comment. It's just not on Facebook; it's on a different website. The way you comment is exactly the same, and in this case, you can choose whether you want your comment to be posted back to your Facebook timeline by checking or unchecking the Post to Facebook box.

Tracking the Past with Friendship Pages

After you've had a Facebook timeline for a while, you'll likely find that you've littered your closest friends' timeline Pages with posts, tagged photos, and invitations. Facebook offers a quick way to see all the communication you've shared with an individual friend over time with the Friendship Page feature.

A Friendship Page collects the timeline posts and replies you've shared with a friend, photos in which you're both tagged, a listing of event invitations to which you've both responded, and the list of mutual friends you share. The Friendship Page even supplies a default timeline picture.

To see the Friendship Page you share with one of your Friends, follow these steps:

1. **Enter the name of one of your friends in the Search box in the blue bar at the top of your timeline page.**

   Typically, you just need to type the first few letters of your friend's first name to generate a drop-down list of friends with similar names.

2. **Select your chosen friend's name in the drop-down list.**

   Look at the top-right corner of their timeline and click the gear icon that appears in the info section of their timeline.

3. **Click See Friendship from the drop-down menu.**

   Facebook automatically generates the Friendship Page, as shown in Figure 7-17, with the most recent posts shared between you and your friend at the top of the Page. Links to shared timeline posts, photos in which you're both tagged, events you both RSVP'd as attending, comments shared on status updates, and shared Likes appear on the left side of the screen. Note how similar this is to your own timeline — it's basically a timeline, but for two people instead of one.

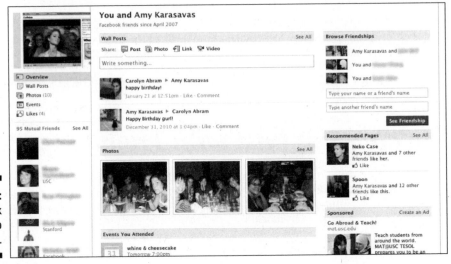

Figure 7-17:
A Facebook
Friendship
Page.

Chapter 8

Just Between You and Me: Facebook Messages

· ·

In This Chapter

▶ Realizing how Facebook's messaging systems differ from other systems

▶ Discovering how to send messages to friends

▶ Chatting with friends instantly

· ·

Chances are, you are someone who communicates with other people online. You may use e-mail all the time, or use instant messaging programs like AIM or Skype. If you have a smartphone, you probably check e-mail and text messages on it as well. Facebook has similar functionality and integrates into all of these programs. In other words, Facebook Messages stitches together e-mail, texting, and instant messaging with a Facebook twist.

One special component of Facebook's messaging system as opposed to other systems is that you no longer have to remember e-mail addresses, screen names, or handles. You just have to remember people's names. The other benefit is that your entire contact history with specific people is saved in one place. The most basic aspect of Facebook Messages is the more traditional message, so I start there in this chapter. After that, I go over the Inbox and what's special about it compared to your other Inboxes. Then, I talk about Facebook Chat before I finish up with a few advanced messaging features like importing e-mail and getting text message notifications set up.

Sending a Message

Figure 8-1 shows the most basic New Message dialog box. A few variations of this box exist, and I cover those as they arise. I generated this one by going to the Messages Inbox and clicking the New Message button.

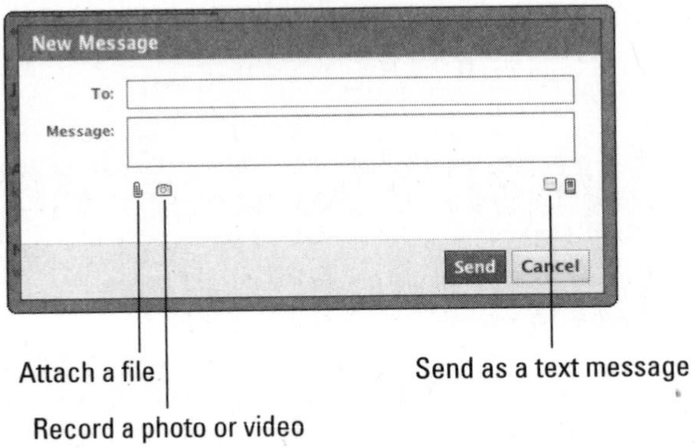

New Message

To:

Message:

Send   Cancel

Figure 8-1:
Send a new
message.

Attach a file   Send as a text message

Record a photo or video

This dialog box has only two fields for you to fill out: a To field and a message box where you type the text of your message. If you're used to using e-mail, this may strike you as a little odd because it doesn't have a cc, bcc, or subject line.

One trait of e-mail is how much it mirrors the formal letters people used to write, whereas now, we all spend a lot of time writing quick notes to the people we see the most. Except for work messages, most of our e-mails are sent to our spouses ("Don't forget dinner with the Joneses tonight,") and our friends ("What are you up to this weekend?"). Given that Facebook is all about friends, and very rarely used for work, you are not very likely to require that subject line.

To address your message, simply start typing the name of the person you are messaging into the To field. Facebook auto-completes with the names of your friends as you type. When you see the name you want, highlight it and click or press Enter. You can type more than one name if you want, and you can also type in the name of a Group you belong to or a Friend List you have created. (For more information on interacting with Groups, check out Chapter 9, and to learn how and when to create Friend Lists, go to Chapter 6.)

You can send a message to someone's e-mail address if they aren't yet on Facebook (although if they aren't yet, it's truly their loss). Simply type the full e-mail address. Separate multiple e-mail addresses with commas or semicolons.

Type your message into the message box. There are no rules around what goes here. Messages can be long or short, fat or skinny, silly or serious — whatever you have to say.

Three icons beneath the message box (refer to Figure 8-1) represent features that are entirely optional and fairly infrequently used, but just in case, here's what they are:

- ✔ **Attachment:** Much as it does in many e-mail programs, the paperclip icon signifies attaching files to a message. Clicking the icon opens up an interface for searching and selecting files from your computer's hard drive. You can attach photos, videos, documents, and so on.

- ✔ **Record Photo/Video:** If your computer has a built-in or attached webcam, click this icon to begin recording a video or taking a photo. Although most messages don't require this, such pictures can be very useful for saying hi to a family member who's far away.

- ✔ **Text Message:** This check box allows you to choose to send a message to a friend as a text message to their phone if it's possible. If you're trying to reach someone *right now*, this can be pretty useful. Don't worry about your friend's messaging charges. This only works if they've opted in to receive these texts from Facebook.

When you're done writing your message, just click Send and be on your way. Your friend will receive the e-mail in their Facebook Inbox, as well as being notified with a little red flag on their Home page. Depending on their account settings, they may also receive an e-mail in their e-mail Inbox letting them know about a message in their Facebook Inbox (yes, it's a little redundant — oh, well).

Messaging Non-Friends

You can message friends on Facebook or people not on Facebook via their e-mail addresses. You can also message a person who is on Facebook even if they're not a friend (if that person's privacy settings allow it). This is particularly helpful when you encounter someone on Facebook whom you'd like to say something to, but are not sure whether you want to add her as a friend. Here are a few examples:

- ✔ **Identification:** Say you search for an old friend and find three people with the same name. One Profile has a clear picture of someone who is definitely not your friend. The second person is in the Dallas network, and you're sure your friend has never lived in Dallas. The third Profile doesn't have a picture, just a placeholder silhouette. From the search results page, you can click Send Message next to the person with the placeholder Profile picture and ask whether you know each other.

- ✔ **Friend of a friend:** For most features on Facebook, you need to be someone's friend or at least in someone's network in order to interact with them in any meaningful way. However, sometimes you have legitimate reasons to contact someone who really doesn't belong on your Friend List. For these interactions, Facebook messaging is perfect.

✔ **Getting to know you:** Pretend you've just joined a new company and you know very few people. Or to really experience this example, go join a new company. You can use Search to find other people at the company whom you'd like to get to know or ask a question, and send them a message on Facebook.

Messaging a non-friend should be treated with caution. If you message non-friends too often, or too many people report your message as unsolicited or unwanted, your account is automatically flagged by Facebook. People who send too many unsolicited messages may have their accounts blocked or permanently disabled. If every person on Facebook could message everyone else, Inboxes would start to fill with impersonal or unwanted messages, eventually making the Inbox too messy to be functional.

You've Got Mail!

Chances are if you send out a message, pretty soon you'll get a little red flag on your Home page letting you know that you've received a new message. When you click the notification, you'll be taken directly to the conversation.

On Facebook, the series of messages between two people is called a *conversation* or *thread*. This is because when you look at a message, it doesn't stand alone; rather, it is added to the bottom of all the messages, chats, and texts you have ever sent each other through Facebook.

Anatomy of a conversation between you and a friend

In Figure 8-2, you can see a conversation between my friend Amy and me.

The most important thing to notice is that the most recent message is on the bottom of the page. Unlike News Feed or the Wall, you scroll up to see older messages. In this case, if you keep scrolling up, you'd see an ongoing conversation that started three years ago, when Carolyn and Amy first became Facebook friends.

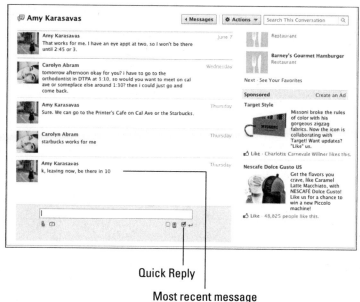

Figure 8-2:
Carolyn
and Amy
converse on
Facebook.

Quick Reply

Most recent message

Although the most recent part of this conversation is about meeting up to get coffee, topics in this conversation have ranged from team logos to information about various coffee shops where the two of us could meet. Unlike e-mail, which is sorted by *what* you're talking about (the subject line), Facebook only sorts by *who* you're talking to.

You may not always be messaging a friend from your computer. You may message a friend from your phone or chat via Facebook Chat (which we cover in the "Chat" section of this chapter). No matter where the message is sent from, it's recorded in this ongoing conversation. Small icons representing a mobile phone, a chat bubble, or an e-mail envelope designate where each message came from, but in reality, that's not important. What's important is *who* you're talking to.

At the bottom of your conversation, below the most recent message, is the message composer. The message box is the same as the one just covered in the Sending Messages section; however, the To field is missing. This is because whom the message is to is already clear. The conversation is with Amy, so any messages sent are going to Amy.

The smaller options are the same, and there is one additional option at the bottom of the conversation. This is definitely a good one to know: the Quick Reply option.

The Quick Reply option (refer to Figure 8-2) allows you to send messages simply by pressing Enter. Some people love this; other people hate it. To turn it on, leave the Quick Reply box checked. If your need a line break in whatever you're writing, press Shift+Enter. Uncheck the box to turn it off. After you do that, a Reply button appears. You can then click that to send your message.

At the top of your conversation page are two buttons (the Messages button and the Actions button) and a search box. The Messages button brings you back to the main Messages Inbox (which is covered in the next section). The Actions button features a drop-down list, as shown in Figure 8-3, with the following options:

Figure 8-3:
Actions to choose for your conversation.

✔ **Mark as Unread:** Choose Mark as Unread to mark the conversation as having unread messages (makes sense, right?). After you choose this option, the main Messages Inbox appears, and the conversation is highlighted in blue.

✔ **Forward:** Choose Forward to send some or all messages from this conversation to other people. Choosing this allows you to select certain messages via check boxes so that you don't accidentally send the whole conversation to another friend.

✔ **Open in Chat:** Opening a message thread in Chat allows you to send messages back and forth with your friend while you're browsing Facebook. It opens a small Chat box (more on that later) at the bottom of the screen. You can then chat with your friend even when you leave the Inbox.

✔ **Archive:** Choose Archive to send your conversation to the archives. Remember, this moves the conversation out of your main Messages Inbox until a new message is sent.

✔ **Delete Messages:** Like forwarding a message, this option allows you to delete some (or all) of the messages from any given conversation. After a message is deleted, you can never get it back.

Just because you have deleted a message doesn't mean your friend has deleted it. So if you send some private information and then delete the message, your friend can still see that information unless he deletes it as well.

✔ **Report as Spam:** This usually doesn't apply to messages you receive from friends, but if you get spam from someone, choose Report as Spam, and the message is moved to a Junk Folder, which is a part of your "Other Inbox."

✔ **Report/Block User:** If someone harasses you through Facebook Messages or makes you uncomfortable, you can block her from being able to contact you and report her to Facebook for her behavior. People who are repeatedly reported for this sort of harassment may be banned from Facebook.

✔ **Move to Other:** The Other Inbox is for messages that aren't as important as your messages from friends. If a conversation with someone doesn't really deserve top billing among the messages you really care about, you can relocate it to the Other Inbox, which we discuss in the "The Other Inbox" section, later in this chapter.

Anatomy of a conversation among many people

You can message more than one person at a time. Doing so creates new conversation between all of the people you message. Everyone can see and reply to the message. So if you send a message to Mike, Molly, and Megan, a new conversation is created. When you're looking at that conversation, you can see all of the messages that have been sent by all the people involved. Figure 8-4 shows a conversation among several friends trying to pick out a location for dinner.

Much like the individual conversation, you can read this exchange from top to bottom, with the most recent message appearing at the bottom of the page. You can scroll up to read earlier messages.

As you're reading, you can see who said what by looking at the names and Profile pictures identifying each message. Each message is separated and has a timestamp so you can see when it was sent.

Below the most recent message is a box for replying. The main thing to remember about group conversations is that you cannot reply individually to members of the conversation. When you reply, all members of the conversation see your reply.

At the top of the page, just like with a one-on-one conversation, is the Messages button to return to the Messages Inbox, the search box to search through the conversation for particular content, and the Actions button with a drop-down list.

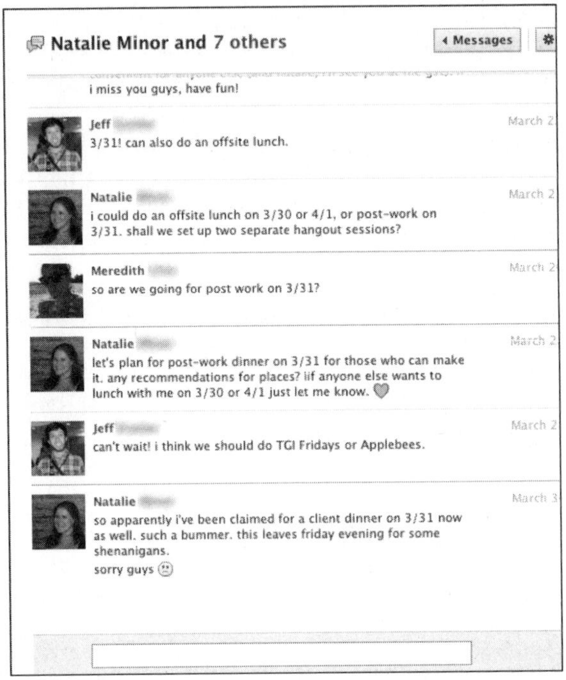

Figure 8-4:
A group
of friends
conversing.

Along with options to mark messages as unread, forward messages, archive messages, delete messages, report as spam, block users, and move to the Other Inbox, the Actions drop-down list for group conversations offers a couple more options not included for individual conversations:

- ✔ **Add People:** If you feel that someone has been left out of the conversation, or if you suddenly realize he should be part of the conversation, choose this to add him. You're asked to enter the name(s) of the person you want to add. The person added can see the entire conversation history, even though he wasn't added until the middle of the conversation.

- ✔ **Leave Conversation:** If a conversation isn't interesting to you anymore, choose this to leave it. If you do leave a conversation, the other people on the thread will see a small notice that you have left.

Inbox

After you're comfortable sending and receiving messages to and from your friends, it's time to learn about the Inbox, where all your messages are collected for easy viewing at any time. Facebook's Inbox is organized a bit differently from traditional e-mail Inboxes.

Most significantly, conversations you are having with friends are kept separate from conversations you are having with non-friends, and messages you receive from Pages, Events, or Groups.

Think about all the things you might receive daily in your e-mail Inbox: You probably get catch-up newsy e-mails from a friend alongside bank statements, newsletters, coupon offerings, and quick notes to the people you might be seeing socially this week. Although these all may be important to you in one way or another, the Facebook assumption is that the ones you care about most are the ones from the people you know best — your family and your friends. The Facebook twist on e-mail is a bias toward your Facebook friends, toward creating a *social Inbox*.

To understand how Facebook Messages work, take a look at how your Messages Inbox is organized on the page. First, navigate to the Messages Inbox from your Home page by clicking Messages in the left side menu. Figure 8-5 offers a snapshot of the Dummies man Inbox.

Figure 8-5:
Welcome to
Facebook
Messages.

You should take note of and understand five segments of Facebook Messages:

- **Messages Inbox:** The main part of this page is dedicated to — you guessed it — your actual messages.

- **New Message button:** Click the New Message button to start writing a new message to a friend.

✔ **Search Messages:** Use this box to find a message from a specific friend or a specific word in the message.

✔ **Left hand menu:** The left side menu displays a number with the amount of unread messages waiting for you. When you click the Messages menu item, the navigation expands to include the Other option.

✔ **Footer area:** Links at the bottom of the page help with more advanced parts of the Inbox.

The Messages Inbox

In the middle column of the page, under the Messages heading, are all of your conversations, organized by friends. Your conversations to and from friends don't require subject lines because they aren't, unlike your e-mail, organized by subject. Instead, these conversations collect messages shared by the person (or people) talking.

Like your e-mail Inbox, your conversations are organized from most recent near the top to older ones toward the bottom of the page. Also at the bottom of the page are little arrows that allow you to page backward through your entire message history. Conversations with unread messages are highlighted in blue.

Figure 8-6 shows a close-up of two conversations in the Messages Inbox. The bottom one is a conversation among many people. You can see the text of the most recent message and the Profile picture of the most recent sender. The top one is a one-on-one conversation with a single friend. A little gray arrow appears next to the text preview to show that I sent the last message. On the right side are the conversation's timestamp and two icons:

Figure 8-6:
Conversation
previews
in the
Messages
Inbox.

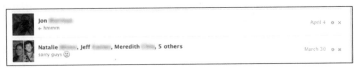

✔ The **conversation's timestamp** is marked on the right side of the conversation preview in gray. This timestamp tells you how long ago the most recent message in the conversation was sent.

✔ The **little circular button** allows you to mark a conversation as read or unread.

✔ The **little X icon** allows you to archive a conversation. *Archiving* conversations allows you to move them to a different part of your Inbox until a later time, when they become relevant to you again.

The Other Inbox

If Facebook Messages brings your social messages front and center, the Other Inbox is for, well, all that other stuff. This might include messages from people you don't know, group messages from events you were invited to, updates from Pages you like, and so on. Figure 8-7 shows an Other Inbox.

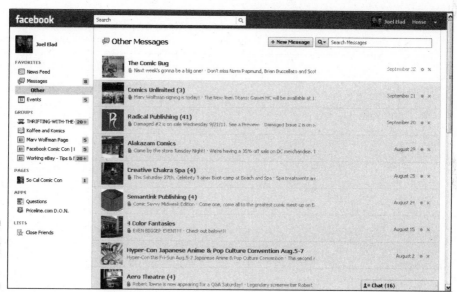

Figure 8-7:
Other stuff goes here.

In many ways, the Other Inbox is exactly like your main Messages Inbox. The conversations are organized by person, Page, or Event. Conversations with unread messages are highlighted in blue. When you click through to view a message, you'll see the most recent messages first.

The biggest difference between the main Inbox and the Other Inbox is that if you have an unread count of messages in your Other Inbox, that number goes away as soon as you view the list of Other Messages. In other words, you can more easily clear all the unread Other Messages just by clicking the

Messages tab from the left side menu and then clicking the Other tab that appears below the Messages tab.

If you have a conversation in Other Messages that you want to be more prominent, click into the conversation, click the Actions button to open the drop-down list, and choose Move to Messages. All the other options are the same as the conversations in your main Messages Inbox.

You can't reply to messages sent by an event or Page. Those are one-way communications. You need to go to the Walls or send individual messages to administrators of those events or Pages if you want to get in touch. You can learn more about interacting with Pages in Chapter 13.

Searching the Inbox

If you're as popular as we suspect you are, your messages add up over time. And if you don't want to go paging through tons of messages to find the one you're looking for, you need a faster way to get to the information you want. That's why at the top of the Messages Inbox, you'll notice a search box. You can search for people's names or for the content of messages.

For example, say you want to find the address of a park where you're meeting with some friends to play Frisbee and you organized this whole outing through Facebook Messages. You can search for the name of the friend(s) on the conversation. As you do this, Facebook tries to auto-complete your friend's name and shows you snippets of recent conversations with her. Alternatively, you type *Frisbee* in the search box and press Enter to get a list of results.

Additionally, you can access advanced search options (see Figure 8-8) by clicking the magnifying glass icon on the left side of the search box to display a drop-down list with the following:

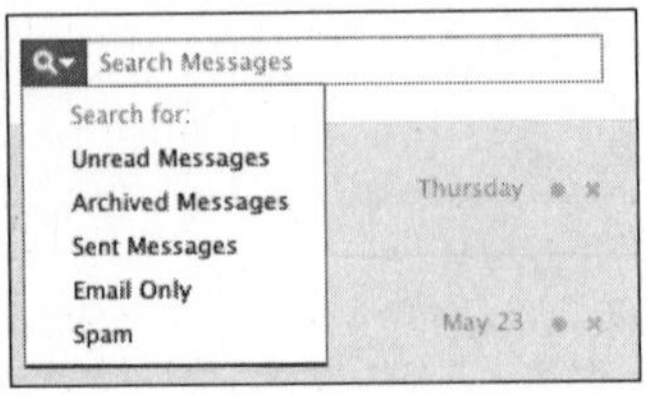

Figure 8-8:
Advanced
search
options
for the
Messages
Inbox.

- ✔ **Unread Messages:** This searches for your search terms in unread messages.

- ✔ **Archived Messages:** This searches your archived messages for the search terms you enter.

- ✔ **Sent Messages:** This searches the messages you have sent to other people for your search terms.

- ✔ **E-mail Only:** This looks only at messages that have come in via e-mail addresses.

- ✔ **Spam:** This searches any messages that have been previously marked as Junk or Spam.

You can also search within a conversation for specific terms. From within the conversation, the search box is in the same place on the page as in the main Messages Inbox; the only difference is that the search box says Search This Conversation instead of Search Messages.

Advanced Inbox

From the main Messages Inbox, you can scroll to the bottom of the page where you see two collections of links:

- ✔ **View section:** This allows you to get to your unread messages or your archived messages whenever you want.

- ✔ **Setup links:** These help you get started on more advanced Inbox options. You can set up text messaging so your messages can go straight to your phone, and you can also create a @facebook.com e-mail address so that your e-mails can go into your Facebook Inbox as well.

If you do choose to claim your Facebook e-mail, Facebook will display available options based on your name. You can also enter another alias that you like. Click Activate Email to finish this process.

Chat

Sometimes you've got something to say to someone, and you've got to say it now. If that someone is not sitting right next to you, try sending her an instant message through Facebook Chat. Chat allows you to see which friends are online at the same time you are, and then enables you to send quick messages back and forth with any one of those people, or have multiple simultaneous conversations with different friends.

Facebook doesn't discriminate when it comes to the way you talk to your friends. Whether a message or a chat, it all goes into your conversation history in your Messages Inbox.

You'll find Chat in the bottom-right corner of any page on Facebook. You'll also find a preview of online friends in the left column of your Home page.

Receiving and sending Chats

Chat is meant to be quick and easy to use. Receiving Chats is simply a matter of being online. When a friend sends you a chat, a small window pops up next to the Chat bar in the bottom right of your screen, as shown in Figure 8-9.

Figure 8-9:
Someone
chatted
with you!

To send a chat message back to them, simply click into the text field at the bottom of the chat window, start typing, and press Enter when you're done. Your message appears below your friend's, just as it does with most IM services.

Because Chat and regular messages are integrated, when you begin a new chat with someone, your chat history is populated with your historical conversations, so your chat window tends to look a lot like a message thread.

Each new chat window lines up next to the other open ones. You can close ones that are not currently active by clicking the X in the bottom bar. You can also go to the message history in your Inbox by clicking the Go to Conversation icon in the bottom bar (it looks like a little square).

To start a new chat with someone, you just need to select their name from the Chat menu. This opens a chat window that you can type in.

Chat options

At the top of each chat window or chat box is a blue bar displaying the name of the person you're chatting with and two or three icons. The one you might or might not have is the video icon, which is covered shortly. The two you will definitely have are the gear icon and the x icon.

The X, farthest to the right, simply allows you to close the chat window at any time. Don't worry about losing the contents of your conversation. Everything said is saved into your Inbox.

The Gear icon, when clicked, opens up a menu of options. These options include:

- ✔ **See Full Conversation:** Clicking this brings you to a view of your entire conversation history.

- ✔ **Clear Window:** If you find yourself wading through too much history at a time, clicking this will give you a blank slate of a chat window. This won't delete the contents permanently, though. Your full message history is still saved in your Inbox.

- ✔ **Add Friends to Chat...:** If you're discussing something with a friend and think that you need the opinion of someone else, you can add them to the chat, and you can all talk as a group (more info in the next section).

- ✔ **Report as Spam...:** If you're getting odd messages from a friend promoting something they wouldn't normally promote, there's a chance their account was *phished*, meaning someone gained access to it that shouldn't have. Report the spam messages to protect yourself, your friend, and other users from having the same thing happen to them.

Group Chat

To get a group chat going, follow these steps:

1. **Begin a chat with a friend by selecting their name from the Chat menu.**

   This opens a Chat window.

2. **Click the Gear icon to open the Chat Options menu.**

3. **Click the Add Friends to Chat option.**

   This opens a text box at the top of your existing Chat window.

4. **Type the name of the friend you want to add into this text box.**

   Facebook auto-completes as you type. As soon as you see your friend's name appear, you can select it. You can add more than one friend at this time if you want.

5. **Click Done.**

   This opens an entirely new Chat window for the group conversation. Any messages sent in that Chat menu are sent to all participants.

The Group Chat window has an additional icon, which may look similar to the Group Icon. Click this icon at any point to add even more participants to your Group Chat.

Video Chat

Video Chat is a fairly new addition to Facebook, which is why you might or might not see the video camera icon at the top of each Chat window. Facebook's Video Chat is actually powered by Skype, an Internet telephone service. If you see the video icon, you can initiate Video Chat with your friends:

1. **Begin a chat with a friend by selecting their name from the Chat menu.**

   This opens a Chat window.

2. **Click the video icon to begin Video Chat.**

   If you've already set up video calling, this begins the call. A pop-up window appears, letting you know that Facebook is calling your friend.

   If you haven't yet used video calling, a pop-up window appears, asking you if you want to set up video calling.

3. **Click Set Up.**

   This initiates a file download. Each web browser and operating system may have slightly different instructions. In general, you need to save the file to your hard drive and run it to complete the set-up.

   After set-up is complete, a new pop-up window appears telling you that Facebook is calling your friend.

4. **Wait for your friend to pick up.**

   When he does, video of him appears in a new window above Facebook. Video of you (what your friend is seeing) appears in the upper corner of this window.

5. **To end the call, close the window.**

Video Chat assumes both people have webcams either built in or installed in their computers. If you don't have a webcam, Video Chat isn't really for you.

Anatomy of the Chat menu

Clicking the chat bar in the bottom-right corner reveals the Chat menu shown in Figure 8-10. Depending on the width of your browser window, this menu may always be open.

Figure 8-10:
The Chat menu.

Search online friends

By default, the Chat menu displays the friends you message and chat with most often, in alphabetical order. A green dot next to their name means they are active on Facebook. A blue crescent moons means they are logged in but aren't currently active. No icon means they aren't currently logged in.

At the bottom of the Chat menu is a search bar. To quickly find the friend with whom you want to chat, or to see if that friend is even online, start typing that friend's name in the search box at the bottom of the Chat menu. As you type, the list of Online Friends narrows to only those with names who match what you've typed. After you see the friend you were looking for, click the name to start chatting. If you get a Friend not Found on Chat notice, it means that person has set her status to offline or isn't signed in to Facebook.

What's a Poke?

On Friends' Profiles, you see a Poke option in the drop-down option of the Gear button (next to the Message button). Since Facebook began, the most common question I've heard is, "What's a Poke?" And since that time, the answer has been, "I don't really know."

I can tell you what it *does,* but I can't tell you what it *is*; it can mean something different to everyone. In some cases, Poke is a form of flirtation. Other times, Poke may mean a genuine *thinking-of-you.* Some people do it just to say, "Hi."

Say your wife Pokes you (maybe her Poke means, "Take out the trash, honey"). The next time you log in to Facebook, on the right side of your Home page, you see a message in the top-right corner of your screen and a notice that *<Your Wife's Name>* poked you. If you click that notice, you have the following options: Poke Back or click the X. Poking Back means she'll see the same notice you got the next time she logs in (except with your name instead of hers). Clicking the X next to the Poke Back option simply removes the notice from your Home page. If you sense the potential for an endless loop, you sense right.

At the top of the Chat menu is the gear icon that signifies an options menu. The top two options are ones that are either on (signified by a check mark) or off. When Available to Chat is on, people can send you instant messages via chat. Turn it off if you don't like interruptions. When Chat Sounds is on, you hear a little noise whenever you receive chats.

The third option, Limit Availability, allows you to fine-tune who can chat with you. Choosing this option brings up the Limit Availability on Chat window, shown in Figure 8-11.

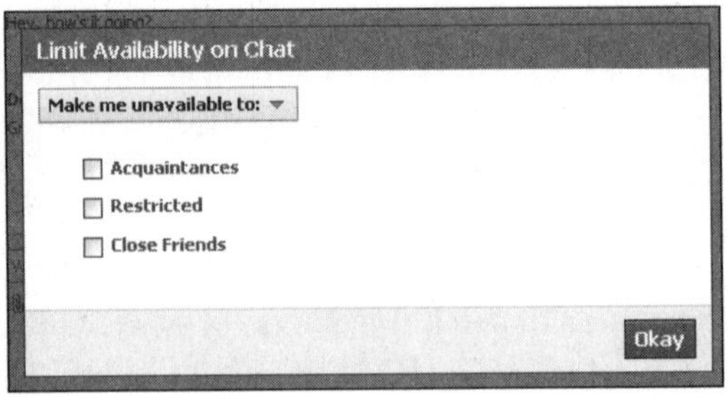

Figure 8-11: Choose who can chat with you.

Chapter 9

Creating and Managing Groups on Facebook

By now, you've probably individually found and linked yourself to your friends. Although they might be more or less equal in your eyes, they are not all the same. I once attempted to make a diagram of my friends and wound up with many categories: Frisbee friends, college friends, grad school friends, hiking friends, friends from work. But then it turned out there were college Frisbee friends, Frisbee friends from work, an unrelated Frisbee team from last year, and, well, you get the idea.

In other words, groups of people exist for all of us in real life. If only there was a way to represent these groups on Facebook . . . why hello, Groups, we were just looking for you.

Groups on Facebook are designed to help you communicate with real-world groups of people, whether that's a big group like Ottawa University's Class of 1958 reunion or a small group like Beach Trip Next Weekend. Like everything on Facebook, you decide who can participate and what they can see.

This chapter starts with the basics: creating Groups, inviting your friends to join, and interacting with them through Groups. From there, I cover the dynamics of managing your Groups through things like notifications and other settings.

Getting Going with Groups

Groups function in large part like a Profile owned by all the people who are part of the Group. To get started with Groups, create one. As your Friend List grows, and as you get involved in more and more activities on and off Facebook, it's inevitable that at some point you will want to create a Group to make sharing with certain people easier. For example, if you like to talk with certain people about certain types of news or if you want to share photos just with family, you can create a Group to facilitate these activities.

Creating your own Groups

As a Group's creator, you're by default the *Group administrator,* which means that you write the Group's information, control its privacy settings, and generally keep it running smoothly. You can also promote other members of the Group to administrators to grant them the same privileges and then they can help you with these responsibilities.

Here are the steps you follow to create a Group:

1. **Click Create Group from the left side menu.**

   The Create Group box appears (see Figure 9-1).

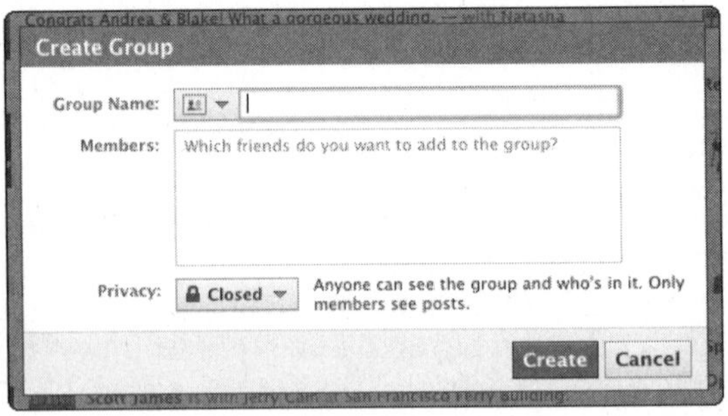

Figure 9-1:
The Create
Group box.

2. **Enter a Group name into the Group Name field.**

   Choose something descriptive, if possible, so when you add people to it, they'll know what they are getting into.

3. **(Optional) Click the arrow next to the Groups Icon (beside the Group Name field) and then click an icon to select it for your Group.**

   You see a variety of icon options, as shown in Figure 9-2. You may find one that represents your Group perfectly. If you don't like any of these, or don't feel like picking, you can always just go with the default silhouette of two people.

Figure 9-2:
Icon-o-rama.

4. **Add members by typing their names into the Members field.**

   At this time, you can add only friends as members. Facebook tries to auto-complete your friends' names as you type. When you see the name you want, press Enter to select it. You can add as many — or as few — friends as you like. If you forget someone, you can always add them later.

5. **Choose the privacy level for your Group.**

   There are three privacy options for Groups:

   - **Open:** Open Groups are entirely available to the public. Anyone can join simply by clicking a join button; anyone can see all the content the Group posts. This type of Group is best for a very public organization that wants to make it easy for people to join and contribute.

   - **Closed:** By default, your Group is set to closed. This means that anyone can see the list of members, but only members can see the content posted to the Group by its members. People can request to join the Group, but admins (like you) need to approve that request before they can see Group info.

   - **Secret:** Secret Groups are virtually invisible on the site to people who haven't been added to the Group. No one but members can see the member list and the content posted. But remember, people who have been added to the Group can also add their friends, so if you are protecting state secrets, you might want to find a more secure method. We recommend carrier pigeons.

6. **Click Create.**

   Congrats, your Group has been created. You can now start sharing!

Sharing with your Group

The whole point of creating or joining a Group is to enable communication, so get started communicating! Ways that you can get involved include posting on the Group Wall, chatting with Group members, creating Docs and Events, and commenting on Group posts.

Posting to the Group Wall is the same as posting to your own Wall or to a friend's Wall. Clicking what you want to share (Post, Photo/Video, or Question) and then following the onscreen prompts is all you have to do to put your content out there.

The important thing to remember is that when you share something from a Group, you're sharing it only with the members of that Group.

If you're a member of a Group, you need to remember that you might not be friends with everyone in the Group. In a big Group, you might actually be sharing with more people who couldn't typically see the things you post.

Although the Publisher works almost the same way across Facebook, all the options are briefly explained here in the context of Groups.

Write Post

Posts are status updates that you share only with the members of a Group (unless the Group is open, in which case anyone can see your post). You might post an update just to say hi or to start a discussion with Group members. To write a post, follow these steps:

1. **Click into the Write Something text box at the top of the Group page (as shown in Figure 9-3).**

   After you click into the box, you see the Post button appear below the text box along with buttons to indicate where you are and which other Facebook members are with you.

Figure 9-3:
What's on
your mind?

> 📝 Write Post 🖼 Add Photo / Video 📊 Ask Question
>
> Write something...

2. **Type whatever you want to say into the box.**

   For the Dummies Group, this might be something like "What do people think of the new Groups?" or "Does anyone know how I can start Group Chat?"

3. **Click Post.**

   Your post appears on the Group wall, and Group members see it in their notifications and possibly in their News Feeds.

If you want to share a link, usually some sort of article, video, or other online content that you want the Group to see, simply type or paste in the complete link to whatever you want to share, along with your thoughts or opinions, into the text box for writing a Post.

Photo or Video

Sometimes, writing a post won't do for the current circumstances. For example, if Carolyn wants her fellow dummies to know that she received the most recent edition of *Facebook For Dummies*, she could tell them by writing a post to the effect of "Hey, dummies, I got my copy of the new book." Or, she could *show* them by doing the following:

1. **Click Photo/Video in the Publisher (at the top of the Group page).**

   The Photo Publisher appears, as shown in Figure 9-4.

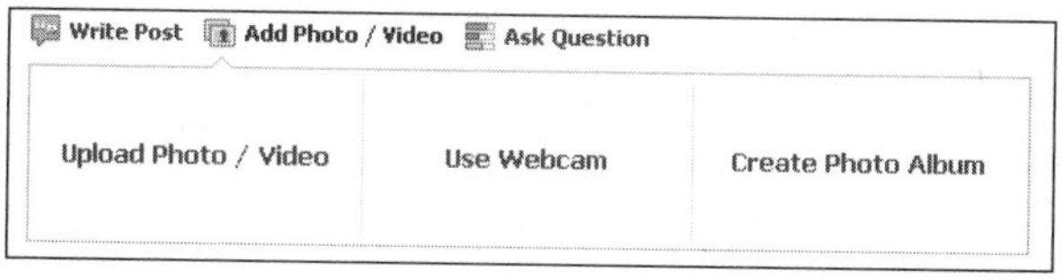

Figure 9-4:
Post a photo
to your
Group.

🖳 Write Post	🖻 Add Photo / Video	📇 Ask Question
Upload Photo / Video	Use Webcam	Create Photo Album

2. **Click Use Webcam (only if you have a webcam).**

3. **Pose for the camera.**

   Remember to smile.

4. **(Optional) Add a comment about the photo in the Say Something box.**

5. **Click Post.**

   The post appears on the Group Wall, and all members (depending on notification settings) are notified about your post. They can then comment and be part of what you are sharing.

Similar to photos, sometimes videos are simply meant to be shared. Maybe you have a video from your most recent Ultimate Frisbee game or from a family trip. This is a great way to share it just with family members and to be certain they are able to see it. To post a video, follow these steps:

1. **Click Photo/Video in the Publisher at the top of the Group Wall.**

2. **Select either Use Webcam (only if you have a webcam) or Upload Photo/Video.**

   For this example, say you want to upload a video you recorded at another time. Clicking Upload Photo/Video expands the Publisher, as shown in Figure 9-5.

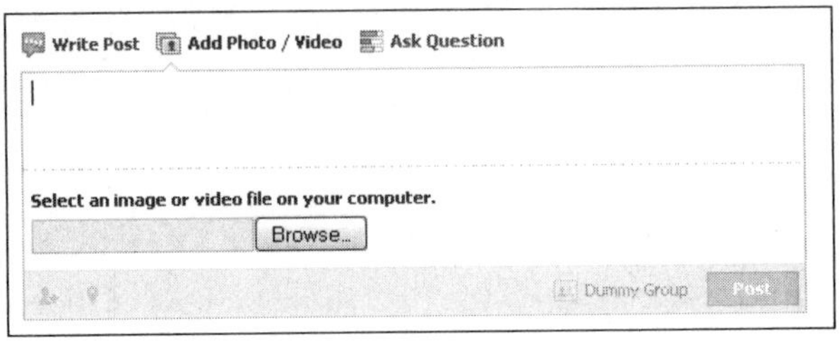

Figure 9-5:
Upload a
video from
your
computer.

3. **Click Browse.**

   A dialog box appears that allows you to select a file from your computer.

4. **Navigate to the video you want and click Select.**

5. **(Optional) Type some thoughts into the box above the Browse button.**

   You might want to explain why you thought the video would be of interest to your fellow members. Or you can say nothing and let the video speak for itself.

6. **Click Post.**

   The video then appears on the Group Wall and in members' notifications and News Feeds.

Ask Question

Using the Question feature is great for polling a Group of people about choices big and small. To poll your Group, follow these steps:

1. **Click Ask Question in the Publisher at the top of the Group Wall.**

   The Question Publisher appears.

2. **Type your question into the Ask Something box.**

3. **Click the Add Poll Options link beneath the text box.**

   This expands the poll options, as shown in Figure 9-6.

4. **Type your first option into the first Add an Option box.**

   Facebook auto-completes these boxes as you type and assumes you are typing in a place, brands, article titles, or other non-friend entities.

5. **Add more options until you're finished.**

   Facebook keeps adding more boxes as you fill up these first few, so just stop when you're ready.

6. **Choose whether people can add more options.**

   A check box labeled Allow Anyone to Add Options controls this setting. Allowing this means people can add more answers to a Poll (so if before people could only choose Dog or Cat, Group members may be able to add Hedgehog as an option) Depending on how big your Group is, this may or may not be a significant choice.

7. **Click Post.**

The question then appears on the Group Wall and in member's notifications and News Feeds. They will be able to vote, Like, or comment on the Question.

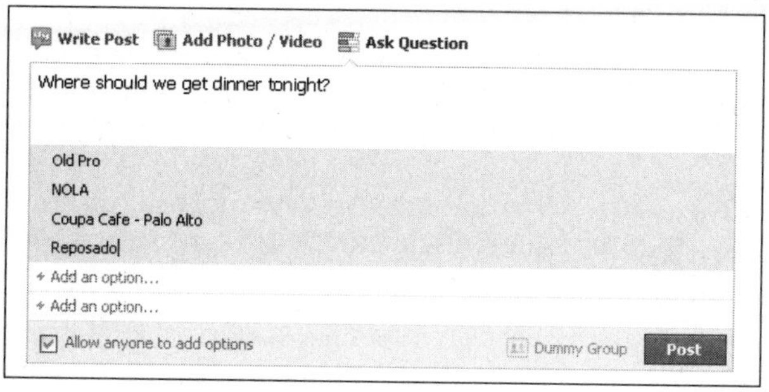

Figure 9-6:
You've got questions? Facebook has answers.

Docs

If you are part of a Group that has real-world things to accomplish — for example, a literary magazine to put out or a wedding welcome letter to create with your family — Docs help you collaborate on these documents. To start a new Doc, click the Docs link below the Group name header in the middle of the screen, create a title (see Figure 9-7), add any content you want, and click Create Doc.

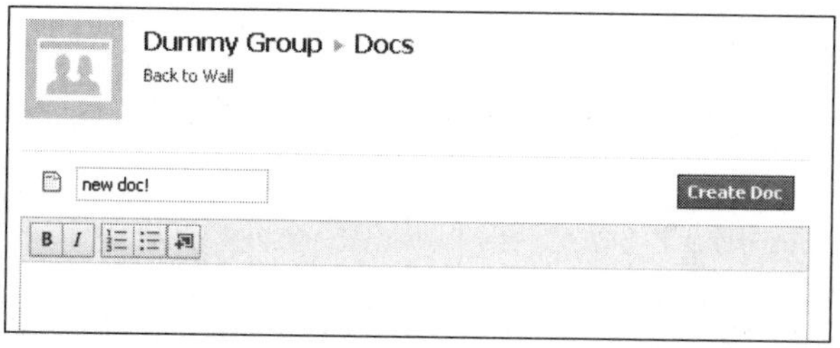

Figure 9-7:
What's up, Doc?

You can always find Docs that have been created by clicking the Doc link below the Group header name in the middle of the screen. Find the Document you'd like to change from the list of documents displayed on the screen and then click the Edit Doc link below its title. You can also leave comments on Docs in order to let Group members know what you liked or didn't like about it.

REMEMBER Docs are a *collaborative* way to write something: As with a wiki, anyone who is a member of the Group can edit and delete Docs that have been created. (A *wiki* is a website that anyone can make changes to. Probably the most famous example is Wikipedia.) So if you've written something you don't want changed in any way, keep it on your own computer.

Event

Your Group may be based around an activity, so Facebook makes it easy for people to plan Events for Group members, whether it's a game of pick-up or a family reunion. To create an Event, follow these steps:

1. **Click the drop-down arrow next to the Gear button on the right side of the Group page and then click the Create an Event link from the list that appears.**

   This takes you to the Create an Event page, shown in Figure 9-8.

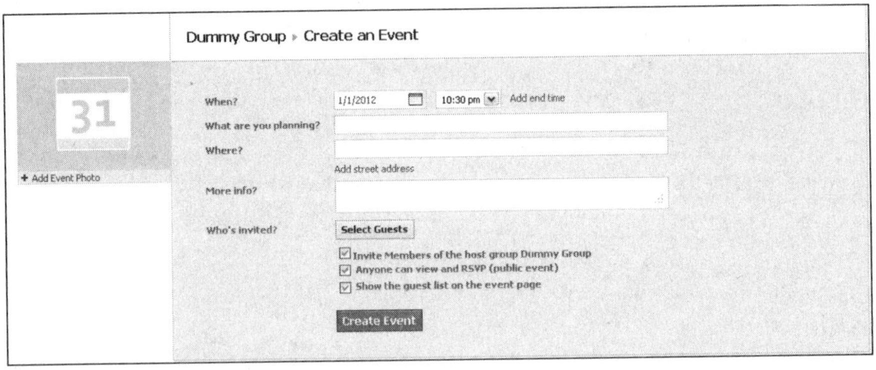

Figure 9-8: Create an Event for Group members.

> Dummy Group ▸ Create an Event
>
> **31**
> + Add Event Photo
>
> When? 1/1/2012 📅 10:30 pm ▼ Add end time
> What are you planning?
> Where?
>   Add street address
> More info?
> Who's invited? Select Guests
>   ☑ Invite Members of the host group Dummy Group
>   ☑ Anyone can view and RSVP (public event)
>   ☑ Show the guest list on the event page
>   Create Event

2. **Fill out the Event information.**

   Give the Event a name, a date and time, and location. For more information about planning Events, check out Chapter 11.

3. **Choose whom you want to invite.**

   By default, an option to Invite Members of the host Group *<Group Name>* is checked. You can also select additional friends from your Friend List to invite.

4. **Click Create Event.**

All members of your Group are invited to your event. As the Event creator, you are automatically listed as attending. The post appears in members' News Feeds and notifications. To RSVP to a Group Event, follow these steps:

1. **Click the Event name on the Group Wall.**

   This takes you to the Event Home page, which shows you more information about the Event, including who has already RSVPed.

2. **Choose I'm Attending, Maybe, or No.**

   All these options are big blue buttons on the right side of the page. To learn more about how to interact with the Event as it draws near, check out Chapter 11.

Chat

One of the most exciting features of Groups is the ability to talk in real-time with other Group members, so you can do something like ask when people are leaving for that Ultimate game.

To chat, simply click the drop-down arrow next to the Gear button on the right side of the Group Home page and then click the Chat with Group link from that drop-down list. This pops open a Chat box, as shown in Figure 9-9.

Figure 9-9:
Chat with Group members.

If you don't want to be bothered, you can always go offline to that Group of people by closing the Chat window.

Comment on posts

Groups are all about getting involved, so don't be afraid to Comment on — or Like or Subscribe to — the posts your friends and fellow members leave on the Group Wall. (If you were added to the Group, after all, they want to hear from you!)

✔ **Comment:** When you see something you have an opinion on, click Comment below the post and let everyone know. (This action subscribes you to subsequent notifications about that post.)

✔ **Like:** When you like anything on Facebook, the person who created that content is notified that you like it. It's an easy and quick way to say "Good job!" when you don't have an active comment to make.

✔ **Subscribe/Unsubscribe:** When you subscribe to a post, you are asking to be notified about all subsequent comments on that post (and, in fact, commenting automatically subscribes you). If a provocative post yields ongoing discussion, you'll always know what's going on.

You might have commented or subscribed to a post that is now going in a completely unrelated direction that you don't care about. If you're bothered by notifications or just find them boring, you can Unsubscribe at any time. The conversation continues without you being notified about it.

Anatomy of a Group

The first thing you see when you visit a Group is its Home page, as shown in Figure 9-10. To get to a Group Home page, just click the Group name in the left side column. If you have a lot of Groups, you may need to click a More link to find the one you want to get to. Just as your Profile provides a summary of you (not to say that *you* could ever be summarized), this page provides an overview of what's happened in the Group recently, including snapshots of the most recent photos, videos, and member comments.

Figure 9-10: Welcome to the Dummy Group.

At the top part of the Group Home page, you see the Group name (in this case, Dummy Group) and the Group privacy level (in this case, Closed). Depending on privacy settings, you may be able to see all of a Group's contents before joining it, even though you can't post new content.

Moving down the central column of the page, you'll see something fairly recognizable: the Wall. People can post content, events, and ideas to the Wall, where other members of the Group can respond via comments. And of course, at the very top of the Wall is a Publisher, where you can write posts, add photos or videos, ask Questions, and create Docs (which are basically wiki-style documents that all Group members can edit).

On the right side of the page are a few buttons, links, and boxes (refer to Figure 9-10). Starting at the top and moving down the page:

✔ **Notifications button:** Click this button in the top-right corner of the page to manage notifications that you receive from this Group and to edit your settings for the group. We discuss these options in the "Controlling Group Overload" section later in this chapter.

✔ **Gear button**: Click the drop-down arrow next to the Gear button to bring up most of your options for this group, including the following:

- **Chat with Group:** Click this link to initiate a Group Chat — in other words, to talk in real-time with all the members of the Group who happen to be online.

- **Create Event:** Click this link to create a new Event for the Group.

- **Edit Group (admins only):** If you are a Group admin, you can click this button to access certain Group settings that only you control. This is talked about more later in the "Being a Group administrator" section.

- **Report Group**: If you feel that this group is violating one of Facebook's policies in some way, you can pick this option to alert Facebook so it can decide whether to close this group.

- **Leave Group:** Turns out the No Boys Allowed Club is kind of dull? Letting your membership in the Community Theater lapse for a season? If at any time you want out, all you have to do is click this link.

If you remove yourself from a Group, you cannot rejoin, and your friends cannot invite you to rejoin.

✔ **Search This Group:** This text box at the top-right corner of the page allows you to search the content of a Group for specific keywords. It only searches text that Group members have entered, so if you're searching for a particular link someone shared, you'll have to find the person who sent it.

Search results within Groups show the context and the keyword, as well as an icon to represent whether the word was found in a comment (quotation mark icons) or an original post (sticky note icon).

✔ **Members box:** At the top of the right column is the Members box (complete with thumbnail Profile pictures). If you want to see all members of a Group, click the See All link in the upper-right corner of the Members box.

✔ **Add Friends to Group box:** If someone adds you to a Group and you know other people who ought to be there, click inside this text box to type in their names and add whomever you want.

Group Dynamics

Now that you know how to create, share, and navigate your way through a Group, it's time to look at some of the long-term things to keep in mind as you join Groups.

Controlling Group overload

Sometimes, especially in larger Groups, you may find yourself a bit overwhelmed by all the notifications (especially if they are coming into your e-mail Inbox, which is how Group notifications are set up by default). To control this, you just need to get comfortable with the Notifications Settings box, which you access by clicking the Notifications button on the Group Home Page, and then clicking the Settings link from the drop-down list. The Settings box is shown in Figure 9-11.

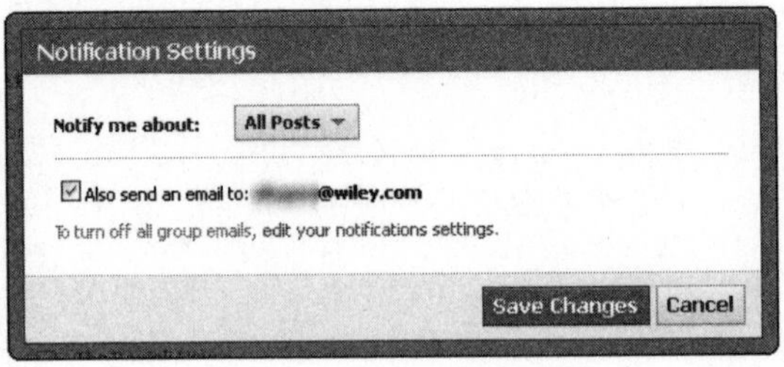

Figure 9-11:
Control notifications and more in this box.

The Notifications Settings box offers several options for receiving on-site notifications (the ones that cause a little red flag to appear in the upper-left corner of your screen). You can choose from the following options:

✔ **All Activity:** This option causes a notification flag to appear whenever any member of the Group posts or comments on a post.

✔ **All Posts:** Because comment threads can often become very long and rambling, this option allows you to see when a new post is created, but not see comments on those posts unless you subscribe to the post, or any other activity to the group.

✔ **Friends' Posts:** In especially large Groups, you might not be official Facebook friends with everyone in the Group, so a good way to filter down to the material you are most likely to care about is only to pay attention to the things your friends post.

✔ **Off:** Some people may only want to read the posts when they choose to look at the Group wall and not receive any notifications from this Group. Selecting Off gives you that silence.

In addition to notifications on Facebook, you can also choose to have these same notifications sent to your e-mail Inbox.

Being a Group administrator

If you are a creator of a Group, you are automatically its *admin* or administrator. Additionally, you can be added as an admin of someone else's Group. After you have members in your Group, you can use the Group member list to remove (and even permanently ban) undesirable members, promote your most trusted members to administrators, or demote your existing administrators (if any) back to regular members.

To get you started in your career as an admin, take a look at the Edit Group page, shown in Figure 9-12. You get to this page by clicking the Edit Group link from the drop-down list you get by clicking the Gear button at the top right of the Group Home page. Does it look a little familiar? It should look a little like your Edit Profile page, albeit with fewer sections.

First, you can add a Profile picture that appears as a thumbnail next to your Group's name, as shown in Figure 9-13. To add a thumbnail, click either the Browse or the Take a Picture button. If you select Browse, navigate to your computer's folders to find your desired photo. After you select the photo, click Open or Save or Select.

Take a Picture works only if you have a webcam installed on your computer.

After you select the image or use your webcam to take a picture, the picture appears on the screen, as shown in Figure 9-13.

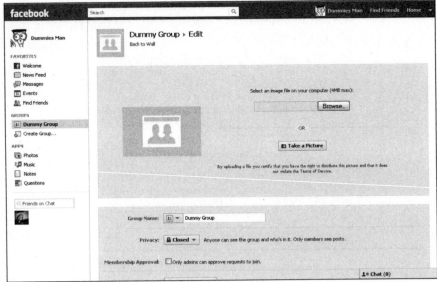

Figure 9-12:
Edit Group
info as an
admin.

Figure 9-13:
Change your
Group's
thumbnail
photo.

You can scroll down to update the Basic Information for the Group, as shown in Figure 9-14. If you're the creator of the Group, this page should look pretty familiar to you. It has many of the same options you had when you created this Group:

✔ **Name:** Edit the Group name here (but I don't recommend pulling the rug out from underneath people by say, changing a Group name from Yankees Fans to Red Sox Fans).

✔ **Icon:** You can change your icon at any time from here.

✔ **Privacy:** The privacy level of the Group can change here. Again, I don't recommend changing a secret Group to an open Group if people are sharing content they may feel is sensitive.

✔ **E-mail Address:** You can register an e-mail address with an @groups. facebook.com domain for your Group that you can then use to share information via e-mail. When members e-mail something to the Group, it appears as a post on the Group Wall.

✔ **Description:** The description of your Group appears the first time new members visit your Group page. So this is a good place to set expectations for what the Group is for and how you expect to use it.

Click Save when you're done editing your Group's information; otherwise, all your hard work will be lost.

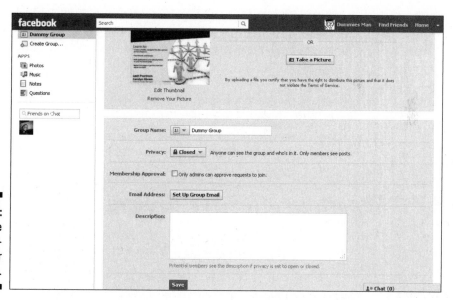

Figure 9-14:
Update the basic information for your Group.

As an admin, you can remove and ban members from the Group, as well as create other admins to help shoulder the burden of admin-hood.

To Edit members, follow these steps:

1. **Below the Group header, in the middle of the page, click the Members link.**

   This takes you to the Members page, shown in Figure 9-15.

Figure 9-15:
Edit Group
Members
here.

2. **To remove members of the Group, click the X next to their names.**

   You need to confirm this. If someone has been posting consistently offensive or abusive content, you can ban them permanently by checking the Ban Permanently box; this means that person can never rejoin the Group.

3. **To make someone an admin, click the Make Admin button besides that person's name.**

   Similarly, when someone is an admin, you can remove their admin status by clicking the Remove Admin button beside their name.

Reporting offensive Groups

If you stumble upon an offensive Group in your travels, you should report it to Facebook so that the company can take appropriate actions. To report a Group, follow these steps:

1. **Click the drop-down arrow next to the Gear button on the right side of the Group's Home page, and then select the Report Group link.**

   You see a form like the one shown in Figure 9-16.

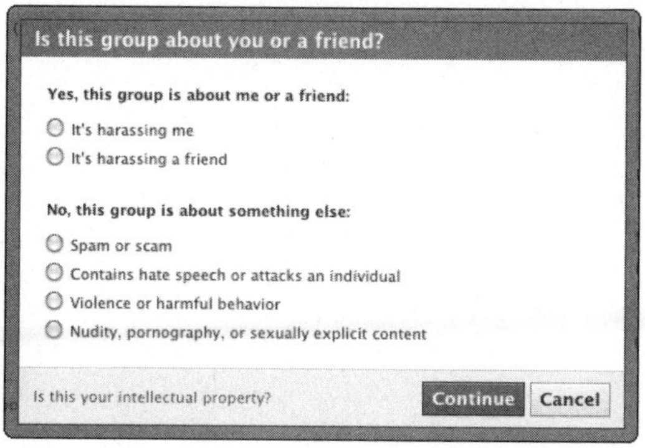

Figure 9-16:
If you find a
Group that
is offensive,
Facebook
is here
to help.

> **Is this group about you or a friend?**
>
> **Yes, this group is about me or a friend:**
>
> ○ It's harassing me
> ○ It's harassing a friend
>
> **No, this group is about something else:**
>
> ○ Spam or scam
> ○ Contains hate speech or attacks an individual
> ○ Violence or harmful behavior
> ○ Nudity, pornography, or sexually explicit content
>
> Is this your intellectual property?   Continue | Cancel

2. **Fill out the report by choosing a reason for the report and include a comment that explains why you feel the Group should be removed.**

3. **Click Submit.**

Facebook removes all Groups that

✔ Contain pornographic material or inappropriate nudity

✔ Attack an individual or Group

✔ Advocate the use of illicit drugs

✔ Advocate violence

✔ Serve as advertisements or are otherwise deemed to be spam by Facebook

Many Groups on Facebook take strong stands on controversial issues, such as abortion or gun control. In an effort to remain neutral and promote debate, Facebook won't remove a Group because you disagree with its statements.

Part III
Out to the Real World and Back Again

The 5th Wave   By Rich Tennant

"I know Facebook is great and you want to be
a part of it. But you're my mom - you <u>can't</u>
be my 'friend.'"

In this part . . .

Okay, Facebook is great — you get it. You use it; your friends use it. It's awesome. But face it: The most awesome thing about friends is actually interacting with them. This part deals with Facebook features that don't replace face time as much as enhance them. Photos allows you to share photos of your life with friends, and Events helps you plan and host events that your friends are invited to IRL (in real life).

I also cover Notes and Questions, which allow you to blog on Facebook and add interactivity to your page with polls.

Chapter 10

Text Ed: Notes and Questions

*I*f the Internet has given us anything, it is the ability to share our thoughts on just about anything and to find answers to just about any question. Facebook is not one to miss out on an Internet trend, especially ones it feels it can offer a social twist to.

In the case of Notes, Facebook's version of a blog, the social twist is simply the ability to keep everything in one place. Presumably, you want your friends to read your blog, so you might as well put it on Facebook, where your friends will be sure to see it. That way they don't need to remember to check a separate website to get your latest news. Additionally, you can tag friends who you are writing about in your notes.

The social twist on Questions, Facebook's application for asking and answering questions, is a two-part process. First of all, it allows people to ask questions that search engines aren't great at answering, like "What's the best brunch place in Palo Alto?" Second-of-ly, it allows you to cull wisdom from the crowds of people on Facebook.

Taking Notes

Notes are blogs. Like blogs, Notes are ways of writing entries about your life, your thoughts, or your all-time favorite songs and then sharing them with your Facebook friends.

The beauty of Notes lies in the ability to blog without needing to distribute a web address to friends so that they can go check out your blog. Instead, your friends are connected to your Profile. Therefore, when you publish a Note, it appears in their News Feeds.

If you already keep a blog, import it into Notes and distribute it to your friends through that application. I discuss how to do this later on in the "Importing a blog into Notes" section.

Writing a note

No specific rules of etiquette dictate the proper length of notes or even the contents of notes. Some people like to keep them short and informative; other people like to take the extra space to say everything they want to say about a topic. Go crazy, or not. Feeling uninspired? Pick a favorite funny memory, awkward moment, or topic that really gets people thinking. A very common note that people write on Facebook is titled "25 Things About Me," where they detail 25 facts about their lives. Getting started on your first note is pretty straightforward:

1. **Go to your Profile.**

2. **In the left side menu, click the header entitled Apps. From the Apps page, scroll down and click the Notes application.**

   This takes you to the Notes page for your Profile. Any notes you've written or received already appear here.

   After you use the Notes application, you should see it in the future under the Apps header on your Profile page, without having to click through to the Apps page.

3. **Click the Write a Note button at the upper right of the page.**

   A blank note appears, as shown in Figure 10-1.

4. **In the Title field, type the title of your Note.**

5. **In the Body field, start writing about whatever interests you.**

   Facebook offers basic formatting options through the little buttons on top of the Body field. You probably recognize these from your word processing programming. The B icon makes text **bold,** the I icon makes text *italicized,* and so on. You can also create numbered or bulleted lists, as well as block quotes. The Preview function within Notes is a good way to figure out whether your formatting is working the way you want it to. To find out quickly whether your HTML tags are working, you can toggle between the Preview and Edit screens.

6. **Tag friends who appear in your note by typing their names into the Tags field.**

   Facebook attempts to auto-complete as you type. When you see the name you're looking for appear, highlight it and click Enter to select it.

7. **Click the Add a Photo link to add photos.**

   I go into more detail about adding photos in the next section.

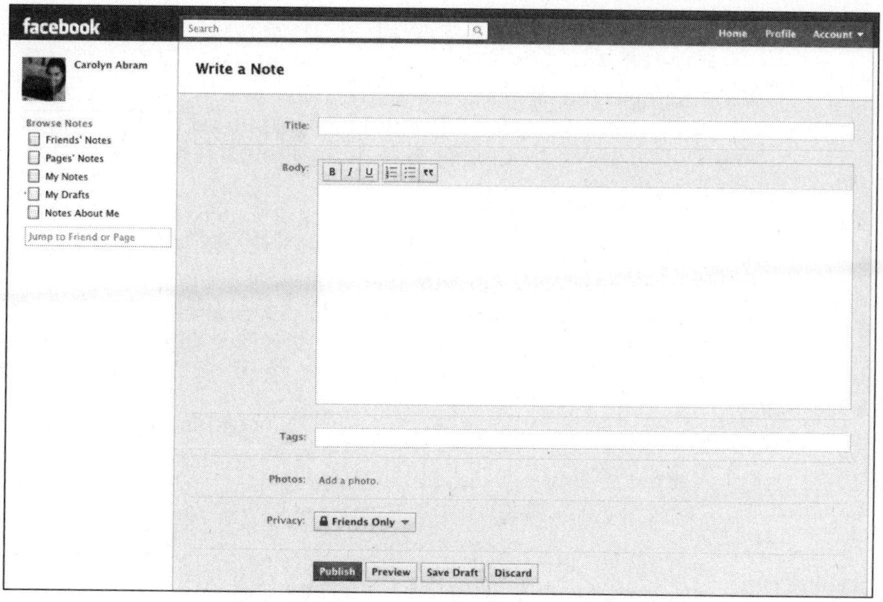

Figure 10-1:
The startling white canvas of a blank note staring at you.

8. **Choose who can see your note using the Privacy drop-down menu**.

   As usual, your options are

   - **Public:** Everyone on Facebook can see this note.

   - **Friends:** Only your friends can see this note.

   - **Custom:** This opens the customize privacy dialog box, which allows you to select specific people who can and cannot see this note.

   - **Lists:** If you've created any custom Friend Lists on Facebook, those lists appear below the Custom option, so you can choose one of those lists to see this note.

9. **After you finish writing, click Preview to view what your note will look like when published. Or click Save Draft if you want to come back to the Note later.**

   Preview opens a preview of the Note, so you can have one last glance-over before you publish it. If you're unhappy with your preview, click the Edit button to return to the Create Note screen.

   You can come back to your draft at any time by clicking the My Drafts menu item. You'll see this on the left column of the page when you come to the Notes tab of your Profile.

10. **When you're happy with your Note, click Publish.**

    Congrats! You shared your Note and your thoughts with your friends. They can now read, like, and comment on your Notes.

Adding photos to a Note

We often hear that a picture is worth 1,000 words; however, that depends on the picture, which is why it is completely optional to include photos within your Notes. If you do choose to include photos, it requires you to add HTML tags to your Note.

1. **On the Write a Note page, click the Add a Photo link.**

   This expands the photo selector, shown in Figure 10-2. You can upload photos from your computer's hard drive as well as import photos from the albums you have already added to Facebook.

Figure 10-2: Options for adding photos.

2. **To choose a photo from your hard drive, click Choose File or the Browse button to find the photos you want.**

   You can add only one photo at a time; therefore, repeat as necessary until you upload all the photos that you want.

   Each photo is given an HTML tag, usually numbered from <Photo 1> to <Photo X>.

3. **To choose a photo from the previous albums, click the album you want and then click the photo from that album that you want.**

   This process adds the same HTML tag, but saves you the step of uploading the photo.

4. **For each photo, add a caption and select how you want the photo to appear.**

   The photo can cover the full width of the Note, or it can be resized and aligned to the left, right, or center, as shown in Figure 10-3.

   The photo tags are put (by default) at the bottom of your Note.

5. **Move the tags (just as you would move text) to where you want the photos to appear.**

Figure 10-3:
Photo
options for
a Note.

6. **Use the Preview button to see how your Note looks.**

7. **To change the look, click Edit, make your changes, and click Publish.**

Importing a blog into Notes

Maybe you've already been keeping a blog, and the thought of moving everything over to Facebook sounds like a nightmare. Maybe you don't want to exclude your friends who haven't joined Facebook from reading all about you. Maybe you like the formatting and photo upload options of a different blogging platform better. Not to worry — Facebook is ready for you.

The following steps show you how to import a blog into Facebook:

1. **Navigate to** `www.facebook.com/editnotes.php?import` **using your favorite browser.**

2. **Enter the URL for your blog in the Web URL box, certify that it's yours by selecting the By Entering a URL, You Represent check box, and click Start Importing.**

   The next page displays a preview of all the existing entries that will be imported into your Notes.

3. **Click Confirm on the left side of the Confirmation page.**

   Your entries are imported, and Facebook checks the feed of your blog every few hours to see whether there are any new entries.

When blogs are imported into Notes, they frequently lose certain formatting or photos that were included in the original. Check your preview to see if these things happen to your blog.

Browsing Notes

When you click the Write a Note button, you get a new set of options in your left side menu relating to browsing Notes.

✔ **Friends' Notes:** This takes you to a collection of all of your friends' Notes, from most recent to the oldest.

✔ **Pages' Notes:** Pages — the Profiles that businesses, brands, and other public figures make to represent themselves on Facebook — may also write Notes to talk about what's going on in their world. You can see all of them, starting with the most recent, by clicking the Pages' Notes menu item.

✔ **My Notes:** This takes you to all of the Notes you have ever written, starting with the most recent. Click a Note's title to see the options to edit or delete it.

✔ **My Drafts:** If you start a Note and didn't finish it, you may want to save it as a draft and come back to it later. Come back to all of your drafts by clicking this menu item.

✔ **Notes About Me:** This takes you to a collection of Notes your friends have written that tagged you. You can always remove tags if you don't like what your friend has said about you. Just click the Remove My Tag link (located under the Tagged box on the left side of the Note's view) to disassociate yourself with the Note. Unfortunately, you can't remove what your friend has written. If you don't like what's been said, you might just want to nicely ask them to take it down.

Asking Questions

Unlike Notes, Questions isn't really about filling out your Profile with content that expresses yourself. Rather, Questions is about learning and gathering more information. There are three main aspects to Questions: asking questions, answering questions, and exploring topics.

Don't be afraid to ask

You can ask Questions from multiple places on Facebook. You can ask them from the Publisher in your Profile, the Publisher on your Home page, and the Publisher on your Group Home pages. To ask a basic question, follow these steps:

1. **Click the Ask Question link in your Publisher of choice.**

   This expands the Questions Publisher, as shown in Figure 10-4.

2. **Click into the text box and type your question.**

3. **Click Ask Question.**

   This posts the question to your Wall and your friends' News Feeds.

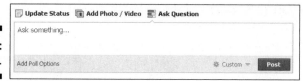

Figure 10-4:
Ask away.

Unlike most posts on Facebook, you can't set privacy on Questions you ask. As your friends answer your Questions, their friends can see it, and their friends can see it, and so on and so on and so on.

Questions with polls can be really useful for making decisions for yourself or for a group of people. Ever tried to get ten people to agree on a dinner location? It can get a bit overwhelming. To create a Question and add a poll, follow these steps:

1. **Click the Ask Question link in your Publisher of choice.**

   This expands the Questions Publisher, as shown in Figure 10-4.

2. **Click into the text box and type your question.**

3. **Click Add Poll Options.**

   This expands the Poll Options boxes.

4. **Type your poll options into the Poll Options boxes.**

   Facebook auto-completes the box with the names of Pages and Places as you type. This can be a little confusing unless you actually are entering restaurant names, in which case, you'll probably get a match.

   As you add more and more options, more and more boxes appear below it. Just fill out as many boxes as you need.

5. **Decide if other people can add options to your poll.**

   If that's okay with you, leave the Allow Anyone to Add Options box selected. Otherwise, deselect it.

6. **Click Post.**

   This posts the Question to your Wall and your friends' News Feeds.

Although Questions are publicly visible, you might ask a Question that you just know one of your friends can answer. When you're looking at a Question, there is an Ask Friends button or link next to the name of the person who asked it. Clicking it expands a type of the Friend Selector, shown in Figure 10-5.

You can choose friends by clicking any part of their name, Profile picture, or the check box next to them. Type names into the search box on top to filter down to just the people you are looking for.

Figure 10-5:
Choose
specific
friends
to ask.

When you've selected all the people you want to ask, click Submit. Your friend gets a notification on their Home page letting them know you want them to answer the Question.

You've got answers

You will mostly see Questions through your News Feed or your friends' Walls. News Feed shows you stories about people both asking and responding to questions. If one piques your interest, either because you know the answer or you want to know the answer, click it to read the entire thing. This generates a Question box similar to that shown in Figure 10-6.

The anatomy of the Question box

The Question box has several parts and they offer a few different options for what you can do next:

- ✓ **Question:** The blue header of the question box shows the original Question asked.
- ✓ **X:** Click the little white X next to the Question title to close this window.

✔ **Asked By:** This section shows who asked the Question. Additionally, in the gray header, you can see how many followers the Question has. You can Share or Report the Question here as well.

✔ **Ask Friends:** The Ask Friends button allows you to redirect a Question to your friends who may know the answer.

What is your favorite pumpkin recipe?

Asked By   9 Followers

Charlotte Carnevale Willner
about 8 months ago · Share · Report   🏴 Ask Friends   +1 Follow

Posts   Friends · Others (15)

Write something...

Natalie Minor
Definitely Paula Deen's Pumpkin Gooey Cakes. But every time I make them, they're much more goo than cake. Still delicious, though.

http://www.foodnetwork.com/recipes/....

about 8 months ago · Like · Comment · Share

👍 Jeff Kanter, Charlotte Carnevale Willner and 5 others like this.

Write a comment...

Figure 10-6:
The
Question
box.

✔ **Follow:** *Following* or subscribing to a Question is a way of asking to be notified of future answers to this Question. When you ask a Question, you automatically follow it. Click the Follow button to begin following, and if you find you are getting too many notifications, you can come back to this screen and click Unfollow.

✔ **Posts:** Posts are the actual answers to basic questions like the one pictured in Figure 10-6. There are actually two views of the Posts section. You can see just friends, or you can see the answers from Others on Facebook. In this example, just one answer is from a friend, and 15 answers are from others.

Question boxes for poll questions look fairly similar, although above the information about who asked the Questions are the actual poll options. The small Profile pictures to the right of each option are your friends who have chosen that answer. Hover over the blue ellipsis to the right of each answer to see how many people have voted. You can see an example of a poll Question box in Figure 10-7.

Figure 10-7:
A poll
Question
with votes.

Adding your answers

To add an answer to a basic Question, you only need to follow three steps:

1. **Click into the Write Something box in the Posts section of the Question box.**

2. **Type your answer.**

3. **Click Share.**

   The original asker and any followers of the question are notified that a new answer is available.

To add an answer to a poll Question, simply click the option you would like to vote for. Some Questions may allow you to vote for more than one option, in which case, check off all the options you want.

Chapter 11

Scheduling Your Life
with Facebook

*T*hink about the worst birthday party that you ever had — the big kickball party during the hurricane when the clown was three hours late and none of your friends showed up because your mom forgot to invite them.

Facebook can't do anything about clowns or the weather (as of publication time), but the invites would've happened if your mother used Facebook Events to plan the party. Facebook removes the hassle of hosting an Event — creating and sending the invites, managing the guest list — and allows you to focus on preparing the Event itself.

Not much of a party planner? No worries. Facebook also handles the planning of smaller, more impromptu Events. You can easily collect a crew for dinner or for Frisbee in the park.

Getting Going with Events

Events is an application built by Facebook. To access its dashboard, click Events in the left menu of your Home page (currently it's right below Messages and right above Find Friends). This brings you to the Events page and opens up additional menu options for Events. The Events page (shown in Figure 11-1) that you land on displays all upcoming birthdays and Facebook Events that have you on their guest lists. This includes Events you were invited to and Events you joined.

To see more information about an Event, click its title to view the Event's Home page, which contains a detailed overview of the Event. Facebook also embeds a summary of the most important information — the Event's date and time, who invited you, and how many people are attending— directly into the Event listing, as shown in Figure 11-2. Wherever you find an Event listing on Facebook — say, News Feed or a Profile Wall — this information is displayed.

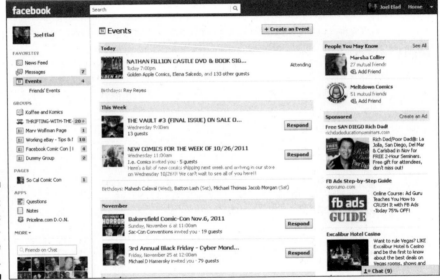

Figure 11-1:
The Events application's Home page.

Figure 11-2:
An Event's listing displays a preview of the most important info.

When you are through looking at upcoming Events, you can also use the submenu on the left side to navigate to your friends' Events.

The Friends' Events page shows you public Events that your friends are attending. In other words, it won't show you any Events that the creators have set as private. If an Event is a big one like a reading or a rally, don't be shy about adding yourself to it. If it's something that seems a little more intimate, like a dinner or a birthday party, you may want to check with your friend or with the host before you add yourself to the guest list.

Anatomy of an Event

An Event is represented on Facebook through its Home page, such as the one shown in Figure 11-3. A Home page evolves throughout the life cycle of an Event. Before the Event takes place, its Home page serves as an invitation and offers critical information for attendees, such as the Event's date and location. An Event's Home page also tracks who will or might attend the Event so that its host can plan accordingly.

Figure 11-3: An Event's Home page.

An Event's Home page is divided into two columns. The skinny column on the left is where the Event Profile picture lives, as well as information about who is and is not attending. The main column in the center of the page displays all the relevant Event information and the Event Wall.

In the main center column, here's what you can learn:

- ✔ **Event Name:** It's big and at the top of the page in black — the name your host has given to the Event.

- ✔ **Inviter (pre-RSVP):** Before you RSVP, you see the name of the person who invited you to the Event right below the Event's name. There's a difference between being invited to something by a good friend and being invited by a more distant acquaintance, so this is good information to know before you RSVP.

- ✔ **Share (pre-RSVP):** The Share link scattered throughout Facebook allows you to share interesting content quickly with your friends, either by sending it to them in a message, or by posting it on your Profile, to your friend's Wall, or to a group Wall. The Share button allows you to share an Event along with a preview containing the Event's name, description, and picture.

- ✔ **RSVP buttons (pre-RSVP):** Across from the Event name, toward the top-right corner of the page, you should see three big buttons: I'm Attending, Maybe, and No. Click the proper button to RSVP.

- ✔ **Attendance Status (post-RSVP):** If you've already said you'll be going to an Event, right below its name, you'll see a sentence reading *You are Attending* (or might attend, or not attending, depending on your response).

    If you want to change your RSVP, click your current attendance status, which is technically a link. This opens a pop-up box with all of the attendance options displayed once again. Choose your new RSVP by clicking your desired response, and then click the RSVP button to save it.

- ✔ **Event Privacy:** Next to your attendance status you'll see a notice about whether the Event is public or private. There's more information about Event Privacy when you learn how to create your own Event in the next section of this chapter.

- ✔ **Event Info:** This area is further divided into convenient sections to show you the when (Time), where (Location), who (Created By), and what (More Info) of the Event.

- ✔ **The Wall:** The Event Wall, like the Wall on your Profile, is where Event guests can leave messages, photos, videos, and relevant links for all the guests to share. In general, the Wall is where people explain why they can't make an Event, or where they express their enthusiasm about coming to an Event.

The left column, which is topped by the Event Profile Picture, contains information about invitations. Assuming you're looking at a Public Event, after you RSVPed, you'll see a button just beneath it that you can click to Select Guests to Invite (refer to Figure 11-3). Clicking this will bring up a Friend Selector that you can use to invite your friends as well. We go over the Friend Selector later in this chapter when we go through the Event creation process.

Just because you *can* invite more people to an Event doesn't necessarily mean you *should.* Make sure your host is okay with you extending the guest list (a good use of the Event Wall) before you blast your whole friend list.

The rest of the left column is dedicated to guests: Who is confirmed as attending, who is maybe attending, who hasn't replied yet, and who has declined to attend. The Attending list is on top and shows you names and thumbnails of guests. If you're not sure if you want to go to a party, this section might help you make up your mind. If you're more curious who *isn't* going, you need to click View on the Not Attending section to view that list.

At the very bottom of any Event page are two useful links:

- ✔ **Export:** You can export Events as calendar events to programs like iCal, Microsoft Outlook, and Google Calendar. Clicking this link brings up a pop-up window that allows you to export the particular Event you are looking at, or export all of your Events automatically (by clicking the Export All of Your Upcoming Events link). For exporting single Events, choose by clicking whether you want to download it as a calendar appointment or send it to yourself as an e-mail.

- ✔ **Report Event:** Hopefully you won't need to use this link often, but if you ever are invited to or see an Event that is harassing, hateful, explicit, or spam, you can report it by clicking this link. A pop-up window appears that lists the possible reasons for reporting an Event. Select your reason by clicking it and then click the Continue button to report it.

Creating Your Own Events

Tired of being a *guest?* Ready to be in charge? Want to host your own Event, have complete control over the guest list, and almost single-handedly decide who among us is *in* and *out?* Let's get down to business — the business of organizing and hosting fun Events. If you're planning an Event that's not happening for a few days or so, start with the Big Events section. If your Event is more spur-of-the-moment, or perhaps has already started, skip ahead to the Quick Events section.

Big Events

Whatever actions have transpired before you log in to Facebook — a conversation about how awesome a surprise party would be, a sudden urge to give all of your friends free food in honor of the season — after you've logged in, creating an Event is easy. To begin, take the following steps:

1. **Click Events in the left column of the Home page.**

   This takes you to the Events Home page.

2. **Click the Create an Event button at the upper-right side of the page.**

   This takes you to the Create an Event page, as shown in Figure 11-4.

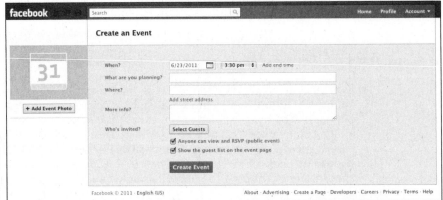

Figure 11-4:
Create your
Event here.

3. **Fill out your Event's info:**

   You can fill out a number of fields:

   - **When? (Required):** By default, Facebook assumes you are an impromptu party planner, so this box shows a party happening later today. Click the calendar icon to change the date, and use the drop-down menu to select a time.

   - **End Time (click Add End Time):** In case you're worried about your guests overstaying their welcome, you can include an end time in your invitation.

   - **What are you planning? (required):** Enter the name of your Event, such as **Jenny's 25th Birthday**.

   - **Where?:** Although it's not required, telling people where to go is generally helpful if you want people to show up. This isn't always the street address, but the name of the venue, like *Mark's house* or *Olive Garden.* Facebook tries to auto-complete the name of your venue as you type. When you see the location's name appear, click it to select it. If it's a Place Page (more on Pages in Chapter 13), Facebook displays a link to that Page so people can find out more.

   - **Street, City/Town (click Add Street Address):** The street address of the location where the Event is taking place. After you expand this section, you need to enter the address separately from the city or town where the Event is occurring. When you type the city or town, the field tries to auto-complete as you type.

- **More Info?** You can include any information you think is relevant in this space — a brief overview of the Event, such as why you're holding it, what the attire is, and why someone should come. This description is one of the first things a guest sees when looking at your Event and determining whether to attend.

4. **Click Select Guests to begin to invite friends.**

   Doing so brings up the Friend Selector (shown in Figure 11-5). Simply click a friend's name or Profile picture to select them. Click again to take them off the list. Use the search box at the top to filter down to a friend by name. When you are done, click Save and Close. You can invite friends who aren't on Facebook by adding their e-mail addresses to the box at the bottom of the Friend Selector.

Figure 11-5:
The Friend Selector helps you invite guests.

You can add a more personal note to invitations by clicking Add a Personal Message at the very bottom of the Friend Selector. Type in whatever the note is, and this will be included in the e-mail invitations that Facebook sends on your behalf.

5. **Choose whether you want a public or private Event using the Anyone Can View and RSVP check box.**

   Public Events are ones that anyone can see and join without invitation. If you aren't holding an exclusive Event, this is usually the right choice because it allows friends you might have forgotten to invite to see the Event and add themselves to the guest list. For parties that you don't want everyone to know about, deselect the Anyone Can View and RSVP box to keep it private. Deselecting the box actually adds a new check box option: Guests can invite Friends. This prevents tons of people from seeing your Event, but still lets guests invite their own friends or significant others.

6. **Decide if you want to show the guest list using the Show the Guest List on the Event Page check box.**

   Keeping your guest list visible is a nice way for friends to know who else is going to an Event. This makes it easy for them to coordinate rides or plan presents, or whatever it is people do before your parties. If you don't want people to see this because of your friends' VIP status, deselect the Show the Guest List on the Event Page box.

7. **Add a photo for your Event.**

   Adding a photo to represent your Event makes it look pretty and inviting to your guests when they see the Event — both on the Event Home page and in invitation requests. Big, official Events often have their flier as the picture. To add an image, follow these steps:

   a. *Click Add Event Photo, which is under the big calendar icon on the left side of the page.*

   b. *Click the Browse or Choose File button to open your computer's standard interface for finding a file.*

   c. *Navigate to (and select) the picture on your computer that you want to use.*

   The picture you choose must meet the file size and type requirements outlined on the page. Currently that is a 4MB maximum. If you're not sure whether your desired picture meets the requirements, select the picture and continue with these steps. Facebook notifies you if the picture you choose can't be used.

   After you've selected a photo, Facebook adds it to your Event.

8. **Click Create Event.**

Event created. Invitations sent. And you didn't have to lick a stamp. You land on your Event's Home page. Welcome home.

As soon as you click Create Event, all of your guests receive the information you just filled out. Double-check to make sure the time, date, and spelling are all correct before clicking.

Did you forget someone? People are asking for directions? Don't worry, you'll learn how to add to and edit your Event in the "Managing Your Event" section.

Managing Your Event

You can do a number of things when you finish creating your Event and people start to join. These actions are visible and available only to you and other administrators. This section outlines the additional power you wield as an Event administrator.

Editing your Event's Info

Need to update the Event time or add info about a dress code? You can do this at any time by clicking Edit Event on the far top right of your Event page, above where the ads in the right column are. This takes you to the Edit Event page. You can edit everything about the Event. Just remember to click Save Event when you are done.

Canceling the Event

As they say, the best laid plans . . . go oft awry. If your life has gone a bit awry and ruined your Event plans, not to worry — it's easy to cancel your Event and send apologies to your guests. After clicking Edit Event in the upper right of the Event Page, you see the now familiar edit Event page, with one addition: a Cancel This Event link in the lower-right corner (sort of parallel to the Save Event button). Clicking Cancel This Event brings up a pop-up confirmation window, as shown in Figure 11-6.

Figure 11-6: Party's off? Cancel it on Facebook.

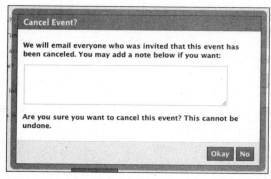

Cancel Event?

We will email everyone who was invited that this event has been canceled. You may add a note below if you want:

Are you sure you want to cancel this event? This cannot be undone.

Okay No

This confirmation window also provides you with a space where you can let your guests know the reason for the cancellation. Write up a short note and click the OK button to confirm that you really want to cancel the Event. This sends an e-mail to all of your guests with the cancellation and your note, so no one accidentally shows up, party hat on, only to be disappointed.

Messaging your Event's guests

Rain delay? Halloween canceled? Keep your guests up-to-date about the Event by sending them a Facebook message. These messages appear in your guests' Facebook Inbox, and, depending on their notification settings, they may also receive an e-mail notification.

To send a message to guests, click the Message Guests button on the far upper-right corner of the Event page, next to the Edit Event button. You're taken to a variation of the standard Compose Message form, shown in Figure 11-7.

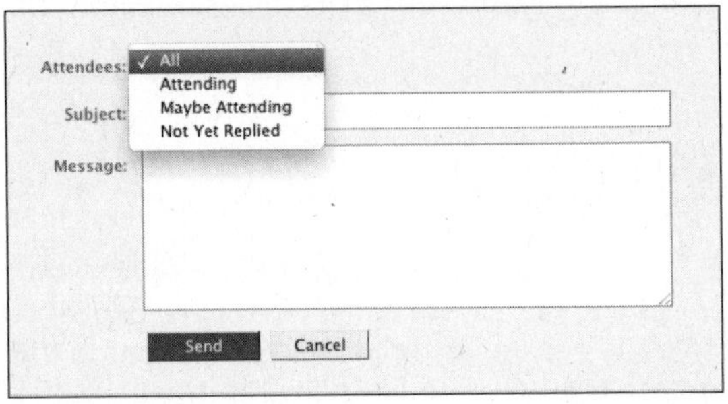

Figure 11-7:
Message all guests?

What's important to note here is the drop-down menu next to the word *Attendees*. Unlike regular messages, where you type in the names of all the friends you wish to message, here you select which segment of your guests you wish to message. You can message All the people you invited, only those Attending (useful for last-minute instructions about the proper way to climb the fence around your building), those who are Maybe Attending (useful for nagging them to, seriously guys, let me know how much food to buy), and those who have Not Yet Replied (see Maybe Attending). After you've selected who is getting the message, type in a subject and a message and click Send.

Your message is sent to your friends' Other Inbox. If that doesn't make sense, check out Chapter 8 to learn all about messages and the inboxes.

Managing your Event's guest list

After guests RSVP to your Event, use the Event guest list to remove (or even permanently ban) undesirable guests, promote your most trusted guests to administrators, or demote your existing administrators (if any) to regular guests.

1. **Click See All next to the Attending section of the guest list under your Event photo.**

   The View Guest List box opens, as shown in Figure 11-8.

Figure 11-8:
The View Guest List box is your one-stop shop for keeping tabs on your current guests and inviting more.

2. **Use the link to the right of each guest name that corresponds to the action you want to take.**

   For instance, to make a member an administrator, click the Make Admin button. As an administrator, the member has the same privileges — inviting people, changing Event info, messaging guests, and so on — that you do.

   You can also use the X to remove a guest from the Event. If you select this option, you can also choose to ban that person permanently so he may not rejoin the Event in the future. Banning someone is useful if the person is posting offensive content or otherwise stirring up trouble.

You can also invite more people by clicking the Select Guest to Invite button underneath the Event photo. This opens a Friend Selector, just like the one you used when creating the Event.

Chapter 12

Filling Facebook with Photos and Videos

· ·

· ·

Many Facebook users share the sensation of getting "lost" in Facebook — not in a bad way, but like you lose yourself in a good book. Often, this happens with News Feed or a friend's Profile. You click an appealing photo, which leads you to an album you like, which leads you to a video from a friend's vacation, which leads you to another friend who has a ton of new notes about her life. And the next thing you know, your editor is tapping you on the shoulder and saying, "Did you finish writing that chapter about photos yet?"

Facebook Photos is the leading photo-sharing application on the web. This may sound surprising because entire sites are dedicated to storing, displaying, and sharing photos; whereas Photos is just one piece of the Facebook puzzle. But as we discuss shortly, the fact that *all* of your friends are likely on Facebook and using Photos makes it a one-stop shop for tracking all the photos of you, all the photos you've taken, and all the photos of your friends.

Facebook Video, which you find within the Photos application, is also a one-stop shop for uploading, recording, and sharing videos with your friends. It enables really cool things like video messaging and video Wall posts. You can show all your friends that brilliant video that formerly languished on your computer. Whether your video is a bunch of people saying, "Oh my gosh, is this video?" or your own indie film, there's a place for it on Facebook.

The idea behind both of these applications is that your photos and videos are at their best not when they are alone in a dark cobwebby closet, but when they are out there being seen, shared, and talked about. As these things become easier to share with your friends, they become more valuable to you.

Managing Photos

Facebook is a great place to keep your photos and videos because you can easily organize them into albums and share them with all the people who may want to see them. You can upload these items for Events such as parties and trips, for a collection of photos to show people, or for a silly video of you and your friends that you took with a cell phone.

From the Publisher, you can click the Add Photo/Video link to post photos. When you do so, you see something like Figure 12-1. This screen gives you options for how you want to upload your content.

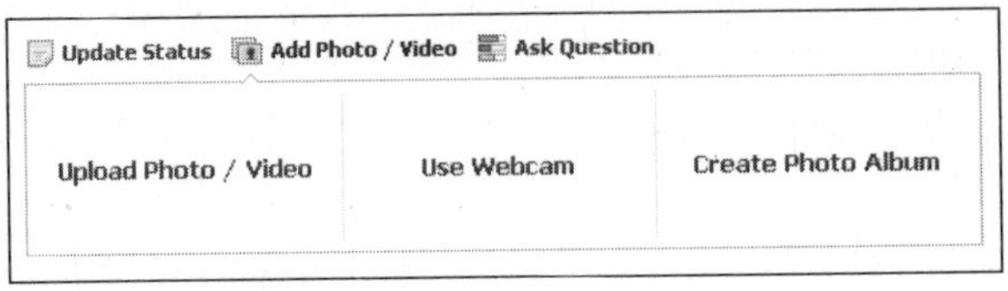

Figure 12-1:
Choose how
you want to
upload your
photos.

The Photo Publisher options include the following, and I'll go through each one at a time:

- ✔ **Upload a Photo or Video:** Use this option if you have one funny photo you want to share by posting it to your Wall. When you upload a single photo, it automatically gets added to an album that Facebook creates called Wall Photos.

- ✔ **Use Webcam:** If you have a webcam built into or attached to your computer, you can take a photo and post it directly to your Wall. When you add a webcam photo, it is automatically added to an album created by Facebook called Webcam Photos.

- ✔ **Create an Album:** Use this option when you want to really show off a series of photos. Choosing this option starts the process detailed in the upcoming section, "Creating an album."

Uploading a single photo

Say you have just one great photo you want to share. To get started, follow these steps:

1. Click Add Photo in the Publisher on your Home page or Profile.

   This opens the Photo options shown in Figure 12-1.

2. **Click Upload a Photo or Video.**

   The Publisher expands to show a Choose File or Browse button.

3. **Click Choose File or Browse (the exact wording may depend on your browser and operating system).**

   This opens a window that allows you to browse your computer's hard drive and select the photo you want.

4. **Click the photo you want to share to select it.**

5. **Click Open or Choose (the wording may depend on your browser and operating system).**

   This brings you back to Facebook. There should be a filename of some sort next to the Choose File button.

6. **Click in the Say Something about This Photo box and type any explanation you think is necessary.**

7. **(Optional) Click the Privacy menu to select who can see this photo.**

   If you've never changed your privacy settings, by default, everyone on Facebook can see this photo if they navigate to your Profile. I usually like sharing my photos with Friends of Friends, but if it's something kind of personal, I only share it with friends. Of course, you can always choose a custom group of people who can and cannot see the photo.

   If you know that most (if not all) of the time you want a limited group of people to be able to see your photos, change the default setting from your Privacy Settings page. This page is covered in detail in Chapter 5.

8. **Click Post.**

   This officially posts the photo to Facebook and creates a post (like that shown in Figure 12-2) that people can see in your Profile and in their News Feeds (provided that they are allowed by your privacy settings to see the photo). By default, this photo is added to an album called Wall Photos, which is basically a collection of all the photos you've ever added individually.

When you log in to your Facebook account and go to your Facebook Mobile page (www.facebook.com/mobile), you see a function called Upload Via E-mail. This function displays your personal upload e-mail address. You can e-mail photos to this e-mail address to upload them to Facebook. The subject line is used as the photo's caption.

Figure 12-2:
Share your
photo posts
with your
friends.

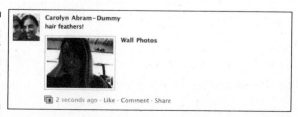

Taking a photo

If you have a webcam, you can always take a photo of yourself to share just what you're feeling at the moment or to illustrate just what's going on around you at that coffee shop you like so much. To get started, follow these steps:

1. **Click Add Photo/Video in the Publisher on your Home page or Profile.**

   This opens the Photo options shown in Figure 12-1.

2. **Click Use Webcam.**

   This expands the webcam interface, as shown in Figure 12-3.

Figure 12-3: Take a photo here.

3. **(Optional) Choose a filter from the menu in the top-left corner of the photo preview.**

   Filters are a way to make your photo a little more silly or fun.

4. **Click the blue camera button in the middle of the frame to take your photo.**

   You'll be able to see the photo you've snapped on the screen. Click the X in the upper-right corner if you want to start over.

5. **Click in the Say Something about This Photo box and type any explanation you think is necessary.**

6. **(Optional) Click the privacy menu to select who can see this photo.**

   If you've never changed your privacy settings, by default, Everyone on Facebook can see this photo if they navigate to your Profile. I usually like sharing my photos with Friends of Friends, but if it's something personal, I share it with friends only. Of course, you can always choose a custom group of people who can and cannot see the photo.

7. **Click Post.**

   This officially posts the photo to Facebook and creates a post that people can see in your Profile and in their News Feeds (provided that they are allowed by your privacy settings to see the photo).

Creating an album

Photo albums are actually some of the posts you are most likely to create and look at on Facebook. Whereas a single photo can share a moment, an album can truly tell a story and spark conversations with your friends. To create an album, follow these steps:

1. **Click Add Photo/Video in the Publisher on your Home page or Profile.**

   This opens the Photo options shown in Figure 12-1.

2. **Click Create an Album.**

   Often this opens an Uploading Tip window. Read it and then click Select Photos to move on. This opens the same interface for exploring your hard drive that you used to upload a single photo.

3. **Select multiple photos by holding the Ctrl or Command button and clicking the files you want.**

4. **When you're done, click Open.**

   This opens the Upload Photos pop-up box shown in Figure 12-4. The progress bar fills with blue as your photos are added.

5. **Fill out your Name of Album and Location.**

   Usually Album Names are descriptive (by default, Facebook names it the date of your upload). Names such as "Wedding!" or "Day at the Beach" usually suffice. You can add more detail later. Location is strictly optional.

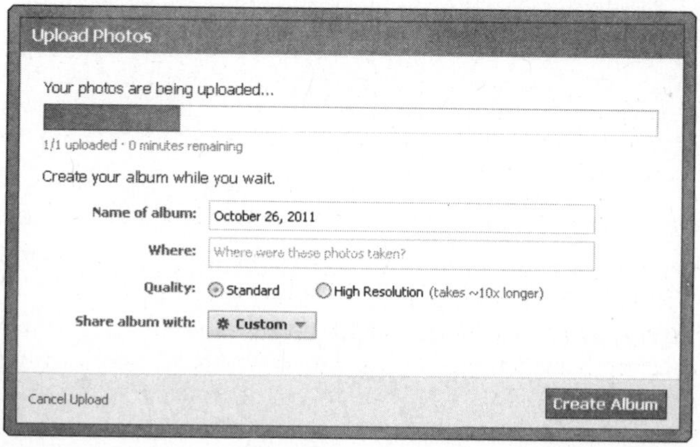

Figure 12-4: Fill out info while your photos upload.

Upload Photos

Your photos are being uploaded...

1/1 uploaded · 0 minutes remaining

Create your album while you wait.

Name of album: October 26, 2011

Where: Where were these photos taken?

Quality: ⦿ Standard   ○ High Resolution (takes ~10x longer)

Share album with: ✱ Custom ▾

Cancel Upload   Create Album

6. **Decide whether you want your photos shown in Standard or High resolution.**

   High-resolution photos obviously look a bit better, but they also take longer to upload. Unless you're a pro photographer or using a truly professional-level camera, Standard Quality is usually sufficient.

7. **Choose who can see the album using the Privacy drop-down menu.**

   As usual, the basic options are Everyone, Friends of Friends, Friends Only, or a Customized set of people.

8. **Click Create Album.**

   If your photos haven't finished uploading just yet, you'll be notified when they do finish. Click the link in that notification to continue on to tagging and arranging your photos.

   If your photos have finished uploading, this brings you to a tagging screen, shown in Figure 12-5, that uses facial recognition to suggest tags.

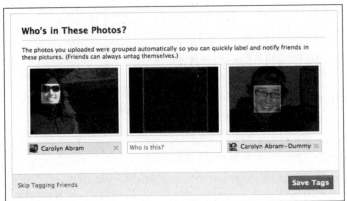

Who's in These Photos?

The photos you uploaded were grouped automatically so you can quickly label and notify friends in these pictures. (Friends can always untag themselves.)

Carolyn Abram   ✕   Who is this?   Carolyn Abram–Dummy ✕

Skip Tagging Friends   Save Tags

Figure 12-5:
Who dat?

Facebook tries to recognize and group similar faces, and then asks you to tag the people in the photos.

9. **(Optional) Type the name of the friend who is in the photo in the Who Is This? box. Facebook attempts to auto-complete your friend's name as you type.**

   You don't have to tag friends in your album; you can always bypass this step by clicking Skip Tagging Friends. However, tagging is highly recommended. It allows your friends to learn about your photos more quickly and share in discussing them with you.

10. **When you're done, click Save Tags.**

    This brings you to the Album View of your album, shown in Figure 12-6.

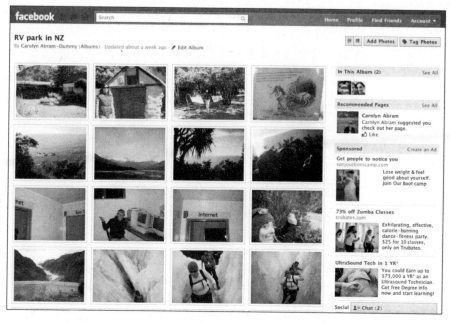

Figure 12-6:
Your album
is ready. No
scrapbook-
ing store
required.

Whew! That was a bit of a marathon. If you need a break or a drink of water, feel free to indulge. Then, when you're ready, read on to find out how to edit your album and the photos in it.

If you are having trouble uploading an album, you can try using the basic uploader. After you click Create Album, an upload photos tip screen appears. Click the Try the Basic Uploader link. You can then name your album and upload one photo file at a time (similar to how you upload a single photo).

What's a tag?

Tagging — the part of Facebook Photos that makes the application so useful for everyone — is how you mark who is pictured in your photos. Imagine that you took all your photos, printed them, put them in albums, and then created a giant spreadsheet cross-listing the photos and the people in the photos. Then you merged your spreadsheet with all your friends' spread-sheets. This is what tagging does. When you tag a friend, it creates a link from her Profile to that photo and notifies her that you've tagged her. Your friends always have the option to remove a photo tag that they don't want linked to their account.

Tagging is most commonly used in Photos, but you can also tag friends in Videos, Notes, and even in comments or status updates. All of these little tags allow your friends to know when you're talking about them (good things, of course) or wanting to talk with them about something.

Editing and tagging photos

After uploading the photos for your album, you have several editing options. You can move photos around, add captions and additional tags, as well as change any info you entered when you set up the album, like name or location. You can also add or remove photos from the album you have created. All of these actions can be done fairly easily from the album view (the grid view of all the thumbnails in your album, shown in Figure 12-6). I'll go through each action you can take from this page and then cover the actions you can take on individual photos.

Edit Album Name, Location, Description, and Privacy

Above the top row of photos is a link to Edit Album, to the right of the little blue pencil icon.

This little pencil icon always indicates that you can edit something. Look for it throughout albums and at the top of your Profile for sections you can edit.

Click the Edit Album link to bring up the Edit Album box, shown in Figure 12-7.

Figure 12-7:
Edit your
Album's
info.

> **Edit Album**
>
> Album Name: RV Park in NZ
>
> Where: Where were these photos taken?
>
> Description: We just wanted to stay the night, then we wound up joining the Dharma Initiative
>
> Privacy: Public ▾
>
> Edit Photos · Delete Album   Save   Cancel

These fields are the same ones you saw when you created the album: Album Name, Location, and a Privacy drop-down box. Additionally, you can now add an album description. This description appears beneath the album view and serves as a summary of what's going on in the album. This might be information about when the photos were taken or some thoughts about the photos in general. Remember to click Save when you're done editing this information.

You can also add or edit your Album Description by clicking the little pencil icon at the bottom of your album view.

Delete an album

While you're looking at the Edit Album box, look for a link in the bottom to Delete Album. If you ever decide, in retrospect, that adding a particular album was a poor choice, you can click Delete Album to remove the whole thing.

If you delete your photo album, all the photos in it will be gone forever, so make sure you want to get rid of it completely before you delete it.

Reorder photos in the album

Chances are that if you added your photos in bulk, they don't appear exactly in the right order. And it's awkward when the photos of the sunset appear first, and the photos of your awesome day of adventure come afterward. To reorder photos, follow these steps:

1. **Hover your mouse over the photo you want to move.**

   The usual mouse icon of an arrow changes to a compass-like shape. A similar image appears in the left corner of the photo you are highlighting.

2. **Click and hold the photo.**

3. **While holding the mouse button down, drag the photo thumbnail to its correct place in the album.**

   The other photos shift positions as you move your chosen photo (shown in Figure 12-8).

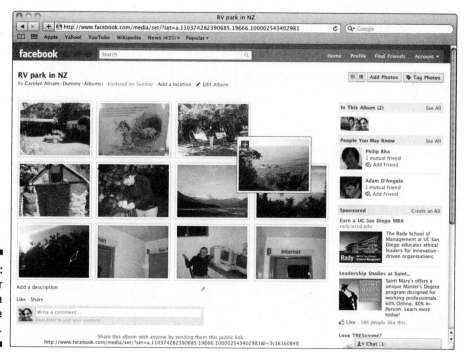

Figure 12-8: Make your album tell a story in the right order.

4. **When the photo is in the spot you want, release the mouse button.**

5. **Repeat with the next photo until your whole album is organized correctly.**

No need to worry about saving. Facebook automatically saves the new order of your album.

Add more photos

After you've created a photo album, you can add more photos to it at any time. Sometimes, depending on how organized the photos on your hard drive are, you may want to add photos in batches anyhow. To add more photos, follow these steps:

1. **Click Add Photos in the upper-right corner of the album view.**

   This opens the same Upload Photos tip that you got when you first created the album.

2. **Click Select Photos to Continue.**

   This opens the interface for exploring your computer's hard drive.

3. **Select the photos you want to add.**

4. **Click Open.**

   The upload process begins, complete with progress bar so you know how long the upload will take.

5. **Click the Done button after the upload is complete.**

   You are asked to tag the new photos you have added.

In addition to the actions you can take on entire album, you can also take actions on individual photos within an album.

Add a tag to an individual photo

If you skipped adding tags earlier, you can always add your tags to individual photos.

1. **From the album view, click the photo you want to tag.**

   This opens the photo viewer, which is a sort of overlay on top of Facebook, shown in Figure 12-9.

2. **In the right side of the top section, click the Tag Photo button.**

3. **Click the face of the person you want to tag.**

   When you hover your mouse over the photo, the cursor turns into a crosshairs icon. When you click a face, it creates a frame and brings up a tagging box, shown in Figure 12-10.

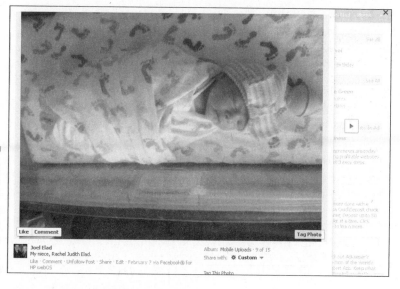

Figure 12-9:
The photo viewer lets you go from photo to photo quickly.

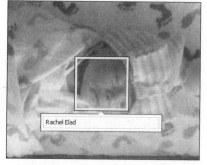

Figure 12-10:
Tagging a friend in a photo.

4. **Enter the name of the person you want to tag into the text box.**

   Facebook tries to auto-complete your friend's name as you type.

5. **Repeat until everyone in the photo is tagged.**

6. **Click Done Tagging.**

   The original Tag This Photo link has become a Done Tagging link. Click it when you're done.

Rotate a photo

Lots of times, photos wind up being sideways. It's a result of turning your camera to take a vertical shot as opposed to a horizontal one. You don't have to settle for this:

1. **From the album view, click the photo you want to rotate.**

   This opens the photo viewer. In the bottom-right corner of the bottom section of the viewer, you'll see two rotation icons — one to turn counterclockwise, and one to turn clockwise.

2. **Click either icon to turn your photo 90 degrees in that direction.**

   You may have to click it more than once to actually get it properly oriented.

Add a description to an individual photo

Just like you can add a description to the album as a whole, you can add descriptions or captions to individual photos:

1. **From the album view, click the photo you want to caption.**

   This opens the photo viewer. Look underneath the top section for your name and Profile picture. There are several links there too: Like, Comment, Share, and Edit.

2. **Click the Edit link.**

   This opens a text box where you can enter your caption.

3. **Enter your caption into the text box.**

4. **(Optional) Add any tags you want about who you were with when the photo was taken (they don't necessarily have to be in the photo).**

   These tags appear in the album caption section as — with <Eric> and <Carolyn>.

5. **(Optional) Add location information about where this photo was taken.**

   Facebook tries to auto-complete your location information as you type.

6. **When you're finished, click Save.**

After you add your caption, the Add a Description link is replaced by the actual description. Click the pencil icon to change the description.

Delete a photo from an album

Maybe you realized that all 20 group shots from the high school reunion don't have to go in the album, or that one photo has a whole bunch of crossed eyes. You can remove photos entirely from an album.

1. **From the album view, click the photo you want to delete.**

   This opens the photo viewer. Look on the right side of the bottom section for a list of links.

2. **Click Delete This Photo.**

   This opens a pop-up window asking if you are sure.

3. **Click Confirm.**

   This brings you back to the album view, now with one fewer photo.

To edit an album at any time, click Photos in the left column on your Home page and then select My Uploads. Click Edit Album beneath the album title you want to modify.

Viewing photos from friends

Although uploading a photo album is a good skill to have, you're actually going to spend much of your time on Facebook looking at other people's albums. As you've already learned, there are basically two ways to view an album (not counting the preview you see in News Feed or on a friend's Wall): the album view and the photo viewer.

Not all albums or photos you view are from albums that your friends created in the ways described previously. Facebook creates albums on behalf of users (like the Wall Photos or Profile Pictures Albums). Sometimes, you'll click a photo of a friend and find you're looking at photos of that friend from a third person's album.

The album view

The album view is the grid of miniature photos that you see when you click the name of an album or click a View Album link. Most average screens can fit about 16 photos in this view, and as you scroll down the page, more and more photos appear until you reach the end of the album.

If you're someone who likes seeing what people are talking about most, look on the top-right corner of the Album View for a series of buttons. The default grid view is selected, but the other button next to it, called Comment View, shows you only the photos in the album that have comments alongside those comments.

Beneath the last photo, you can read the album description (if there is one). There are also Like and Share links. If a friend has posted an album of really fun or beautiful photos, clicking Like on the whole album lets them know that you enjoyed seeing it. Clicking the Share link allows you to post the whole album to your own Wall, send it to a friend as a message, or post it to a group Wall.

There's also a comment box (it says Write a Comment in the text box) at the bottom of the album view. Type your comment text into it and press Enter to leave a comment on the album as a whole.

Photo viewer

The photo viewer is an overlay on top of Facebook that allows you to quickly browse photos and leave comments. The top part of the viewer is where the photo actually is. Clicking anywhere in the photo viewer screen progresses the album from start to finish, although you can also go back by clicking the gray arrow on the left side of the viewer.

The bottom section of the photo viewer provides some information and several ways for you to interact with a photo. A close-up of this section is shown in Figure 12-11.

Figure 12-11:
The bottom
section of
the Photo
Viewer.

This section includes the following information about what you're viewing:

- ✔ Album Name and who it's been shared with.
- ✔ Album Creator or Owner (that is, whose album it is).
- ✔ Which photo you're looking at and how many photos are in the album.
- ✔ Who is in the photo (that is, who has been *tagged* in the photo).
- ✔ Any captions or descriptions that the owner has added.
- ✔ Names of people who have liked the photo. (You can add your name to this list simply by clicking Like.)
- ✔ Any comments people have left on the photo. (You can add your own comment simply by typing into the comment box and pressing Enter.)

Additionally, this section contains five action links:

- ✔ **Tag This Photo:** Just as you can tag your own photos, you can tag friends' photos. Your friend, as well as any people you tag, is notified that you added a tag.

✔ **Add Location:** You can update your photo to indicate where the picture was taken, and Facebook tries to tag it with a location in its database.

✔ **Download:** You can download specific photos to your computer if you want to save them for another use.

✔ **Make Profile Picture:** If you are tagged in a photo, this link allows you to turn it into your Profile picture. You'll be able to crop photos that you make into your Profile Picture, so if there are more people than just yourself in your photo, you'll be able to focus on just you.

✔ **Delete This Photo**: Again, hopefully this won't be something you do often, but if you decide that you don't want this photo in your album anymore, you can delete it using this link.

If you're tagged in a photo and you don't want to be, look next to your name for a link to Remove Tag. Clicking this removes the tag from the photo, and your friend will be unable to retag you.

Looking at the Profile Picture album

Facebook creates an album of all your Profile pictures automatically. It's named the Profile Picture Album. Every time you upload a new Profile picture (see Chapter 2) it's added to the Profile Picture Album.

You can access this album by clicking your current Profile picture from your Profile. This takes you to an album view, where you can see all your past Profile pictures. You can caption, tag, reorder, and delete photos simply by clicking the photo you want to edit.

You can automatically turn any photo from this album back into your Profile picture by clicking the Make Profile Picture link beneath the left corner of the photo. You also see this link beneath any photo in which you are tagged.

Working with Video

Too often, videos wither away on hard drives or cameras or even on mobile phones. The files are big and they can be difficult to share or e-mail. Facebook seeks to make sharing videos easier. So film away and then let everyone see what you've been up to. To add video to Facebook, you want to start from a Publisher. There's one at the top of your Home page, the top of your Profile, and at the top of group pages (in case you want to share a video with a group).

Click the Add Photo/Video link to get started. This opens up the Photo and Video Publisher, shown in Figure 12-12.

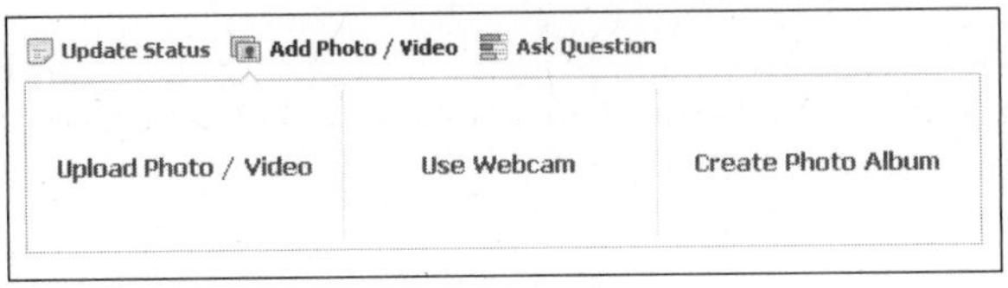

Figure 12-12:
The Photo
and Video
Publisher.

Update Status	Add Photo / Video	Ask Question
Upload Photo / Video	Use Webcam	Create Photo Album

Recording video

If you have a webcam either built into or attached to your computer, you can record videos straight to Facebook.

1. **Choose Add Photo/Video in the Publisher.**

   This opens the Video Publisher, shown in Figure 12-12.

2. **Click Use Webcam.**

   This expands the Publisher and turns on your webcam. By default, it will be in photo mode, so click the tripod icon button to switch to video. You should see yourself (or wherever your webcam is pointed) within the Publisher, as shown in Figure 12-13. Note that you aren't yet recording.

Figure 12-13:
The Record
Video
screen.

Say something about this video...

Share

3. **Click the red button in the middle of the screen to start recording.**

4. **Click the button again to stop recording.**

5. **Press Play to watch the clip and make sure you're happy with it.**

   If you don't like it, click Reset and start over.

6. **(Optional) Type any explanation or comment into the Say Something About This Video box.**

7. **(Optional) Select who can see this video using the Privacy drop-down menu.**

   As usual, your basic options are Everyone, Friends of Friends, Only Friends, or a Customized group of people.

8. **Click Post.**

   The video is posted to your Wall and may appear in your friends' News Feeds.

Just as you can record video straight to your Profile from the Publisher, you can record video straight to your friends' Profiles and straight into messages that you send from the Inbox. From the Inbox, or from your friend's Wall, click the Video icon (it looks like a camcorder on a tripod) to attach a video and then follow the preceding instructions. When you're done, send or post the message with video as you would a normal message or Wall post.

Uploading video

Uploading a video to a website includes going out into the world, recording something, and then moving it from your camera onto your computer. We're going to assume you've already done that part and are now back to being sedentary in front of your computer. Now, to upload a video to Facebook:

1. **Choose Add Photo/Video in the Publisher.**

   This opens the Video Publisher, shown in Figure 12-12.

2. **Click Upload Photo or Video.**

   This expands the Publisher to reveal a Choose File or Browse button.

3. **Click the Browse or Choose File button.**

   This opens a window to explore and navigate your computer's hard drive.

4. **Select a video file from your computer.**

   This brings you back to Facebook, where now there should be a file name of some sort next to the Choose File button.

5. **(Optional) Type any explanation or comment into the Say Something About This Video box.**

6. **(Optional) Select who can see this video using the Privacy drop-down menu.**

   As usual, your basic options are Everyone, Friends of Friends, Only Friends, or a Customized group of people.

7. **Click Post.**

   Facebook opens a new browser window where your video upload can be tracked. Because video uploads can sometimes take a while, you can go back to Facebook and browse around there or go to another website without fear of interrupting your upload.

After your Video has finished uploading, the upload window displays a yellow notice letting you know that it's done. From there, you can click the Close and Edit Video button to move on to editing and go back to your original browser window.

If your browser blocks pop-up windows, you may have some trouble with uploading videos to Facebook. Add Facebook to the exceptions for your pop-up blocker (from your browser options) to make your life a little easier.

Editing and tagging videos

When I talk about editing videos that you've added, I don't mean the kind of fancy editing that editing software like Final Cut Pro might do. Rather, you're editing how these items are displayed and seen by your friends.

To get to the Edit Video screen, click the blue title of the Video and then look beneath it for a list of action links. Click the Edit This Video link. This brings you to the Edit Video page, shown in Figure 12-14.

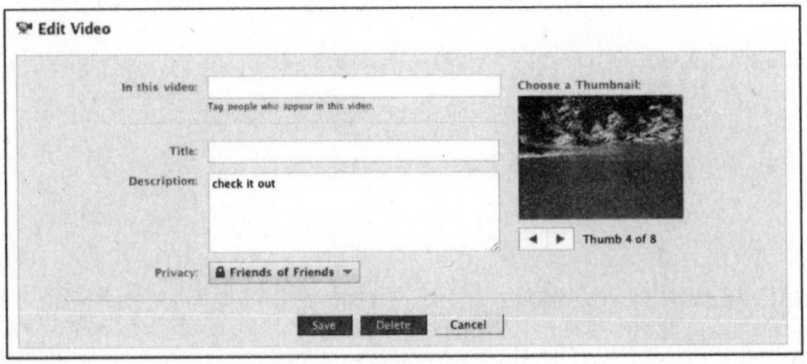

Figure 12-14: The Edit Video screen.

Edit Video	
In this video:	Choose a Thumbnail:
Tag people who appear in this video.	
Title:	
Description: check it out	
	Thumb 4 of 8
Privacy: Friends of Friends	
Save Delete Cancel	

The Edit Video screen has several fields to fill out; most of these are optional:

- ✔ **In This Video:** This option is similar to tagging a photo or a note. Simply start typing the names of all the friends who are in the video and then select the correct friends from the list that displays. Your friends are notified that they've been tagged in a video and can remove the tag if they decide they don't want to be forever remembered as *The one who got pied in the face.*

- ✔ **Title:** Name your video. You can be artsy and name it something like *Boston Cream Meets a Bitter End* or something descriptive like *Pie in the Face.* If you don't choose a title, the video is automatically titled with the timestamp of when you recorded or uploaded it.

- ✔ **Description:** This field is for you to describe what's happening in your video, although frequently videos speak for themselves.

- ✔ **Privacy:** Your privacy options for videos are on a per-video basis. Thus, you can choose that everyone sees *Pie in the Face,* but only certain friends (with strong stomachs) see *Pie-eating Contest.* These are pretty much the same options listed in the "Discovering Privacy" section later in this chapter. For all-around privacy info, be sure to read Chapter 5.

- ✔ **Thumbnail:** On the right side of the Edit Video page is a thumbnail or a still from the video. This thumbnail is what displays to friends in the preview of the video they see before clicking Play. You can change the thumbnail by clicking the arrows to see other possible thumbnails.

Click Save when you're done filling out these fields.

Viewing Videos

You'll mostly encounter videos in your News Feed, where they'll look something like Figure 12-15.

Figure 12-15: A post about a video.

From here, simply press the big blue play button to start the video. It expands within your News Feed so you can actually see what's going on. You can Like, Comment, or Reshare the video.

While the video is playing, you can pause it by pressing the space bar, and you can enlarge the video to fill up your entire screen by clicking the squarish-looking button in the bottom-right corner of the player. (It expands as you hover over it to show you that the video will expand, too.) Press the Escape button on your keyboard to leave full screen mode.

Viewing Photos and Videos of Yourself

When I say *photos and videos of yourself,* I'm referring to photos and videos in which you're tagged. Maybe you tagged them yourself, or your friends may have tagged you. The first place your friends will likely encounter photos of you is in the row of thumbnail photos at the top of your Profile. Clicking any of these photos opens an album of Photos of You. People can click through a full history of photos of you (that they can see, of course).

Another common way to see all the photos of you is to click the Photos tab beneath your Profile picture. Most of your friends can also get to these pages, but the photos and videos they can see may differ. For more on this, see the upcoming "Discovering Privacy" section.

The Photos tab displays photos and videos of you. Remember, if a photo or video of you has a tag that you don't like, you can always remove that tag.

Note: If there's a photo or video you don't want on Facebook at all, even after you've removed the tag, get in touch with your friend and ask him to remove it.

Generally, your friends can comment on any of your photos or videos, and you can comment on any of theirs. You can delete comments you leave as well as any comments on your photos that you don't like or think are inappropriate. You can see all the comments on one of your albums by navigating to that album and clicking the Comments view button in the top right of the page.

Discovering Privacy

While Privacy is covered in detail in Chapter 5, it is worth going over a few settings again now that you really understand what it is you are choosing to show or not show to people.

The two relevant privacy settings in terms of your photos and videos are privacy settings on a per-album/per-video basis and those related to photos and videos in which you're tagged. The interaction between your friends' Tagged Photos privacy settings and your Album Settings can sometimes be a bit confusing, so I'll try to keep them distinct.

Album and video privacy

Each time you create an album or add a video to Facebook, you can use the Privacy drop-down menu to select who can see it. These options are as follows:

✔ **Public or Everyone:** This setting means that anyone can see the album. It doesn't necessarily mean that everyone *will* see the album, though. Facebook doesn't generally display your content to people who are not your friend. But if, for example, someone you didn't know searched for you and went to your Profile, they would be able to see that album.

✔ **Only Friends:** Only confirmed friends can see the photos or videos when you have this setting.

✔ **Custom:** Custom privacy settings can be as closed or as open as you want. You may decide that you want to share an album only with the people who were at a particular Event, which you can do with a custom setting.

 Another way to control who sees an album or video is to share it through Groups. So, for example, a video of your kids playing might be of interest only to people in your family. If you have a group for your family, you can share it from the Publisher on the Group wall, and then only people in the group will be able to see it.

By default, when you start using Facebook, albums and videos you add are visible to everyone. If you aren't comfortable with this, remember to adjust your privacy settings accordingly when you add new photos and video. You can also go to the Privacy page and change the setting for "Your Status, Photos, and Posts" to a more comfortable setting.

Privacy settings for photos and videos of yourself

The beauty of creating albums on Facebook is that it builds a giant cross-listed spreadsheet of information about your photos — who is in what photos, where those photos were taken, and so on. You're cross-listed in photos that you own and in photos that you don't own. However, you may want more control over these tags and who can see them. To control this, go to the Privacy Settings page from the Account menu and click Edit Settings next to the How Tags Work section. This expands a pop-up window. The settings to pay attention to in the context of photos and videos are Profile Review and Profile Visibility.

Turning on Profile Review allows you to review all the tags people add of you before those photos, videos, and other posts are actually added to your Profile. You can reject tags for photos you don't like or don't want to be associated with. Remember, just because you reject a tag doesn't mean the photo won't be added to Facebook; it just means you won't be officially marked as in it. If you really don't want a specific photo or video on Facebook, contact the friend who uploaded the content and ask them to take it down.

Profile Visibility controls who can see the content you're tagged in after you've approved the tags. In other words, just because you've approved a tag, it doesn't mean you want random people able to see those photos and videos. I keep my Profile Visibility for tags set to Friends of Friends, but if you're more shy, Friends is a good setting for this.

Sharing albums with non-Facebook users

If all your friends and all the people you want to see your photos are already on Facebook, sharing photos is easy. You can see their albums, and they can see yours, all in one place. Tags and News Feed help people know when new photos are posted; comments let people talk about those photos. However, most people have at least a few friends who aren't on Facebook, but you can still show them your photos.

From the album view, go to the bottom of the page, where you see the Public link. Copy and paste this link into an e-mail, blog, or a website on the Internet, and anyone who clicks that link can see your album.

Part IV
Pages, Games, and Mobile

The 5th Wave   By Rich Tennant

"I know it's a short profile, but I thought 'King of the Jungle' sort of said it all."

In this part . . .

1 warn you upfront: By the time you've made it to this part, most people wouldn't refer to you as a "dummy." In fact, your friends are possibly already calling you for help with Facebook. Now that you understand the basics of Facebook, you can take it to a whole new level, with new features and new ways to use it when you're out and about.

In both the real world and Facebook, you interact with businesses, brands, bands, and causes every day. In this part, I deal with Pages, which let you represent and interact with public figures and other entities on Facebook.

Also in this part, I cover how you can take Facebook everywhere you go using Facebook Mobile, as well as how to make your Facebook experience richer through the use of third-party applications and games. Hang on to your hats; this is going to be fun.

Chapter 13

Creating a Page for Promotion

*P*icture your town or city. Besides the occasional park or school, it's primarily made of buildings in which people live (like houses) and buildings in which people buy things (like stores). When you drive around town, you see all sorts of activities happening — whether people are throwing a Frisbee around, arguing politics over a cup of coffee, or working out. The world we live in is composed of people, the stuff they do, and the stuff that they need or want. People have real connections to all this stuff: the shops, the brands, the bands, the stars, the activities, the passions, and the restaurants and bars — everything that's important. Facebook is all about people and their real-world connections, including the connections that aren't just friends.

Facebook offers a way for these non-friend entities to be represented as part of your life: *Facebook Pages.* "Page" is a pretty common word on the Internet, so I always capitalize the *P* in Pages when talking about these official ones. There are two types of Pages: *Community Pages,* which are collectively managed and curated by its fans; and *Official Fan Pages,* which are managed and curated by official representatives of any business entity.

This chapter is all about understanding the world of Pages. If you just want to know what these things are that you've been Liking and that have been showing up in your Profile and News Feed, check out the next section, "Pages and You." If you are looking to represent your small business, brand, band, or anything else on Facebook, start with the "Do I need a Page?" section and read on from there.

Getting to Know Pages

When you're thinking about interacting with Pages of any sort, the most important thing to keep in mind is that they are just like the Profiles of your friends. However, you don't friend Pages; you Like them. And when you like a Page, it doesn't get to see your private info. You can do many of the same things with Pages that you can do with friends — write on their Walls, tag them in posts, and so on.

Anatomy of an official Fan Page

The anatomy of Pages should feel pretty familiar to you — they're meant to be just like Profiles. So if you read Chapter 6, most of the following will be a good refresher. Figure 13-1 shows a sample Facebook Page from *The New York Times*.

Figure 13-1: *The New York Times's* Facebook Fan Page.

Here's the anatomy of a Fan Page, across the top from left to right:

✓ **Profile picture:** Just like you and your friends, Pages choose one photo to represent themselves across the site. Usually, it's a logo or an official press photo.

✔ **Like button** *(not pictured):* Before you become a fan, you will see a Like button to the right of the Page's name. Click this to connect with the Page (see the "Connecting and interacting with Pages" section for more on this topic).

✔ **Row of Photos:** Thumbnail photos the Page has added also appear in a row above the Wall.

✔ **Wall (and Publisher):** The Wall is the heart of a Page — it's where the Admins can post updates and where fans can leave Wall posts and comments. Pages may or may not have a publisher here, although most choose to let their fans interact on the Wall as if they were friends (although often the Publisher on Pages has fewer options than on your Profile, usually just Post, Photo, and Link). You'll be able to see the posts from both the Page and from its fans on the Wall.

The following appear down the left-side menu:

✔ **Tabs:** Pages have many of the same tabs that your Profile does: Wall, Info, Photos, and Notes. Pages do have a few more options in terms of adding custom tabs to represent themselves. In some cases, this may be a tab for a coupon or offer; it might be a tab for a custom application.

✔ **Fans:** The number of people who like this Page is tallied on the left side. Facebook is also offering counts for the number of Fans who are discussing this Page or checking in to a physical location.

✔ **Likes:** Pages can Like other Pages, and any ones they've listed as a Like appear here.

✔ **Action links:** At the bottom of the Page are links that you need only occasionally. They are still important to know about because they include both a Report page, which you use to report an offensive Page or one that violates your intellectual property, and Unlike, which you use to remove your affiliation with a Page. You'll also find links here to create your own Page (as well as a Create a Page button on the top-right corner) and to subscribe to posts via SMS or RSS. If you're a Page owner, you'll also see links to Add to My Page's Favorite.

Community Pages

Community Pages, or Pages that don't have one official Admin, are fairly new additions to the Facebook universe. These tend to represent a wider range of things, from basic activities to political statements. Often, the object represented by Pages is something that simply can't be owned by a corporation or individual — things like "sleeping" or "Ultimate Frisbee" or *Pride and Prejudice* (though, interestingly, a new movie version of *Pride and Prejudice* would almost certainly have an Official Page, as opposed to a Community Page).

A sample Community Page is shown in Figure 13-2.

Figure 13-2:
The
Community
Page for
Ultimate
Frisbee.

Community Pages differ from Official Pages in key ways. First and foremost, they don't have a Wall. Instead, they have a Related Posts tab, which shows posts your friends have made mentioning a particular topic or idea, as well as Related posts (posts set to Everyone) that people across Facebook have made. Additionally, Community Pages often pull basic info from sites like Wikipedia to explain the topic they are representing.

As we mentioned, Community Pages are fairly new to Facebook, so they will probably develop additional functionality over time. In the meantime, they function mostly as badges on your Profile, added to your Activities and Interests section.

Connecting and interacting with Pages

Wherever you go on Facebook, and in many places across the entire Internet, you'll see links and buttons prompting you to Like something. You can Like photos, statuses, comments, articles, websites, videos . . . if it's online, you can probably Like it.

You can also Like Pages. And doing so is the way that you become a *fan*, a person who Likes a particular Page. Being a fan accomplishes a few things:

✔ **Gives you a News Feed subscription:** After you Like a Page, you may start seeing its status updates and other posts in your News Feed. If you don't like what you're seeing, you can always hide that Page from your News Feed. To do this, hover over a post in News Feed; then click the small x that appears over it. This opens a menu where you can select "Hide all by <Page>."

✔ **Updates subscription:** Liking a Page subscribes you to receive *Updates*, which are basically messages from Pages. These Updates go to your Other Inbox so they don't interfere with the messages from your friends.

✔ **Provides access to the Wall:** Just as when you add a friend, Liking a Page lets you write on its Wall, usually with the ability to add photos, links, and videos. Not all Pages allow fans to post on their Wall, but many do.

✔ **Displays the page you Liked on your Profile:** It's important to keep in mind that when you Like a Page, it appears in the Activities and Interests section of your Profile, and by default, this section is visible to Everyone.

So what does this all mean for you? Basically, when you Like something, you're starting a relationship with it that can be as interactive as you want or as hands-off as you want. Frequently, people Like a lot of Pages simply as a signifier or badge on their Profiles. Just because you Like the TV show *Modern Family,* you might not care about articles about it, or interviews with the cast. And that's fine. On the other hand, if you like reading those sorts of things, or interacting with other fans on the Wall, you can do that as well. It's a pretty flexible system.

Creating a Facebook Page

A Facebook Page isn't equivalent to an account. Rather, it's an entity on Facebook that can be managed by many people with their own distinct accounts. This section takes you through all the steps of Page creation, administration, and maintenance.

Do I need a Page?

In other words, should I be creating a Facebook Page for my <small business/ band/charity/coffee shop/school/and so on>? The short answer is probably. Facebook Pages, at their most basic level, are for anything that's not an individual person and can even be useful for individual people who are celebrities or who have a public presence beyond their friends and family.

So whether you have a small consulting business, are fundraising for a local organization, are a politician, or are a member of performance troupe, creating a Facebook Page can work for you. You *do* need to be an authorized representative of any larger entity (for example, you shouldn't create a Page for a local congressperson unless you are working for her). But assuming that part is all squared away, you're ready to learn how to create and manage a Page.

Creating your Page

Before you get started, I recommend you read the Pages Terms at www.facebook.com/terms_pages.php. First of all, the Terms clarify some of the expectations for owning a Page and who can create a Page for their business. There are also a few notes about who can see your content when you create a Page and age restrictions on your Page. I cover all of these topics throughout this chapter, but the Terms provide a nice summary. If you violate these Terms, your Page may be disabled, which will be very bad for your business. On the same note, if you create a regular Profile to do the work of a Page (as I describe here), that Profile will almost certainly be disabled for violating the Statement of Rights and Responsibilities (which you can read at www.facebook.com/terms.php).

If you haven't already created an account on Facebook, we highly recommend that you do that first before creating a Page (although you don't have to). If you don't want to, you can still create a Facebook Page. If you take that route, you'll have to take the additional step of entering your e-mail address and creating a password for your Page's account.

Pages can have multiple Admins (or Administrators). If you plan to have other people managing the Page you're creating, they can do so from their accounts. There's no reason to share the e-mail address or password with anyone. In fact, doing so violates the Statement of Rights and Responsibilities. So use your real e-mail address and birth date; don't create a fake e-mail just for the Page. This information won't be revealed to anyone else, and it makes your future interactions on Facebook much easier.

1. **Navigate to** www.Facebook.com **and log in with your username and password.**

2. **Scroll down until you can't scroll any farther and then click Create a Page in the footer menu.**

   This brings you to the Create a Page screen, shown in Figure 13-3.

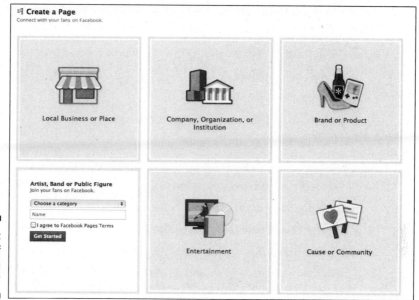

Figure 13-3:
What kind of
Page do you
need?

3. **Click the category your Page falls under.**

   You can choose from the following:

   - Local Business or Place: Place pages have integration with Facebook's mobile check-in service, which I talk about in Chapter 15.

   - Company, Organization, or Institution

   - Brand or Product

   - Artist, Band, or Public Figure

   - Entertainment

   - Cause or Community

   When you choose your category, a registry field appears. (The Artist, Band, or Public Figure category was chosen in Figure 13-3, for example.)

4. **Choose your subcategory from the Choose a Category menu.**

5. **Enter the Name of your Page into the Name text box.**

   When you name your Facebook Page, it's important that you sign up with the exact name of your business, just as you need to sign up for Facebook with your real name.

Good examples of names for hypothetical Facebook Pages are

- Amazon
- Anthony's Pizza
- Stephen Colbert
- Buffy the Vampire Slayer

Bad examples of Facebook Page names are

- Amazon's Facebook Page
- Anthony's Pizza at 553 University Ave.
- Stephen Colbert, Politician & Comedian Extraordinaire
- Buffy the Vampire Slayer Is Awesome

6. **Click the check box to agree to the Facebook Pages Terms.**

7. **Click Get Started.**

Facebook prompts you to add a Profile picture and start gathering fans. You can skip those steps and Facebook will bring you to your Page, which is currently a blank template with a series of prompts for getting set up, shown in Figure 13-4.

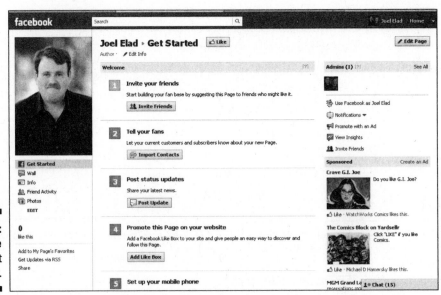

Figure 13-4: Your Page is almost ready.

If all the excitement has gotten the best of you, continue on to customize your Page right away; the next section guides you through that process. If you plan to take a break, you need to know how to get back here. The fastest way is simply to search for your Page name in Search. Because you're the Admin of it, it should be one of your top results.

Getting started

In this section, I go through the steps Facebook takes you through to get your Page set up. These are all located on the Getting Started tab, and the steps will disappear as you complete them.

Step 1: Add an image

Much like getting your own Profile set up, the first step to take on your Page is getting a Page Profile picture in place. Facebook prompts you to Upload an Image from your computer. Click that link and then click Choose File or Browse to select an image from your computer's hard drive.

When the photo has been successfully uploaded, it appears in place of a big question mark on the left side of your Page.

Step 2: Invite your friends

One of the first steps in starting your Facebook account was to get yourself some friends. This is even more important for Pages: Without fans (the Pages equivalent of friends for a Profile), your updates and information won't reach anyone. A good place to start looking for fans is to suggest your Page to your own friends. Click Invite Friends to select friends you wish to suggest your Page to. Your friends see this suggestion on the right side of their Home page. They can choose to either Like the Page (which makes them your fan) or ignore the suggestion.

Step 3: Tell your fans

If you already have any sort of e-mail list you use, you can import it. It's basically the same thing as the Friend Finder, only in this case you should consider it a Fan Finder. Click Import Contacts to start using the Fan Finder. This sends Facebook notifications to anyone who's already on Facebook and e-mails to anyone who Facebook can't find.

Step 4: Post Status Update

Updates and posts are how your fans learn what's going on with you because these updates will most likely wind up in their News Feeds. Make them interesting and engaging to get conversations started.

Step 5: Promote your Page on your website

If you don't already have a website, this option isn't for you. But if your band, business, or whatever it is has another home on the web, you can link it to your Facebook Page by adding a Like box. There are several implementations of the Like box, but they all provide a way for visitors to your website to become fans of your Page on Facebook, which gives you a way to stay in touch with them even when they aren't looking at your website.

Step 6: Set up your mobile phone

This step isn't necessary for all Pages, but it's a good one to be aware of. It lets you use your mobile phone to post status updates and mobile uploads to your page. Mobile uploads can often be the most engaging posts: think of a photo of a group of people cooking at a soup kitchen, or a status update about how busy the store is with everyone taking advantage of your new coupon. These are the types of updates that keep your Page fully human.

Using your Page

After completing the previously described steps, click the Wall tab from the left side menu of your Page. This should look pretty familiar to you. It's a lot like a Profile, with a Profile picture, Wall, Info, and Photos tabs in the left side menu. You'll also see a Wall with a Publisher. The right column is taken up with administrative links for managing the Page.

The Wall

If you have a personal account with a Profile, the Wall will feel very familiar. It's the constantly updating list of posts you've added to Facebook. Check out the Wall for Oreo brand in Figure 13-5 to get a feel for how a Page can use its Wall to showcase what's new and exciting.

The Wall is where people who have connected to you land when they visit your actual Page. The content you publish on your Wall also feeds into their News Feeds, assuming they've subscribed to your posts. In other words, it's a very important place to represent yourself honestly and engagingly through constant updates.

In Chapter 4, I describe the Wall in detail as a place that tells the story of you. That story still needs to be told for you, even when you represent something else. People are going to want to hear from you and to learn about you, and the place they go to do that is your Wall.

As a Page Admin, the most important part of the Wall to understand is the *Publisher.* The Publisher, as shown in detail in Figure 13-6, is where you and fans create the posts that actually appear on the Wall.

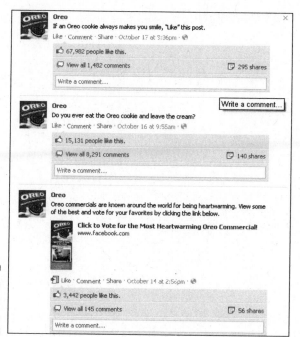

Figure 13-5:
Oreo on
Facebook.

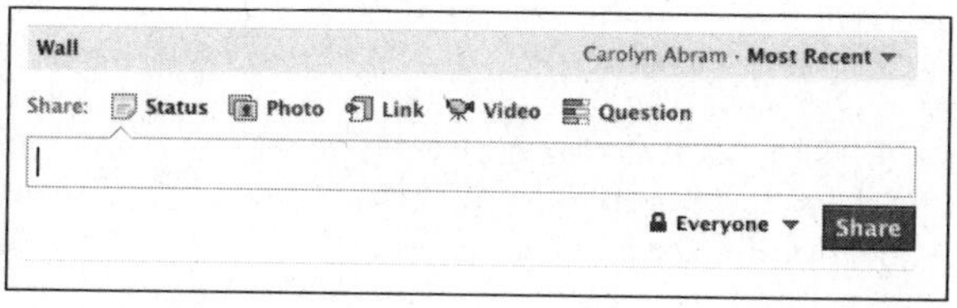

Figure 13-6:
Use the
Publisher to
send posts
out to fans.

The most basic post you can make is a *status update*, a short text post letting people know what's going on, what you are up to, thinking about, and so on. To write a status update, follow these steps:

1. **Click Status or straight into the text box in the Publisher**

2. **Type your update in the What's on Your Mind? text field.**

3. **(Optional) Target your update by clicking the lock icon to the left of the Share button.**

   Status updates from you as an individual have privacy rules about who can and can't see them. Status updates from you as a Page have *targeting* — limitations for who can see which posts. By default, Everyone can see all posts, but you can also choose Customize from the drop-down menu, which opens a pop-up window shown in Figure 13-7.

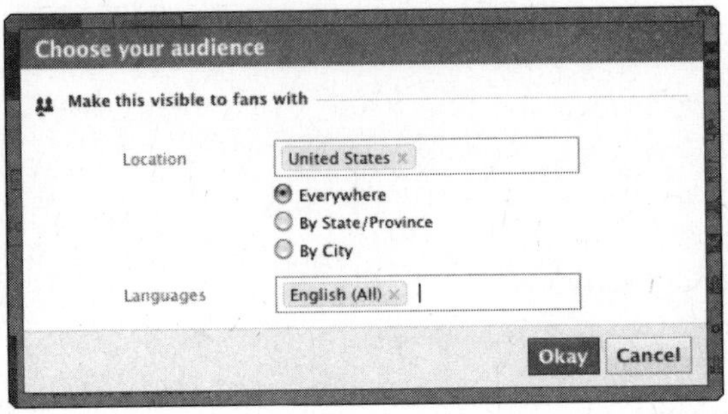

Figure 13-7:
Target your
posts to
specific
groups of
fans.

Choose your audience

Make this visible to fans with

Location	United States ×
	◉ Everywhere
	○ By State/Province
	○ By City
Languages	English (All) ×

Okay Cancel

You can target posts to people by location or by language. This is really useful if, for example, your band is going on tour and you want to let people in a specific area know you're going to be there. Language targeting can also be useful if you have an international presence.

4. **Click Share.**

The post you've created appears on your Wall and in your fans' News Feeds.

In addition to posting status updates, you can post photos, links, videos, and Questions to your fans. You can learn more about asking questions and polling people in Chapter 10.

By default, people who have Liked your Page can post on your Wall and Like and comment on your posts. This is a chance to engage with your customers and fans. If someone asks a question, answer it. If they report that they had a problem with your product or experienced bad customer service, let them know that you're listening and will do your best to correct the problem.

Information

In addition to the Wall tab, your Page has an Info tab where you can share some of the more basic information about your Page. This may be something like hours of operation (if you're a business) or contact information or information about the cause you are promoting.

To edit the information that appears in your Info tab, click the Edit Page button in the upper-right corner of the Page. This brings you to the Edit Page screen, shown in Figure 13-8.

Just like the Edit Profile page, the different sections you can edit appear down the left side of the Page. Editing your Page has to do with managing settings as well as managing what people see. To edit what people see in your info, click Basic Information.

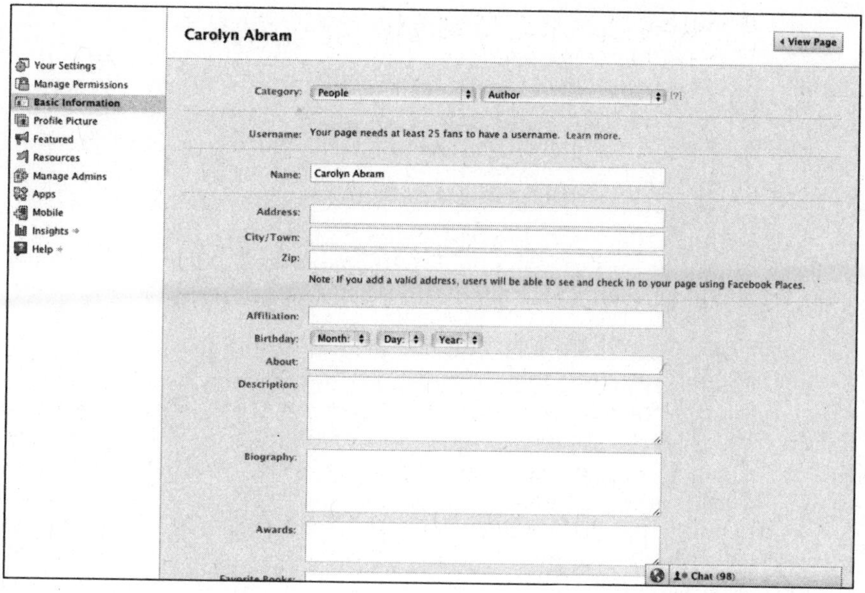

Figure 13-8:
Edit your
Basic
Information.

Each Page has slightly different fields to fill out based on the category you selected when you created your Page. Most are pretty self-explanatory. You can always change the category of your Page using the drop-down lists at the top of the Page.

Usernames

Usernames are specialty URLs for directing people to your Page. A specialty URL might be something like www.facebook.com/carolynabram or www.facebook.com/facebookfordummies. In other words, it's a way to direct people to your Page without worrying about them finding you in search. You need to have at least 25 fans before you can create one, but after you reach that threshold, click the Create a Username for this Page? link in the Basic Information tab of the Edit Profile page.

This brings you to the Create Username page. Here you can select from your Pages and then enter the username you'd like. If the username is available, you're asked to confirm that it is the username you want.

After you select a username, you can't change it. Make sure you've spelled it exactly how you want it and are very happy with it before you click Confirm.

Other Page tabs

After you return to the main view of your Page, you'll see several tabs listed down the left side. In addition to Wall and Information, your Page has a number of different tabs that people can visit. Although not all Pages have all of these, here are a few of the most common tabs.

Photos

Use the Photos application to publish albums for your fans to enjoy. If you own a restaurant, you may want to take photos of your most popular dishes, creating one album for breakfast, one for lunch, and one for dinner. Bands may publish albums from their various concerts and events. Brands may use photos to show off people engaging with their products. For example, Nike might show women in Nike shoes, Starbucks might show a kid with whipped cream on his nose, and Blockbuster might show friends watching a movie. Add photos by clicking the Photo link in the Publisher (remember to make sure you're on your Page's Publisher, not on your Profile's).

If you choose, you can set the Photos application to allow people who've connected to you to add photos to your Page (you can do this from the Manage Permissions tab of the Edit Page screen). These photos are shown in a separate section from the photos you add, which helps viewers distinguish the content you're adding to your Page from what your fans add. Publishing photos is often a great way to keep your Wall looking really diverse and to generate interesting posts to go into your subscribers' News Feeds.

Events

If you ever host any kind of event for your business, you'll get a ton of value from using Facebook Events. Stores create Events for their big sales, comedians create Events for their shows, and clubs create Events for their special-party nights. To create an Event, click the pencil icon in the upper-right corner of the Events box on the Control Panel. Choose Edit from the menu that appears. This takes you to the Create Event page, where you can fill out the info and upload a photo (see Chapter 11 for more details on Event creation). Finally, send a message to all your subscribers informing them about your Event.

Discussion board

Many Pages come with a discussion board where your fans congregate and discuss topics relating to your Page. It's like a more organized version of the Wall. With the Discussion Board on your Page, users can instantly start topics and respond to others.

Video

Just like with Photos, you can upload videos to your Page. For example, a coffee shop may show a video of a barista making a fancy drink, a singer may show clips from a recent concert, and a movie theater may show clips from an upcoming film. The online shoe retailer Zappos has added some pretty funny videos that include interviews and short skits done by its employees. It's a great way to put a human face on a brand. You can add videos from the Publisher, which you can discover how to do in Chapter 12.

Applications

Photos, Events, and Video are applications that Facebook has built to integrate with Pages and Profiles alike. But what about specific features for specific types of Pages and specific needs? What if you want people to get access to coupons at all times? Or you're a band and want information about all of your albums to be discoverable? Well, as they say, there's an app for that. Facebook has the ability to integrate with applications built by developers outside of Facebook.

Rather than browsing the Application Directory for good applications, some Page administrators check out their competitors' Pages to see what kinds of applications seem to be working well for them. If you do this and see one you like, search for the application in order to add it to your Page.

Lots of musicians use an app called BandPage (by RootMusic) to display a music player at the top of their Pages' Walls. Or, you could add a Welcome tab with customized content using Static HTML. When you find an App you want to use on your Page, go to that App's main page and click the Go To App button. Then, authorize the app and select the Page you want to add it to.

Using Facebook as your Page

After you start to get going with your Page, you may choose to "switch" into your Page. In other words, you can use Facebook as if your Page, not you, were the main user. Your Page has its own News Feed, where you can catch up on your Page's favorite Pages and leave comments as your Page. You will have easy access to your Page-related tools and settings on the left side of your Home page, instead of getting distracted by your friend's photo of her trip to Greece.

Switching into your Page (you can see a sample switched Home page in Figure 13-9) is especially useful for big companies or brands who want to have a full-time presence on Facebook. This way, the notifications coming in are all about your Page, instead of mingling with the personal stuff.

From your Page, click the link in the right column to Use Facebook as <Page Name>. This switches you into using Facebook as your Page. Click the link again to switch back.

Switch back to your personal account from the Account menu in the big blue bar on top of every Facebook page.

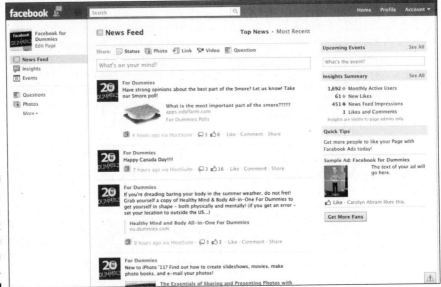

Figure 13-9:
Using
Facebook
as a Page
instead of a
person.

Managing Your Page

As the creator (and therefore Admin) of your Page, you have a lot of control over how people see and interact with your Page, as well as the ability to designate additional Admins. You control most of these options from the Edit Page screen. To access it, click the Edit Page button in the upper-right corner of your Page.

Your settings

The top section of controls on the Edit Page screen has two different controls you can turn on or off:

- ✔ **Posting Preferences:** This check box lets you decide whether the posts you make from the Publisher on your page come from you personally or from your Page. For example, on the Facebook For Dummies Page, I could make posts come from Facebook For Dummies (the Page) or from me (Carolyn Abram).

- ✔ **E-mail Notifications:** This check box lets you decide whether you want e-mail notifications about posts or comments on your Page. Depending on how busy your page is, this might get overwhelming to keep on, so remember where it is in case you need it later.

Manage Permissions

The Manage Permissions section of the Edit Page screen controls who can get to your Page and how they can interact with it:

- ✔ **Page Visibility:** This check box allows you to make your Page visible to Admins only. This is most useful if the Page is under construction because you're adding some new stuff to it. Don't accidentally leave it in this state when you're done making updates or your fans won't be able to find you.

- ✔ **Country Restrictions:** Leaving this box empty means everyone everywhere can see your Page. Entering specific countries means only people in those countries can see your Page.

- ✔ **Age Restrictions:** By default, anyone on Facebook can see your Page. If your Page deals with adult products or themes, you may want to consider age restrictions. There's a specific Alcohol-Related option in the drop-down if your Page is related to alcohol products.

- ✔ **Wall Tab Shows:** You can choose from two options here: All Posts or Only Posts by Page. In other words, you can choose whether people can see posts from fans mixed in with posts from your Page, or just the posts from your Page. Even if you choose Only Posts by Page, people can click to see posts from fans.

- ✔ **Expand Comments:** The Expand Comments check box means comments on posts are automatically visible (instead of people needing to click to see them).

- ✔ **Default Landing Tab:** You can choose which tab people will land on when they come to your Page. You may want people to see your Wall right away or you may want them to get the info first. You can also choose any tabs you've added via applications.

- ✔ **Posting Ability:** These three check boxes allow you to choose whether you want people to be able to post to your Wall, add Photos to your Page, add tags to your Photos, and add Videos to your Page. I highly recommend selecting at least the first box: Without interaction, your Page won't feel as Facebook-y. (And yes, *Facebook-y* is a word. Look it up.)

- ✔ **Moderation Blocklist:** If your page is seeing a lot of debate, and some of it is simply offensive or not productive, you can create a moderation blocklist. If words added to the blocklist are found in a post, the post is automatically marked as Spam.

- ✔ **Profanity Blocklist:** You shouldn't need to come up with your own blocklist for the most commonly offensive terms (none of which I can print here as an example for you). If you want at least a little sanitization of your Wall and Discussion boards, you can turn this to Medium. If you want it to be as PG as possible, turn it to Strong.

Even with your blocklists on, you should still be diligent about checking your Wall, Reviews, and Discussion Boards for the types of offensive language that can't necessarily be caught by these automatic systems.

- ✔ **Delete Page:** If at some point you decide you don't want your Page anymore, you can delete it here.

Basic Information and Profile Picture

I've already covered the Basic Information and Profile Picture sections, but come to them to change what appears on your Info tab and your Page's picture. You can also hide or unhide the row of photos at the top of the Wall from the Profile Picture section.

Featured

As a Page, you can Like other Pages. Then, you can feature particular Pages by adding them to the Featured Likes. The Likes you feature always appear in the left column of your Page, beneath all the tabs and the number of people who like your Page.

You can also feature yourself or other Page Admins by selecting the ones who always appear in the featured section on the left column of your Page.

Resources

The Resources section basically provides you with some helpful links to things like the Best Practices, to make your Page engaging, or a link to Twitter (so when you update Twitter, you also update Facebook). If you find yourself with questions that this chapter doesn't answer, this section is a good place to go to get more answers.

Manage Admins

The Manage Admins section displays a list of current Admins and allows you to remove them. You can also add additional Admins by typing a name or e-mail address into the text box. Remember to click Save Changes when you're done.

Apps

The Apps section allows you to see the applications your Page is using. If you no longer use some of these applications, click the X to the right of them to remove them. Note that Photos, Events, Notes, and so on are all considered applications. Facebook considers these integrated applications, so you can remove these applications just like any others.

Some apps may have a little link underneath that says Link to This Tab. Clicking this link provides you with a URL you can share. When people click that link, they go to that specific tab on your Page, as opposed to the Wall, which is where people go by default.

Mobile

The Mobile section gives you information about the various ways you can use your mobile phone to control your Page. If you attach a particular mobile phone number to your Page, you can use that number to update your status and post photos.

Additionally, if you have many different Admins who want to post updates on the go and who have smartphones, you can use your Page's Mobile E-mail to e-mail posts to your Page. Each Page gets a special e-mail address (usually one that's hard to memorize, so be sure to save it to your contact list). Your Page Admins can then e-mail photos or status updates to that address, and they are added to the Page.

Insights

The little arrow icon next to the Insights item in the left menu of the Edit Page screen signifies that it takes you away from the Edit Page screen to the Insights page. Insights are a way of tracking metrics about your Page. Insights are covered in more detail in the "Insights into users" section later in this chapter.

Help

Clicking this tab takes you to the Help Center, where you can search for answers to specific answers you couldn't get answers to here.

Know-It-All: Finding Out Who Is Using Your Page

Within 48 hours of publishing your Page, you start to see exactly how people are engaging with it. From your Page, look on the right side for a link to View Insights. Clicking that link brings you to the Insights page, where you can see valuable metrics about how people are interacting with your Page. By default, you land on an *overview page* for that Page, which gives you feedback about the current success of your Page. By default, you see two main graphs about your Page's metrics — information about users and information about interactions. You can adjust whether you see a week's worth or a month's worth of data at a time, as well as change the date range to a point in time in the past.

Want to do your own analysis of the data? Click the export button to export raw Facebook data into an Excel spreadsheet, where you can make your own custom reports.

Insights into Users

The first graph on the overview page is about users. Clicking See Details brings you to the Users Insights page (shown in Figure 13-10). Insights on Users focus on Likes (or fans) and Activity from those people. At the very top of the page, you see information about New Likes (in other words, how many new people have liked your page in the last week or month), Lifetime Likes (total number of fans), and monthly active users.

Active users are people who have viewed or interacted with your Page in the last month. Although getting a lot of people to Like your Page is a good goal to have, it's important to balance it with having an interesting and engaging Page that people want to come back to.

There are five graphs on the Users Insights page:

- ✔ **Active Users:** This graph breaks down your daily, weekly, and monthly active users. Remember, an active user is defined as one who looks at or interacts with (commenting, Liking, and so on) your Page.

- ✔ **Daily Active Users Breakdown:** This graph lets you delve further into how people are interacting with your Page. Are they just looking? Or are they Liking posts? Or leaving Wall posts themselves?

- ✔ **New Likes:** This graph shows you the trend in Likes, and from where people are Liking your Page. This lets you know if your Page is spreading virally or due to something like an e-mail blast you sent out.

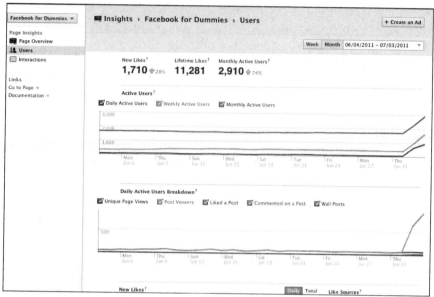

✔ **Demographics:** This graph shows the gender and age breakdown of your fans, as well as the countries, cities, and languages in which most of your fans fall.

✔ **Activity:** Activity is actually broken into two graphs: Page Views and Media Consumption, which is the number of photo and video views in addition to audio listens. You can also see here the tabs that people visit on your Page and the external referrers (websites outside of Facebook that link to you).

Insights about Interactions

The second graph on the overview page is about Interactions. Clicking See Details brings you to the Interactions Insights page, shown in Figure 13-11.

The two big numbers at the top of the page here correspond to the number of times a post you made was viewed in the time period you specify, and the number of Likes and comments left on posts you created.

The Daily Story Feedback graph shows Likes and comments in correspondence to date so you can check to see which posts generated the most feedback. Additionally, any *unsubscribes* — people hiding you from their News Feed — are reported here. If you're getting a lot of unsubscribes, you may be annoying people, so think carefully about what and how often you are posting.

Figure 13-11:
The
Interactions
Insights
page.

The Daily Page activity graph compares how often all the different types of interactions are happening, so you can see if you're getting more Wall posts than reviews.

To modify the graphs you're looking at, use the check boxes at the top of each graph to change how many different things you're tracking at one time.

Promoting your Page through advertising

Creating and maintaining a Page on Facebook is free. However, if you want to promote it more aggressively or bring attention to a specific Event, you can consider running advertising on Facebook as well.

Creating an ad on Facebook consists of three main steps after you click Promote with an Ad on the right column of your Page:

1. **Create your ad:** Ads on Facebook have fairly standard formats. Your ad needs a title or headline, body text of fewer than 135 characters, and an image. You also need to have a link ready for where you want your ad to take people when they click it.

2. **Target your ad:** Here is where advertising on Facebook can become most efficient. You can target an ad based on location, age, and gender, as well as by likes and interests. Narrowing down the people who see your ad to those people who are likely to want your product or service makes your advertising more effective. Say your band has a performance you'd like to promote. You could walk around town distributing flyers, but wouldn't it be better if you only gave flyers to people who like the type of music you perform or like similar artists? That's what Facebook ads allow you to do. You can type in virtually any terms and

use them to get your ads in the right hands. Depending on what you're promoting, you can also target your ads to your fans, to your non-fans, or to friends-of-fans.

3. **Budget and schedule your ad:** You can spend tons of money on your ads or very little. Facebook's ad system is a cost-per-click auction model. In other words, you set a bid for how much you'll pay for a click. Your ad goes into rotation with other ads based on the targeting you chose, and you only pay for the number of times your ad is clicked (it's up to Facebook to show it enough times to get more clicks). You can set a maximum daily budget so you won't ever be surprised by how much you're spending. You can schedule your ad to run continuously or to stop after a certain date.

Remember, the key to effective Facebook advertising is knowing what you want to accomplish with your ads. Do you want more fans of your Page? Do you want to distribute a coupon to get more customers in the store? Do you want to bring attention or solicit donations for a cause? Knowing the answers to these questions helps you create and target the best ads.

Chapter 14

Games, Apps, and Websites on Facebook

In This Chapter

▶ Understanding what applications are and how they work on Facebook

▶ Seeing how applications can enhance your Internet experience on and off Facebook

▶ Discovering good, trustworthy applications

*I*f you're familiar with Apple's iPhone commercials, you've probably heard the phrase "There's an app for that." In iPhone-land, an app is a kind of program you add to your phone that suits your particular needs. It might help you track what you eat, or it might be a game you can play alone or with friends.

Well, Facebook has its own ecosystem for apps and games that it calls *Facebook Platform*. Platform is a way to give developers who don't work at Facebook the ability to incorporate Facebook information and interaction into the programs they build. In turn, you can use these programs within Facebook to enhance your interactions with friends.

This chapter covers the basics of playing games and using other apps on Facebook. If you want some recommendations for good games and apps, check out Chapter 16.

Understanding What an App Is

For a long time, Facebook was the only company that could build apps for Facebook. And it did; it built Photos, Videos, Notes, Events, and Groups. All these are considered applications because they use the same core set of information to function: the connections between you and your friends. Building these apps on Facebook made them easier for people to use and also better. Photos and Videos are great because of tagging — the connections between the people in them. Events and Groups are great because the invite lists are easy to access, and you know who everyone is. Additionally, the News Feed and ticker help spread information about photo tags and events and so on, meaning more people can find out about cool things.

When Facebook opened up Facebook Platform, it enabled third-party developers anywhere to build applications that fit into Facebook as easily as Facebook Photos fits in. So an application is any sort of Facebook integration into websites, games, and software.

The thing to remember about apps and games is that, for the most part, they weren't built by Facebook. Why does this matter? Because sometimes, some apps might behave differently than Facebook does. First of all, things may look or function differently. And, unfortunately, sometimes the apps you use that may be less inclined to offer you a useful product and more inclined to spam you (and your friends) or do shady targeting with your information. That's why when you use applications, you need to authorize their use of your information, and why you should learn how to get rid of applications that are behaving badly.

Getting Started: Request for Permission, Sir

Before you can start using most applications within Facebook, you need to grant the applications permission to interact with your timeline, account, and information. Most applications achieve this through the Request for Permission page, shown in Figure 14-1.

The Request for Permission page, shown in this example with the application Words With Friends, has five sections:

- ✔ **Access My Basic Information:** Your *basic information* here is the directory information about you that Facebook requires to stay public: your name, timeline picture, gender, user ID, Friend List, and networks, if applicable. Additionally, any information that is visible to Everyone is counted as public information. If you allow this application permission, it is able to access all of this information. (You can learn more about controlling this information at the end of this chapter, or in Chapter 5, where I cover privacy in detail.)

- ✔ **Send Me E-mail:** By default, when you click Allow, games and apps can store your e-mail address in their servers, as opposed to accessing it through Facebook's servers as it does the rest of your information. This allows you to establish a direct relationship with the app because the developers can always get in touch with you, without Facebook acting as an intermediary.

  Giving your e-mail to an application means you can get e-mail newsletters and other updates direct from the source without logging in to Facebook. However, if you aren't sure about an application's trustworthiness, you can click the Change link, shown in gray beneath the Send Me E-mail icon. Doing so expands an option to send you e-mails through an anonymous source or *proxy* e-mail, as shown in Figure 14-2.

  If at any time you don't want to share your e-mail address with a certain application anymore, you need to unsubscribe from their e-mail list through *them* as opposed to through Facebook.

- ✔ **Post to Facebook As Me:** This permission allows an application to post status updates, photos, and other content to your timeline. These posts may then appear in your friends' News Feeds and tickers. An example of a post might be something like Figure 14-3. Here, Bejeweled Blitz is showing off Amy's achievement in the game to her Facebook friends. You can remove this permission later on if an application is posting too much or posting spammy stories on your behalf.

Figure 14-2:
Send
e-mails to
your contact
e-mail or
to a proxy
e-mail.

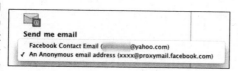

Send me email
Facebook Contact Email (@yahoo.com)
✓ An Anonymous email address (xxxx@proxymail.facebook.com)

Figure 14-3:
Posts
gain atten-
tion for you
and for the
application.

✔ **Access My Data Any Time:** Some applications need access to your Facebook data even when you're not on Facebook to properly function. For example, a desktop application like Facebox (a Mac app that alerts you when you've received a new Facebook message) needs access to your messages to determine when you receive a new message. Most of the time, this information is used to improve your experience within an app or game by ensuring the information about you and your friends is current.

✔ **Publish Games and App Activity:** Granting this permission means apps or games can publish your scores, achievements, and other app-specific activity to Facebook, where it will likely appear in the app ticker (a feature I discuss later in this chapter).

Other permissions

You'll encounter the five permissions described previously most often, but there are two additional permissions you'll occasionally come across. I briefly explain these permissions as well:

✔ **Access My Timeline Information:** Here, Facebook defines *Timeline Information* as any part of your timeline or account that is restricted in any way — in other words, things that are set to any privacy level lower than Everyone. Applications such as Groupcard — an application that helps you send personalized greeting cards to a friend from multiple friends — need access to some of these things in order to create personalized greeting cards for your friends. Applications are required to list every piece of information they need access to. Pay attention to what fields applications ask for access to and make sure the fields they ask for jibe with what they purport to do.

✔ **Access Information People Share with Me:** This gives an application permission to access information about your friends' game and app activity (if their privacy settings allow) to customize your experience with the app.

If you've reviewed the requested permissions, trust the application, and are excited to get started, click Allow.

You might be wondering how you'll find the apps and games you wind up using. Mostly, you'll find them through friends. Friends may send you invitations or requests to join in a game they are playing. You'll also be able to see your friends' app activity in multiple locations on the site, such as your News Feed or the App and Game Request pages. You can also find apps by searching for them by name (say, if you heard about a really cool app from a certain *For Dummies* author) in the Search box in the blue bar on top of each Facebook page.

Now What? Using Applications

Because there are so many different applications answering so many different needs, it's difficult to tell you what to do next. However, there are some common prompts and on-screen actions. Read on to find out what form these might take.

Application Home pages

For the most part, after you've allowed an application access to your information, you'll be taken to its Home page. You can see a sample Home page, for Bejeweled Blitz, in Figure 14-4. Its Home page basically prompts you to start playing the game. When I say that applications "live" inside Facebook, this is what I mean — the game's home is beneath the main Facebook menu (the blue bar on top), as opposed to on another site entirely.

From Facebook's perspective, all it's doing is providing a blank space for applications to do their things, which is why it calls any page generated by an application a *canvas page.* Canvas pages vary widely from application to application, but generally they direct you to take some sort of action. This might be playing a game, promoting a cause, or taking a quiz.

Bookmarks

The left menu on your Home page displays shortcuts to various parts of Facebook: messages, friends, photos, and so on. As you begin playing games and using other applications, bookmarks appear in the Apps section of this menu. The ones you use most often are highest up. Click the More link to see all of your apps and games.

You can add an app to the Favorites section of you left menu by hovering over the app's name from the Apps section and clicking the pencil icon that appears to the left. Select Add to Favorites from the drop-down menu that appears.

Invitations and Requests

You can invite friends to Events; you can also invite friends to play games or support causes. These are actions you always have to make a special effort to do, regardless of whether the application was built by Facebook.

Figure 14-4:
The Home
page for
Bejeweled
Blitz.

Additionally, after your friends are playing the same game as you or using the same application, you can send them requests for specific actions. For example, within many games, you can send requests to people for specific items they may have accumulated through their own play.

Most games prompt you to invite friends to play with you fairly frequently. The beauty of games on Facebook is that you can play against your friends, which means they can be opponents in word games, generals in your online armies, or tellers in your online banks. Figure 14-5 shows the confirmation dialog box that you need to approve to send an invitation. That dialog box shows what the actual invitation will look like.

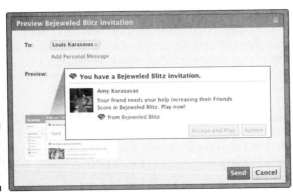

Figure 14-5:
Sending
requests.

Extra Credit

Lots of games on Facebook allow you to purchase virtual goods within the game. For example, if you haven't yet gotten to the level needed to unlock an advantage in Bejeweled Blitz, you could purchase that advantage (five extra seconds!) for a dollar or two. Some games create their own currency which you buy, and some use Facebook Credits.

Facebook Credits is a payment system built by Facebook that other applications can incorporate into their service. Purchasing Facebook Credits is a way to purchase goods without sharing your credit card information with a million different game developers. Each Facebook credit costs ten cents, so one dollar gets you ten credits. Games may require different numbers of credits for different items.

Using Facebook outside of Facebook

Imagine all the things you do on the web. Maybe you buy gifts for friends at Amazon. Or perhaps you blog or like to comment on blogs that others write. Maybe you look up movie reviews. Maybe you rent movies through sites like Blockbuster or Netflix. You do any number of things, all of which could be better if your friends were there.

Luckily, Facebook offers websites multiple tools to make the time you spend on their site more meaningful. There are four main ways to use Facebook on other websites, and each interacts with your account and information a little differently.

Log in with Facebook

The first way to improve your web experience is to eliminate the need to create and register a brand new account for every Single. Web. Site. Ever. The web forms that ask for your name, your e-mail, and subsequent prompts to upload a profile picture and find friends — these are things of the past. As an example, check out how you can create a new account on Quora, a question-and-answer site.

When you go to the Quora sign-up page at www.quora.com, you'll notice that it features the fact that you can register by using an existing Facebook or Twitter account. Clicking the Connect to Facebook button brings up the familiar Request for Permission screen, shown in Figure 14-6.

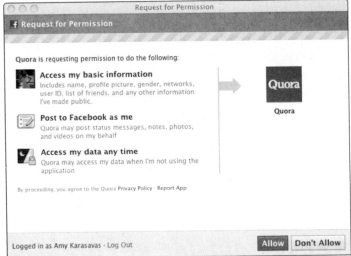

Figure 14-6:
Connect
your
Facebook
account
with Quora.

Notice a few important things about this screen. My name is already display-ing at the bottom of the screen because I was logged in to Facebook when I clicked the Connect prompt. If you aren't logged in to Facebook, you see a Facebook log-in screen in this space, where you have to enter your Facebook login e-mail and password. Also, if you share a computer with other Facebook users, make sure that the name displaying in the bottom of the dialog box is, in fact, yours.

The second thing to remember is that Quora is basically asking you for the same information as the Request for Permission screen for an app or game on Facebook — in order to work, this site needs access to your Facebook info. For the most part, sites that use Login with Facebook need this info for legiti-mate purposes, but you should still make sure you trust the site that you're using before you click Allow. WellknownMcgoodreputation.com? Probably okay. SleazyMcSpamerson.com? Maybe do a little more research first.

Figure 14-7 shows the final screen of this sign-up process. Similar to appli-cations on Facebook, Quora builds its own list of users' e-mails so you can enter any e-mail you want here if you don't want it using the one Facebook supplied (remember, that was part of the permissions you allowed). Additionally, Quora asks you to create a password so that in the future, you can log in just using your e-mail address and password. The sign-up process will be slightly different for each site that uses social plug-ins, so don't worry if the site you're using has a slightly different look and feel than Quora.

Each time you return to a site like Quora, you'll be able to log in by clicking the log-in button. You may also see mini thumbnail photos of friends who have previously logged in or registered through Facebook.

Figure 14-7:
Finish
signing up
by creating
a password.

Social plug-ins

Wish you had a better sense of whose Yelp reviews you could trust? Looking for a movie recommendation? Don't actually like dealing with strangers on the web? Welcome to *social plug-ins*.

A *social plug-in* is the term used to refer to applications that live on other websites. These plug-ins may or may not be similar to the applications you use within Facebook; however, you do not need to allow access to your Facebook information in order for a social plug-in to work (you do, however, usually need to be logged in to your Facebook account). It may be more accurate to say that these plug-ins use a Facebook link that you establish to make your experience on their sites more social. These sorts of plug-ins have already been touched on throughout this book — Liking and commenting on other websites, for example.

Here's a more complete list of some of the integrations for social plug-ins you may see as you use the Internet.

Like and Send

With social plug-ins, you can Like virtually anything, anywhere on the web. Facebook has made it very easy for companies to add Like buttons to their online content. You can see a great example of this on the articles of popular news site Salon.com (www.salon.com). Alongside every article is the Like button, as well as statistics about who has Liked it. If any of your friends have Liked something, you'll see their names in addition to the number of Likes. If you like something, it is shared on Facebook on your timeline and in your friends' News Feeds and tickers. You can see a Like button and its News Feed post counterpart in Figures 14-8 and 14-9.

Figure 14-8:
The Like button on a post on Salon.com.

Figure 14-9:
A News Feed story about an article Amy liked.

Any content you Like off of Facebook is shown on your Facebook timeline and may appear in your friends' News Feeds. If liking a controversial article might make waves with some of your friends, you can instead choose to share it as a link and set privacy on that share.

For certain sites, a Like box, such as the example in Figure 14-10 from the website www.postsecret.com, shows recent updates from the website's Facebook Page as well as a sampling of people who like the Facebook Page.

Similar to Like, some websites feature Send buttons. Likes are shared publicly through timelines and News Feeds. Sending something allows you choose just a few friends to share it with privately. Your friends receive the content you send in their messages Inbox in Facebook.

Comments

Figure 14-11 shows a comment box powered by Facebook. In theory, any blog, whether a big name or just your friend's little hobby, can add a comment box so people can quickly sign in and leave comments. This usually is preceded by a log-in screen.

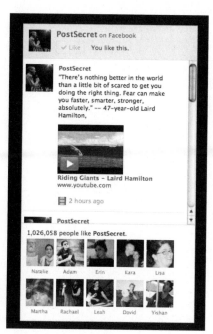

Figure 14-10: The Like box.

Figure 14-11: Comment on a blog using Facebook.

Feeds

Virtually every news site is a feed of updating posts, so it makes sense that you might want some help from your friends in understanding what to read or pay attention to. A few types of stream plug-ins help with this:

✔ *Recent Activity* **or Activity Feed:** Recent Activity boxes on websites display recent actions taken by your friends on the website in question. In Figure 14-12, you can see an example of Recent Activity — in this case, friends queuing and Liking various TV shows on www.hulu.com.

✔ *Recommendations* **or recommendation streams:** Recommendations shows similar information to recent activity, although instead of what's most recent, it shows what's been Liked by the most people in order to show what you might like as well.

Figure 14-12:
Friends'
Recent
Activity on
another site.

> ✔ ***Live streams* or *status streams*:** Live streams are a very popular integration for various television channels to use during live broadcasts. The first implementation of live streams was actually during the 2008 presidential inauguration of President Obama, and since then, the live streams of status updates have created an online interactive component to everything from live sports to the Oscars and other award shows.

Friends

As I've said over and over again, everything is better when your friends are there. That's the philosophy of those websites that display a count of friends who have in some way connected their accounts with their Facebook accounts.

Instant Personalization

Instant Personalization is Facebook's way of connecting accounts to trusted partners on behalf of its users. There are only eight partner sites at the time of this writing: Bing, Pandora, TripAdvisor, Yelp, Rotten Tomatoes, Clicker, Scribd, and Microsoft Docs.

Unlike social plug-ins or login, Instant Personalization requires little work on your part. You go to a partner site for the first time and you'll receive a notification on the screen that Instant Personalization is at work. Instant Personalization automatically shares your public information (name, timeline, picture, gender, networks, and other info you've shared with Everyone) with that site. In other words, the partner site doesn't have to wait for you to click a log-in button. As soon as you arrive, you are logged in. The idea of Instant Personalization is to make the social aspect of these websites completely seamless. As you use the Internet radio station Pandora, for example, you see which of your friends like the artists and songs that appear on your screen. You can instantly find all the people on Yelp whose reviews matter most to you: your friends.

If you don't use any of the partner sites mentioned and don't like the idea of your information being shared in this way, you can opt out of Instant Personalization. Go to the Privacy Settings page, click the Edit Settings link next to Apps and Websites, and then click the Edit Settings button next to Instant Personalization. Deselect the check box at the bottom of the page that appears.

Social Apps

Recently, Facebook announced a new variety of applications that grant other services and websites direct access to your timeline and News Feed.

Social apps are different from social plug-ins, login, and Instant Personalization in that you can grant them a one-time blanket permission to automatically share your activity on the site to your timeline. The first time you authorize the application, you'll see a permission screen similar to Request Permissions that lists which pieces of your Facebook information the application needs to function. If you agree to allow access, click the Add to Timeline button, and the app will be able to post to your timeline every time you take an action on their site. A popular example of a social app is *The Washington Post* Social Reader. Every time you read an article on *The Washington Post*'s website at www.washingtonpost.com, a story with the article's name is posted to your timeline. Remember that anything posted to your timeline can appear in your friends' News Feeds and tickers.

Interacting with content your friends post via social apps does not require you to leave Facebook. Click any active link from a social app post, such as an article title, to open that content within Facebook.

Mobile plug-ins

If you have an iPhone or other smartphone that uses apps, you can connect your Facebook account with mobile apps. Mobile versions of games like Words with Friends use this to help you find friends to play with. Photo-editing apps like Instagram use this to help you share cool photos with friends. You need to approve applications on your phone the same way you do on the web.

Managing Your Applications

Depending on how you wind up using applications and how you feel about the ones you've added, there may come a time when you want to change some things. After you reach that point, there's one place you need to be: the Apps, Games, and Websites Privacy page.

You can get to this page by following these steps:

1. **Click Privacy Settings in the Account menu, the white downward-facing arrow, from the big blue bar on top.**

   This takes you to the main privacy page.

2. **Click Edit Settings next to the Apps and Websites heading.**

   This takes you to the Apps, Games and Websites privacy page, which has four sections:

   - **Apse You Use:** This is the section I discuss in just a second. It's where you go to control what information apps are getting about you.

   - **Info Accessible Through Your Friends:** When your friends use other websites and applications in conjunction with Facebook, they may find it useful to see their friend's (that is, your) information. An example of this is a birthday calendar application, which may alert them when a friend's birthday is on the horizon. In this section, you can determine the information about you that your friends can allow sites to access. If you want your friends to be able to use a birthday reminder website to remember your birthday, you may want to allow them to give your birthday to the sites they trust. If you never want any application having access to some of your information, such as the notes you write, for example, deselect that check box and your friends won't be able to import that information into their applications.

   - **Instant Personalization:** Instant Personalization is a way of instantly linking your Facebook account to partner sites. If you don't want Facebook doing this on your behalf, opt out here.

   - **Public Search:** This listing refers to a limited view of your timeline that anyone can see if he searches for your name in an external search engine such as Google. Your Public Search Listing shows a portion of the content you've made available to everyone.

From the Apps, Games, and Websites Privacy page, you can get to the App Settings page, shown in Figure 14-13, by clicking the Edit Settings button next to Apps You Use. By default, when you arrive, you see the applications that you've used most recently. To the right of each application's name are two links: Edit and a little X. The X can be used to remove an application entirely. Clicking it removes your authorization of it, meaning that application won't have any access to your info. If you want to use it again, you need to go through the request for permission screen again.

Clicking Edit expands the page to show you what permissions you have previously granted to the application and which you can revoke if you desire. You can also see the last time the application accessed your information and what they accessed at that time.

All of these settings should look familiar; they are the same fields you see in the Request for Permission dialog box. If you don't like how an application is behaving, you can remove certain permissions. Sometimes app and game developers require that certain permissions be granted. In other words, the app is saying, if we can't use this info, we can't function. In that case, the only solution from your perspective is to remove the application entirely and stop using it.

If you are editing a specific app, head to the App Activity Privacy drop-down menu, which contains the familiar Audience Selector. Use the Audience Selector to choose who can see your activity from that app.

App Settings

You have authorized these apps to interact with your Facebook account:

Hulu	Less than 24 hours ago	Edit	×
Salon Registration	Less than 24 hours ago	Edit	×
Quora	Less than 24 hours ago	Edit	×
Rdio	October 3	Edit	×
Spotify	October 3	Edit	×
OM NOM NOM	More than 6 months ago	Edit	×
iPhoto Uploader	More than 6 months ago	Edit	×
Presence	More than 6 months ago	Edit	×

Figure 14-13:
The App Settings page.

Opting out

If you've been reading this chapter and you're getting more and more queasy about the idea of using games and apps, you can consider opting out of using Facebook Platform entirely. This isn't a step I personally recommend because applications can be a lot of fun and very useful.

But if you are very protective of your information, you can effectively turn off Platform. From the Apps, Games, and Websites Privacy page, look at the bottom of the Apps You Use section for a Turn Off All Platform Apps link. Clicking this link brings up a pop-up window with a list of all the apps you currently use. You then need to select the ones you want to disable, which, in this case, is all of them. You can't disable just a few and still opt out of Platform entirely. When you have selected all the apps, click the Turn Off Platform button. This keeps all applications from accessing your information, even through your friends. It also keeps you from being able to play games and use apps that your friends recommend.

Controlling what you see from friends

You know that aunt you have who shows up for family events wearing crazy hats and talking a little too loudly about everyone? More than one family member may have listened to her lecture on the virtues of macrotastic vitamin supplements and responded simply with, "To each, her own." Similarly, you may have some friends on Facebook who just don't have the same taste as you when it comes to applications. Maybe they take a ton of quizzes, which flood your Home page with information you don't find particularly enlightening. Or maybe they are always challenging you to games of Scrabble, and you've been boycotting that game since that one time you got two triples in one word and knew you would never top yourself. Here are a few tips that will keep your Facebook just the way you like it:

- ✓ **Block an application:** If you find an application offensive or it keeps sending you some sort of invites, you can block it. From its invitation or request, click the x button next to the request. A yellow box appears with a confirmation. Within the yellow box is a Block <App> link. This prevents the application from being able to contact you at all, even if your friends are using it. You can always unblock an app from the Block Lists section of your Privacy pages.

- ✓ **Ignore a Friend's Invites:** Remember that crazy aunt? She may be sending you invites or requests from multiple hat-related applications. Click the X next to the request or invitation. When the yellow confirmation box appears, click the Ignore All Requests from <Friend Name> link. You can still be friends, but you won't receive all the annoying invites anymore.

- ✓ **Hide from News Feed:** If your Home page is inundated with some type of post that you just don't like to look at, use the Hide links (which you can find by clicking the caron in the upper-right corner of that post when you mouse over it) to hide all posts for that application. Alternatively, if all the annoying posts are coming from one person using many different applications, you can hide that person from News Feed.

Game Requests and App Requests

The App and Game Request Pages live in the Apps section of the left menu of your Home page. The layout of the App and Game Request pages is mostly the same and serves as a destination for responding to app requests and invites as well as a portal for discovering popular apps your friends use.

- ✓ **Requests:** Various applications (as you've learned by now) may prompt you to send requests out to friends to bring them into your game or app. These might be requests for items or for something else. The requests are at the top of the page so you can respond to them quickly.

- ✔ **Top Games/Apps:** This section displays a list of applications that are popular, interesting or appealing to you based on three different factors.

- ✔ **Recommended:** Apps recommended by your friends and the Facebook community.

- ✔ **Newest:** The latest apps added by developers.

- ✔ **Friends Using:** Apps a number of your friends use organized by most to least.

- ✔ **Featured:** On the right side of the page are games or apps that Facebook has chosen to highlight. These games are often some of the most popular that the platform has to offer, so this is a good place to start looking for a new game. If one looks interesting, you can click the Play Now link beneath its name to get started right away.

The app ticker

A special app ticker, shown in Figure 14-14, lives on the right side of every canvas page. This ticker behaves exactly like the Home page ticker — it continuously refreshes with real-time stories, and you can click any story to expand it — but the stories are only about friends using games and apps on Facebook. The goal of the app ticker is to make your experience with apps and games more social by facilitating interaction with your friends. For example, if I notice a friend and I are playing Words with Friends at the same time, I might decide to send her a game invite, knowing that we could begin the game immediately.

The top of the ticker contains space for five app bookmarks so that you can switch to another app with one click. These are the same five apps that show up on the Apps section of your left menu. Red notifications on the bookmarks indicate that you have a request or message regarding that app. If you can't see an app, click the aggregate icon at the far right of the top row to see a list of all bookmarks.

You can control who sees your app activity in their app ticker from the App Settings page. Note that if you choose Only Me from the audience selector for a specific app, no one will be able to see anything about your interactions with that app.

There are a few options for removing a story from your app ticker. Click a story to expand it and then click the caron in the upper-right corner. From the drop-down menu, you can choose to remove a post, stop receiving stories about someone playing an app, or hide all stories from an app.

I know this sounds silly, but games on Facebook are incredibly addicting. I could tell you how much time was lost writing this chapter due to the discovery of Words with Friends and the relapse into Bejeweled Blitz, but it would be so, so shameful. Suffice it to say, remember to shower and change your clothes every once in a while.

Figure 14-14:
The app
ticker.

Signs of a trustworthy application

As you explore games and applications, you will come upon Request for Permission screens frequently. Before you click those buttons, you should make sure you trust the application. To determine that, check out the Application's profile Page by clicking its name from Search Results or from the Request for Permission page (the Application's name is a link on that page).

An Application's profile Page is a rich source of information that helps you know whether the application will behave in a way that is respectful of your information and of your friends. You don't want an application that uses your photos in ways you don't like, nor do you want an application that's going to spam your friends every time you sneeze. Here are some things to look for:

✔ **Your Friends are using it:** The first mark of a good application is that your friends are using it. This usually means it's fun, useful, and generally good. One note of clarification: When I say your Friends, in this case, I mean *the Friends you interact with most on Facebook*. If that guy you met that one time (TGYMTOT) sends you an invitation and you think, "Weird, I haven't spoken to TGYMTOT on Facebook in ages," there's a good chance that this is a bad application using nefarious methods to get invitations sent.

  ✔ **Its reviews are generally positive:** You can see an overall rating of an application in the left column of its Fan Page. Also, click the Reviews tab. There you can see ratings as well as explanations of those ratings. Lots of comments like "Spammed my friends" or "Too slow" should tip you off that this may not be a good experience.

  ✔ **It provides some level of support:** Whether through FAQs or responding to timeline posts, good applications respect their users and try to at least help them out a bit if they get stuck. Now, some applications may be developed by one guy in a garage, so their level of support may not be as high as one developed by a big corporation, but the gesture is what signifies a good application.

App Support

Providing support is one of the traits of trustworthy applications. There is any number of reasons you might need some help in the process of using a game or an app. Many of them are the same problems you encounter on Facebook: harassment, spam, something not working or being broken. However, because apps and games are often built by outside developers, Facebook itself can't help you with these problems. You will need to contact the developers of whatever app or game you are using. To get in touch with them, follow these steps.

1. **Navigate to Facebook's Help Center by clicking Help Center from the Account menu, the downward-facing white arrow, or by directing your browser to** www.facebook.com/help.

   This brings you to Facebook's Help Center. It has a search bar at the top for typing in keywords and questions and a few different sections in the right column to help you browse more easily.

2. **Click the Games and Apps link at the bottom of the page.**

   This displays a list of all the games and apps you've used. Each name is a link.

3. **Click the game or app you need help with.**

   Each app or game has different protocols for helping you. When you click some, they take you to an outside website or forum where you can search for answers to your questions or solutions to your problems. Others, when clicked, display a pop-up window where you can submit information about your issue.

If an app or game is doing something really bad, you can also report it to Facebook. Reasons for reporting an app would include things like pornographic content, misleading or deceptive content (promising free iPods in exchange for you taking an action, for example), or using your information without your permission in ads. From any page within the app, scroll down to the bottom and click the Report App link. Select the Report radio button and click Continue. You'll then be asked to provide more information about why you're reporting the app and what it's done wrong.

Chapter 15

Facebook on the Go

*T*hroughout this book, you've been discovering how Facebook enriches relationships and facilitates human interaction. Nevertheless, what can Facebook do to enrich your relationships while you're *not* sitting in front of a computer? Life is full of beach weekends, road trips, city evenings, movie nights, dinner parties, and so on. During these times, as long as you have a mobile phone, Facebook still provides you a ton of value.

Don't take this as license to ignore a group of people you're actively spending time with to play with Facebook on the phone (unless, of course, you *want* to ignore them). Moreover, don't think you can tune out in class or in a meeting to Poke your friends. But knowing the ins and outs of Facebook Mobile actually enriches each particular experience you have — while you're having it. With Facebook Mobile, you can show off your kids' new photos to your friends or broadcast where you're having drinks, in case any of your friends are in the neighborhood and want to drop by.

Facebook Mobile serves another function — making your life easier. Sometimes you need *something,* say, a phone number, an address, or the start time of an Event. Maybe you're heading out to have dinner with your friend and her boyfriend whose name you can't, for the life of you, remember. Perhaps you hit it off with someone new and would like to find out whether she's romantically available before committing yourself to an awkward conversation about exchanging phone numbers. (Just a heads-up: This conversation can be awkward even *if* you find that person is single. Facebook can do a lot for you, but not everything.)

In this chapter, I make an additional foolish assumption: I assume that you have a mobile phone and know how to use its features. If you don't have a phone, you may consider buying one after reading this chapter; this stuff is way cool. Mobile texts simply require that you own a phone and an accompanying plan that enables you to send text messages. Facebook Mobile requires a mobile data plan (that is, access to the Internet on your phone). Facebook applications require that you own any one of the several types of phones that Facebook can currently support.

Is That Facebook Mobile in Your Pocket . . . ?

In many ways, using a mobile phone can augment your experience of using Facebook on the computer. This first section is about how you can easily add information to and get information from Facebook when you're not physically in front of the computer. These features are primarily for people who do most of their Facebooking on the computer, but sometimes interact through their phone.

Getting started

This chapter teaches you almost everything you need to know about using Facebook with a mobile device. However, if you ever find yourself asking questions about it while near a computer but *not* near this book, you can go to www.facebook.com/mobile for much of the same information. To get started with Facebook Mobile, you first need to enter and confirm your phone number into the settings page:

1. **Choose Account Settings from the Account menu in the upper-right corner of the big blue bar on top.**

2. **Click the Mobile tab on the left side of the page.**

3. **Click the green Add a Phone button.**

   This opens the Activate Facebook Texts dialog box.

4. **Choose your country and your mobile carrier.**

   If your carrier isn't listed, sadly you may be out of luck for using Facebook from your mobile phone.

5. **Click Next.**

   This brings you to Step 2, which you actually have to do from your phone.

6. **From your phone, text the letter F to 32665 (FBOOK).**

FBOOK texts you back a confirmation code. This can take a few minutes, so be patient.

7. **Enter your confirmation code into the empty box.**

8. **Choose whether you want your phone number added to your Profile via the Add This Phone Number to My Profile check box.**

   Personally, I find it very useful when friends share their mobile numbers on Facebook because it allows me to use Facebook as a virtual phonebook. But if you're not comfortable with that, simply deselect the check box.

9. **Click Next.**

   This confirms your phone and brings you to set up for Facebook Texts. Your phone also receives a confirmation text with some instructions.

Mobile Texts

After your phone has been confirmed, Mobile Texts are the most basic way to use Facebook on your phone. You don't need a camera on your phone or a smartphone to get use from Mobile Texts. Using just a simple SMS (Short Message Service) or text message, you can update your status to let people know where you are and what you're up to.

Here are the various actions you can take on Facebook via SMS:

- ✔ **Update your status** by typing your status into the text message. You can type in any sort of phrase and it will appear on your Facebook Profile and in your friends' News Feeds with a little mobile icon next to it so people know you're on the go.

- ✔ **Add a new Facebook friend** by sending **Add** and the person's name. Using your phone to immediately friend a person you meet is less formal than exchanging business cards, less awkward (and more reliable) than exchanging phone numbers, and gives you more flexibility later for how you want to get in touch. However, remember that by friending someone from your phone has all the same implications as friending someone from your computer, so add wisely.

- ✔ **Subscribe to a friend's status updates** by sending the word **subscribe**, followed by your friend's name. If you have a few friends who you like to hear absolutely everything from, this is a great way to keep up on the go. If you subscribe to a lot of friends' statuses, make sure you have unlimited texting; otherwise, charges could pile up quickly.

- ✔ **Unsubscribe from a friend's updates** by sending the word **unsubscribe** followed by their name. Remember the last paragraph, where I said that charges for subscribing to a friend's status could pile up quickly? If you realize you want fewer people's statuses coming straight to your phone, just unsubscribe from the ones you don't want to see on your phone.

✔ **Stop getting texts** by texting the word **stop.**

✔ **Restart getting texts** by texting the word **on**.

What's all the buzz about?

An old wives' tale claims that when you feel your ears burn, someone is thinking about you. Here's a slight modification: Someone, somewhere, is thinking about you when your phone starts vibrating. Turning on Facebook Mobile Texts means that you can be notified via SMS when someone Pokes you, sends you a Facebook message, comments on your photos and notes, writes on your Wall, or requests to be your friend.

To activate Facebook Mobile Texts, go to the Mobile tab of the Account page; click Edit next to the Notifications section and then select the Text Notifications are On radio button. You can see the Mobile tab in Figure 15-1.

The Notifications section of this page also allows you to control the following options:

✔ **Receive text notifications from friends only**

The text notifications you get can be modified from the Notifications tab of the account Page (more on that in a minute). The Receive Text Notifications from Friends Only check box here controls whether you receive text notifications of message from friends only. This means that if, for example, you get texted whenever you get a new message, you can choose to only receive texts about messages from friends. Messages from strangers won't be texted to you.

✔ **Text times**

You can specify what time you prefer to receive text notifications so, for example, if someone Pokes you at 2 a.m., you don't have to wake up for it. (Maybe you *only* want to know who's trying to Poke you at 2 a.m. No judgment here.)

Additionally, you can opt to not receive text notifications (via the Do not send SMS notifications check box) while you're actively using Facebook because that can get a bit redundant.

✔ **Whose Status Updates Should Go to My Phone?**

This is another entry point for specifying which of your friends' statuses you want sent to your phone. Simply type the name of the friend you want to subscribe to into this text box and press Enter.

If you subscribe to the status of someone who doesn't spell very well but is conscientious about it, you may receive several texts as he tries to get his status just right.

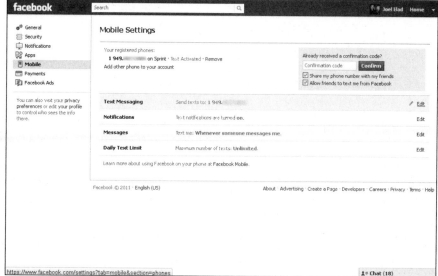

Figure 15-1:
Set up your
preferences
for receiving
notifications
on your
mobile
phone.

The Daily Text Limit section allows you to modify the number of text messages you receive per day. If you have a mobile plan for which you're charged per text message (and you're exceedingly popular), use the settings that limit the number of messages Facebook sends you per day. Otherwise, you might have to shell out some big bucks in text message fees.

Mobile notifications

From the Account page, you can also jump into your Notification settings, where you can control which notifications go to your e-mail account and/or to your phone.

From the Notifications tab, you can see recent notifications you've received, as well as all possible notifications, sorted by application and feature. Click Edit next to each section to decide which notifications will be sent to your e-mail account or to your phone. An expanded section of the Notifications tab appears in Figure 15-2, showing the Facebook section of notifications. After you've activated mobile texts, this screen displays one column with check boxes next to each type of e-mail notification.

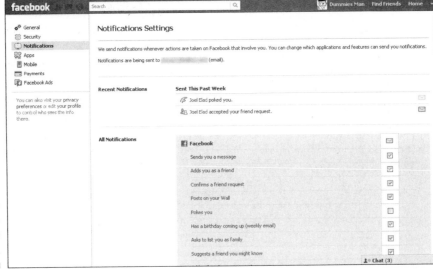

Figure 15-2:
Control
mobile
notifications
from the
Notifications
tab.

Mobile uploads

Two types of people can be found at social events. You find the scrapbookers who always remember to bring their fancy-schmancy camera to every gathering. (You know who they are because they tell you to smile a lot or sometimes say "Act natural.") Then there is the person who never intends to take photos but who, when the birthday girl blows out her candles, the host spills wine on himself, or someone arrives wearing a hilarious slogan tee shirt, is ready with the mobile phone camera. (Hey, it captures the moment, right?)

For the scrapbookers of the world, Facebook Photos was built for you, and you should make sure to read Chapter 12 to get the most out of photos. After the social gathering, plug your camera into a regular computer, weed out the bad photos, and upload the rest to a photo album. However, if you're the mobile photo taker, Facebook Mobile Photos is for you. With mobile photos, you have no time for weeding, editing, or second thoughts. Mobile photos pave the way to instantaneous documentation.

Here's how to upload a mobile photo:

1. **Make sure you have a phone with a camera and you know how to use it to take a picture and/or take a video.**

   If you're unsure, check your phone's instruction manual or ask just about any teenager.

2. **Go to** www.facebook.com/mobile **and look beneath Upload Photos via E-mail for a personalized e-mail address.**

This e-mail address, of the form aaa111parsec@m.facebook.com, makes it possible for you to upload photos to your Profile from your phone. Optionally, you can click Send My Upload E-mail to Me Now. From there, you can ask Facebook to either e-mail you the address or text it to your phone. Either way, you want to add that personal e-mail address to your phone's contacts so you can easily message it in the future.

3. **Wait for something hilarious or beautiful or awesome to happen and then take a picture or video of it.**

4. **Send an e-mail to the address you just found with the picture or video attached.**

   The subject line is the caption, so choose wisely.

5. **(Optional) To make any edits or changes to your mobile photos, go to your photo albums and click the Mobile Uploads album. To make changes to your video, go to the Video application and edit there.**

   Note that the default visibility of your mobile uploads is Everyone.

Using Facebook Mobile

Viewing a web page from your phone can be extremely difficult because the information that is normally spread across the width of a monitor must be packed into one tiny column on your phone. Facebook is no exception to this, which is why the very first tip in this section is this: Never go to www.facebook.com/ on your mobile phone. You'll regret it.

But fear not, you still have a way to carry almost all the joys of Facebook right in your purse or pocket. On your mobile phone, open your browser application and navigate to m.facebook.com — a completely new window in Facebook designed specifically to work on a teeny-tiny screen.

If you use an iPhone, or one of a few other select phone types, entering www.facebook.com/ redirects you to iphone.facebook.com, which I talk about in more detail in the upcoming "Mobile Apps" section.

The first time you arrive at m.facebook.com, you're asked to log in. After that, you never (or rarely) have to reenter your login information unless you explicitly select Logout from your session, so be sure you trust anyone to whom you lend your phone.

If you plan to use the Facebook Mobile site frequently, we recommend that you have an unlimited data plan that allows you to spend as much time on the Mobile Web as you like for a fixed rate. The Facebook Mobile site is nearly as comprehensive and rich as the computer version. You can spend hours there and, if you're paying per minute, spend your life savings, too.

Mobile Home

After you log in, you see the mobile version of the Facebook Home page. Although the design of the mobile site is somewhat based on the design of the regular website, it has some significant differences. Some of the differences exist simply because of less space; the mobile site must cut to the chase while allowing you to get more information on a particular topic.

The other differences arise because people using Facebook on a mobile phone often have different needs than those at a computer. For example, one of the first pieces of information you find on a friend's Profile is her phone number (if she has it listed) because if you're looking up someone on a mobile phone, you may be trying to contact her by phone.

To follow along with this section, you can navigate to m.facebook.com on your web browser. Just imagine what you see on about one-tenth of the screen.

The Mobile Web page is shown in Figure 15-3. In this section, I detail what you see on the Mobile Home page; we cover the other pages in the following sections.

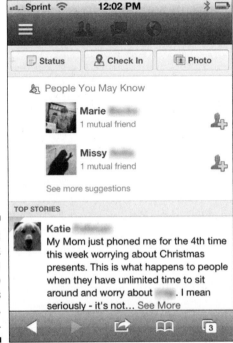

Figure 15-3:
Facebook
Mobile
Home, also
known as
m.facebook.
com.

From m.facebook.com, you'll see these items in your Mobile Home page:

- **Facebook menu (three horizontal lines):** The three horizontal lines at the top-left corner of the screen represent the drop-down menu with links to the usual Facebook suspects: News Feed, Messages, Places, Events, Friends, Groups, Notes, Settings, and Help.

- **Friend Requests, Messages, and Notifications:** The three icons across the top of your screen are used throughout the Facebook experience: Friend Requests, Messages, and Notifications. Any unread instances in each category will be marked with the red flag, just like when you log onto your Facebook account from a PC. Tap any of these icons to review that category.

- **All Stories:** This button, at the top right of the screen, opens a list where you can choose whether to read All Stories, Status Updates, Photos, Links, Pages, Events, Videos, or the activities of a defined List or network of Facebook friends.

- **New Notifications and Birthdays:** When you reach the mobile site, you find whether you have any upcoming Events or notifications right at the top of the Home page. These links only appear if you have something waiting for you. You will also be notified if any of your friends are celebrating their birthdays today, so you can easily hop over to their Walls and wish them a happy day.

- **Status button:** When you use Facebook from your mobile phone, you're probably not sitting at your home office, workplace, or school. You may be trapped in jury duty, hanging with friends at a bachelorette party, or waiting in line for a roller coaster. Facebook makes it super-easy to update your status so you can spread the news the moment you're doing something that you want people to know or when you want people to meet you.

- **Photo button:** If you want to upload a photo to your Facebook account, you can tap this button and either use your built-in camera to take a photo (or video) or pick a photo from your mobile device photo library to upload to your page.

- **Check In button:** If you want to let people know where you are, through Facebook, tap the Check In button to check in with your location and share that status on your Wall.

- **Mobile News Feed:** Shows you the most recent stories that you would see on your computer. As you scroll down, you'll get more and more stories, so you can keep reading to your heart's content.

Mobile Profile preview

Profiles on Facebook Mobile are designed differently than Profiles on the regular site. As we mention in the previous section, a lot of information from specific applications may be absent from your Profile. Moreover, the structure is ordered such that the information you're after is closest to the top. When you arrive at any mobile Profile, you see the most usable and actionable subset of the available information. A See Full Profile link at the bottom gives you access to the rest.

Access to information on mobile Profiles is the same as on the regular site — when you look at your Profile on the mobile site, you see your information, but that doesn't mean everyone has access to it. They have access only to what you specify via the privacy settings on the regular site:

- ✓ **Wall:** When you visit a friend's Profile, you land on their Wall tab, where you can see their most recent posts, whether that's a status update or a photo. You can also see how many people Liked or commented on their status, and you can add to those counts yourself by doing the same. You can also use the text box to leave a post on your friend's Wall to say hello.

- ✓ **Info tab:** To see the Info tab, you likely have to click the link to it located above Profile picture. This shows the same information you can see on that person's Info tab on the normal site, but reordered to be mobile-friendly. Contact info is right at the top of the Info tab because when you look someone up on a mobile phone, you're often after a number or address. If the person has his phone number listed here, you can select it to start the call.

- ✓ **Photos tab:** Also above the Profile picture is a link to go to a Photos tab. This allows you to see all your friend's photos by album.

- ✓ **Profile picture and Info:** The first thing you see is their current Profile picture. You can also see some of their most basic info such as where they work and where they went to school.

Mobile Inbox

The Mobile Inbox functions the same as the Inbox on the regular site, but you access it in a compacted view. In the Mobile Inbox, your messages are sorted by the time the last message on a thread was sent. Each thread includes the sender's name, the date or how recently the message was sent and a snippet of the message.

When you enter into the mobile thread, similar to regular Facebook, the newest message is at the bottom with the Reply box beneath it. At the top of the message is a drop-down menu with action links. You can Mark Read/Unread, Delete, Mark Spam, Move to Other, Archive, or Forward. The Mark as Unread link is particularly handy because often you read a message on your mobile phone, but don't have time or energy to type a response right then. Marking it as Unread reminds you to respond when you return to your computer.

Mobile Apps

Mobile Web and Mobile Texts are generally pretty flexible systems. You can use them from almost any type of phone, with any sort of plan, and they generally look and work the same way. However, mobile apps are a different breed. They are tailor-made by Facebook for specific devices, and the way they work from device to device can differ greatly depending on factors like whether there's a touch screen or not. Right now, Facebook has apps available for the following phone types: iPhone, Palm, Sony Ericsson, INQ, Blackberry, Nokia, Android, Windows Phone, and Sidekick.

The mobile app for each device may look and operate differently. The following section focuses on how the Facebook for iPhone app works, which looks identical to the mobile browser interface for Facebook. If you don't use an iPhone, play around with your own phone; chances are, there are a lot of similarities.

iPhone Layout

The Facebook app for iPhone is organized exactly like the mobile home page for Facebook, as shown in Figure 15-3 before. When you tap the top-left corner (represented by the three horizontal bars) of the screen, you see the drop-down menu to access the different parts of Facebook, as shown in Figure 15-4.

✔ **Profile:** This menu option takes you to your own Profile. In general, Profiles are organized into the same Wall, Info, and Photo tabs as Profiles on the site; however, each is abbreviated, and any additional tabs that might exist on the real Profile aren't on this version of the website. The Info tab has only basic and contact information. To add something to your Wall, you can use the Share photo or Write Post button located above your Profile picture.

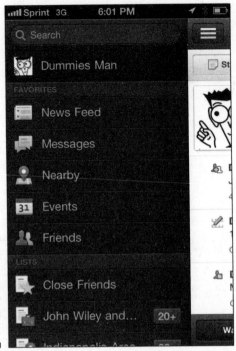

Figure 15-4:
Facebook for iPhone menu for user Joel Elad.

✔ **News Feed:** News Feed is the same News Feed you see on your computer screen, a constantly updating list of what your friends are up to at this moment. You can comment on and Like posts from News Feed, as well as using the Publisher there to add your own status update or mobile upload.

✔ **Messages:** This is where you access all your messages. From here, you can compose a new message, delete a message, or reply to one. You will also see the number of unread notifications as a number on the right side.

✔ **Nearby:** This is an aspect of Facebook that lets you use your phone's GPS to share or check in where you are with your friends. It's so special that it gets its own section. If you see a number next to Nearby, that shows the number of friends that have checked in close to you recently.

✔ **Events:** This lets you get to any Events you've RSVPed to. This is incredibly useful when it turns out neither you nor your significant other remembered the exact street address of the dinner you're going to.

✔ **Friends:** The Friends section of the iPhone app should feel fairly similar to your phone's contact list. You can scroll through your friends from A to Z or search them from the search box at the top of the list. Any friends who have phone numbers listed have a big phone icon next to their names. Tap the phone icon to initiate a text or phone call.

✔ **Groups:** This lets you interact with any groups you are a part of. This way you don't miss out on discussions when you're out and about.

✔ **Apps:** This brings you to your own Facebook apps, like Photos, Notes, and anything you installed on your Facebook account that would work on a mobile device.

✔ **Pages and Lists:** These last two options let you go directly to any Pages on Facebook that you follow or any Lists of friends or acquaintances that you have created using Facebook.

At the bottom of the menu is the Account option. This lets you update your Account or Privacy settings, reach the Help center, or log out of your account.

Posting from the iPhone

To update your status from the iPhone, follow these steps:

1. **Start the Facebook app or use your mobile browser to go to Facebook.**

   This brings you to your News Feed. There are three buttons at the very top of News Feed: Status, Photo, and Check In.

2. **Click Status.**

   This expands a large text box, shown in Figure 15-5.

Figure 15-5: iPhone status updates start here.

3. **Type in your status.**

4. **(Optional) Click the gear icon to choose who can see this status update.**

   You can choose from the usual options (Everyone, Friends of Friends, Only Friends) as well as choosing from any lists you've created.

5. **Click Post in the upper-right corner.**

   The post is added to your Wall and your friends' News Feeds.

Given how great the iPhone's camera is, chances are you may want to add a photo to Facebook. Here's how to do that:

1. **Start the Facebook app or use your mobile browser to go to Facebook.**

   This brings you to your News Feed. There are three buttons at the very top of News Feed: Photo, Status, and Check In.

2. **Click Photo.**

   This brings up a menu with two options: Take Photo or Video, or Choose from Library. If you choose to take a photo, your phone's familiar camera interface opens up. Point and Shoot and click Use if you are satisfied with it.

   If you choose from your library, the phone brings up icons of all the photos saved on your phone.

3. **Tap on any faces in the photo to tag them.**

   This brings up a black text box at the top of the screen. Begin typing in a friend's name until you see the name appear in the menu and then tap to select that person.

4. **Tap Next.**

5. **Write a caption to go along with the photo.**

   Type your caption into the Say Something About This Text Box that appears.

6. **Tap Post.**

   The photo is then added to your Wall, and your friends will be able to see it in their News Feeds.

Remember, part of the greatness of Facebook on your mobile phone is that you can share the things that are happening to you as they happen. Don't be shy about documenting the funny/cool/interesting foibles of your daily life.

Checking in to Places

These days, most mobile devices have some sort of GPS functionality built in. This means you, via your phone, can always locate yourself on a map automatically. Facebook Places is a way for you to connect to your friends around where you are.

Facebook Places works like this: when you go someplace using your Facebook app or Facebook Mobile, you choose from a list of possible locations. These might be restaurants or parks or buildings. Facebook generates this list based on the location it's getting from your phone. When you select a location, you *check in* to that location. Checking in basically means actively telling Facebook that you're there. Facebook won't share your location unless you check in.

You can tag friends in your check-ins, or add photos or a few words about what's going on. After you've checked in, your friends can see where you are in their News Feeds. If they're out and about and also using Facebook on their phones, they can see if they are near you.

Checking in to Places leads to all sorts of nice serendipitous encounters. When I was in Boston recently, I checked in to a few different restaurants. An old friend I hadn't seen in ten years sent me a message asking how much longer I'd be in town. I didn't even know she had moved to Boston. We had brunch the next day.

To check in from your iPhone, follow these steps:

1. **From your Facebook screen, tap Check In in the upper right corner of the screen.**

   This brings up a list of nearby places. These places may range from official businesses (Peet's Coffee) to people's homes (Carolyn and Eric's Place) to shared spaces (Dolores Park, San Francisco Airport Terminal 2).

2. **Tap the name of the place you'd like to check in to.**

   If you don't find what you're looking for, type in the name of the place you want to check in to and search for it. If it's not found, Facebook brings you to the Add a Place page, shown in Figure 15-6, and you can click Add to add the place to the list.

3. **(Optional) Type a comment into the Check In box.**

   The Check In screen appears, as shown in Figure 15-7. Check-ins with comments tend to feel a lot like status updates, with a little additional information.

4. **(Optional) Tap the Tag Friends link to tag friends.**

   This brings up your list of friends. Tap the ones you want to tag. Remember, some people are very private about their location information, so it's considered appropriate to ask people before you tag them. Tap Done when you're done tagging.

5. **Tap the Post button.**

   This officially marks you as "here." The check in is added to your Wall as activity. Your friends can see it in their News Feeds, where they can comment or Like your check in, or maybe even pop by to say hi.

Part V
The Part of Tens

The 5th Wave
By Rich Tennant

"That's the problem-on Facebook, everyone knows you're a dog."

In this part . . .

In the earlier parts of this book, I talk a lot about hypothetical situations. So, to ensure that you have some concrete examples of what's really happening on Facebook, here is the Part of Tens.

In this part, I don't make claims about what's the *best* of anything on Facebook because every experience is unique. However, you can see how much your taste matches mine by checking out my favorite applications. Additionally, you can see how Facebook has made an impact on people's lives — and how it might just have an impact on yours. In case you forgot some of what you read earlier (I know, it's a lot of info), I include some of the most common questions we get from our family and friends. And finally, I have a special section of tips for parents with teenagers.

Chapter 16

Ten Great Games and Apps

Traditionally, Facebook has focused on offering the most general types of functionality that just about anyone would find useful. But, in life, different people have different needs and desires. Students like to know what courses their friends are taking. Athletes sometimes trade exercise tips; some record their workouts. Foodies often swap recipes. Music lovers share new music discoveries; movie buffs rate and review films. In an attempt to be all things to all people, Facebook has empowered the masses to add all the specialized functionality that can transform Facebook from a general social network into a specific, tailored tool for managing one's lifestyle — no matter what that lifestyle consists of. This specialized functionality includes all of the previous examples, tools for students, business people, hobbyists, families, and more. Here's a variety of applications (all of which were built by outside developers) that I think are good examples of what Facebook has to offer.

To find any of these applications, just search for their names from the search box in the big blue bar on top. Then, go to their *Application Page* and click the Go to App button. If you need a refresher on how to start using Apps, check out Chapter 14.

Typing Maniac

On the surface, measuring the speed of one's typing sounds like something only professional stenographers would want to know. However, Typing Maniac, a game available to be played on Facebook, tests that theory. As words float down the screen, you must type them before they hit the bottom. As you move up the levels, the words get longer and move down the screen faster.

Of course, the part of the game that is most entertaining is that you can track your progress among your friends. As Typing Maniac posts to your timeline about your progress from caveman to alien, your friends are alerted and can start to compete against you. We strongly suggest that you not use this game as a "break" from work because you will never want to stop playing.

Bejeweled Blitz

Bejeweled Blitz is a fairly simply matching game. You try to make groups of three from a chart of jewels. The fun part comes in when you compete with your friends (whose scores are always looming to the right). You can then choose to share your high scores on your timeline, and you can even post video replays of your brilliance.

CityVille

CityVille is one of the many games created by the people at Zynga. Other Zynga games you may have heard of include FarmVille, FrontierVille, Mafia Wars, and many, many others. CityVille's premise is that you are the founder of a city, and it's your job to build the basics so that people will move in and make your city great. You start out with a few residences and then build up until you earn enough to create skyscrapers, public parks, and high-rise apartment buildings. You can appoint friends to be members of your local government and you can be a tourist in their cities. Your achievements get posted to your timeline for your friends to see.

The Zynga games are often known for their addictive nature, their entertainment, and, unfortunately, sometimes spamming people's friends. As you're playing CityVille and FarmVille, make sure you pay attention to your timeline and the number of posts the games make to it. You can remove posts you don't want or report spam by clicking the caron (downward-pointing triangle) that appears on the right corner of the post when you hover your mouse over it.

Word Challenge

Word Challenge is a game that presents you with a series of letters and asks you to make as many word combinations as possible. The longer the words you get, the more time gets added to the round. Bonus rounds require you to discover a friend's name within a series of letters. You can then see how you stack up against your friends and post any new high scores to your timeline.

Groupcard

Groupcard is an application that replicates the real-world experience of passing a card around to be signed at a party. Groupcard allows you to choose a card type and the basic look and feel of the card, and then invite others to sign it. Each person who signs it can select a variety of fonts, as well as pull from his photos to find an appropriate one to send with the card. After everyone has signed, the card then gets "sent" to its intended recipient.

Book List Challenge

Book List Challenge is a really simple application that asks you how many of the 100 Great Books (as determined by the BBC) you have read. Your response is then shared with your friends, and they can take the quiz as well.

Book List is one of many quiz applications that you may come across as you use Facebook. Quizzes can be really fun depending on the types of quizzes you find. They can range from "Which character from classic Disney cartoons are you?" to "Which alien from Tatooine is your soul mate?" The results can then be shared on your timeline and in your friends' News Feeds. Lots of times these quizzes have been created by other users, and only the template for them was created by the application developer.

Carpool, by Zimride

The Carpool application allows people to offer and request rides to wherever they need to go. It can be used to organize regular carpools to and from work (especially useful when people at your company have actually joined your workplace network) or to find company for longer, one-time road trips.

There are plenty of other services online that people use to find rides, but what's great about the Zimride Carpool application is that you can use it to really check out who you'll be sitting next to for several hours. Do they have mutual friends? Mutual interests? You can go into the drive well prepared.

Museum of Me, by Intel

The Museum of Me is a beautiful Facebook application that mostly happens outside of Facebook. Connect Facebook with Intel's Museum of Me, and Intel pulls timeline information to create a beautiful virtual museum that is all about you. As you move through the rooms, you can see photo memories of your friends, geographic representations of them, and more. The music makes it that much more nostalgic. After you've toured the museum, you can post an album of photos of the museum back to Facebook. Especially for people who've been using Facebook for a few years, this makes a great trip down memory lane.

Visual Bookshelf

So, if the presence of multiple book and word-related games and apps hasn't yet tipped you off, I am a big nerd. Add Visual Bookshelf to the list of nerdy and wonderful apps I love. Visual Bookshelf allows you to share with friends what you are reading. You can see what your friends are reading, post reviews and ratings for the books you have finished, and geek out on books to your heart's content. Have you ever been unable to find something good to read? This app helps you solve that problem more seamlessly than any book club could.

Last.fm

Last.fm is a radio website. You choose music stations based on artists you like, and last.fm streams music to your computer. If you choose to log in to `Last.fm` by connecting it with your Facebook account, `Last.fm` instantly pulls the names of artists you like from your Facebook timeline. Additionally, you can connect with your Facebook friends and see what they are listening to. It takes all the work out of setting up your favorite radio stations. You just log in and you're ready to go.

Chapter 17

Ten Ways Facebook Uniquely Impacts Lives

Sometimes people are dismissive of Facebook, saying, "I keep up with my friends by calling them and visiting them. I don't need a website to do that for me." This is true. However, Facebook doesn't replace real friend-ships — it supplements them. You can still communicate and share informa-tion with your friends without Facebook; however, it's easier and faster to do it with Facebook. Some things are always a part of life; Facebook just makes them better, faster, and stronger.

Keeping in Touch with Summer Friends

I once spent a summer leading a troop of seventh graders into the wild. After two weeks of backpacking, kayaking, climbing, and bonding, the kids were given a big list of e-mail addresses and phone numbers, said their good-byes, and were packed off to their respective homes. I, about to head out west to work at Facebook, lamented the fact that the kids were too young to be on Facebook because they almost assuredly would lose that sheet of paper. I quickly friended my co-counselors (who were all old enough to be on Facebook) and kept up with them through photo albums, notes, and the occasional Poke war. As an added bonus, years later, when my co-counselor needed a reference, he knew exactly where to find me.

Not just for me, but for thousands of high school students, the best-friends-for-the-summer — who had a tendency to fade away as school and life took over — are now a thing of the past. Camp friends immediately become Facebook friends, and on Facebook, no one gets lost. Plus, it's easy to share the memories of a fun summer via Facebook Photos. If you're interested in finding out what's new with your camp friends, they're only a click away. Additionally, it's easy to plan camp reunions without needing to find everyone's new info.

Preparing to Head Off to School

Everyone has a story about leaving for college. Whether they're dropping off a child or an older sister or heading off themselves, people remember some form of anxiety, nervousness, or blinding fear of the unknown. Who were these people in the hallway or sharing the bathroom? Who was this so-called roommate?

Now, college students go off to school having been introduced to their future dorm mates, roommates, and residence assistants via Facebook. Students can list their residences and easily pick out the people they'll most likely meet on the first day, thus dulling the fear that they won't know anyone.

In the time between acceptance letters and orientation, college freshmen spend their time posting on timelines, friending, and getting to know their future classmates. Therefore, they join groups and support one another through a big transition. Suddenly, school is less scary.

Going on Not-So-Blind Dates

Ever been a matchmaker? Ever had a particularly difficult "client" — a friend who has a million requirements for "the one"? Ever been embarrassed because you didn't realize just how picky your friend was until after the date? Enter Facebook. Now, "He's smart, funny, has a great job, lots of cool hobbies, a nice family, and nice friends" can be condensed into a Facebook message with a shared timeline. From there, both parties can decide based on the timelines — looks, interests, or the combination of all the information — whether they want to go on a date.

Some of our friends have gone so far as to say, "No timeline, no date." Given the circumstances, this is reasonable. Not only do you get a little window into a person's world, but you also prepare for talking about the various interests and activities that you see there. This way, "So I saw you like snorkeling. Where does one do that when you live in Idaho?" can be a much better conversation starter than, "So, what do you do?"

Think of it as *far-sighted* dating rather than blind dating.

Meeting People in Your New City or Town

Many people are making themselves comfortable this way in new cities around the world. I got the following message from my friend, Shelby, who was living in Abuja, Nigeria, at the time:

> *So I was friends with this Marine in Liberia. We lost touch when I left Liberia. He joined Facebook two weeks ago, and requested me as a friend. We started talking again. He put me in touch with a friend who works for the U.S. Consulate in Lagos, Nigeria. I Facebooked her. She found my blog address on my Facebook timeline, and forwarded it to her friend who works for the U.S. Embassy in Abuja.*
>
> *Tonight, I went out with this girl from the Embassy and a bunch of other Embassy people. And I have plans (finally!!) for a couple of days next week with these people.*
>
> *And all of this is because of Facebook.*

Shelby's story is just one example of how Facebook makes moving less of an ordeal — a neighborhood is waiting for you when you arrive.

Reconnecting with Old Friends

Long-lost friends. The one who got away. I wonder whatever happened to her. Have you heard about him? These are just some of the ways people talk about the people they somehow lost track of along the way. Whatever the reason for the loss, this sort of regret can be undone on Facebook. Finding people is easy, and getting in touch is, too.

Many recent graduates exclaim that going to a reunion is unnecessary — you already know what everyone is doing five years later; you found out from Facebook. But even for the not-so-young alums, the Find Classmates and Find Coworkers features provide a direct line to search anyone who's on Facebook that you remember from way back (or not so way back) when.

Facebook gets e-mails every so often about people who find birth parents or biological siblings on Facebook. However, the majority of the time, people are looking for and finding their old classmates and reminiscing about the good old days. Better yet, they are reigniting a spark in a friendship that can last far into the future.

Keeping Up with the 'rents

Face it: Keeping your parents in touch with everything that's going on is difficult. However often you speak, it sometimes feels as though you're forgetting something. And visits often feel rushed, as though you don't have enough time to truly catch up.

Facebook Photos and Video applications are two of the best ways to easily and quickly share your life with your parents. Because you can upload photos so quickly, they can feel as though they were present at the <*insert activity here*>. Whether a dance, party, or concert, it's as though you came home and immediately called to tell them about it.

For new parents, Facebook is invaluable for connecting kids with their grandparents. There are few things grandparents like more than photos of their grandkids being brilliant, and you can have those in spades on Facebook. The more generations you have on Facebook, the more fun it can be for all.

Facebooking for Food (or Jobs)

If you've ever found yourself job hunting, you probably are acquainted with the real-world version of *networking*. You ask friends for their friends' numbers and job titles; you take people out to coffee; you go on interviews; you decide whether the company is right for you; you repeat the whole process.

Although finding the right job hasn't gotten any easier with Facebook, a lot of the intermediate steps have. Asking your friends for their friends' info is as easy as writing a note. Better yet, scan through your friends' networks to see whether any of them are working at companies that interest you. After you receive some names, send them a Facebook message (or e-mail, whichever is most appropriate) to set up the requisite "informational coffee date."

After interviewing, a great way to get information about a company is to talk to people who work there. Use Find Coworkers to search people who've listed that company in their timelines.

The only caveat to this approach is that you're now using Facebook to represent a professional portion of your life. If you contact people via Facebook and they feel a little uncomfortable with the content in your timeline, whether that's your timeline picture, a recent status that can be easily misinterpreted, or a timeline post from a friend that reveals just a little too much information, it could make a bad first impression — just as if you'd shown up to the interview in torn jeans and the shirt you slept in. As a well-educated user of

Facebook (because you *have* read all previous 16 chapters without just skipping directly to this one, right?), you're well aware of the myriad privacy settings that enable you to tailor what different parties see and don't see. However, if anything on your timeline might be particularly misunderstood, simply hide it until you sign your offer letter.

Facebook for Freedom

If you were watching news articles about the "Arab Spring" sweeping through the Middle East in early 2011, you would have heard frequent references to Facebook and Twitter. Young people in Egypt did a lot of their communication and coordination through Facebook. Although Facebook wasn't the source for the revolution, it was an invaluable tool in making it successful (and helping people stay in touch with family across the world who might be at risk of violence).

Facebook has always been impressive at gaining support for important causes. Whether it's a monk-led protest in Myanmar, raising money to support Haiti after the devastating earthquake, creating a massive rally in Colombia denouncing a terrorist organization, or raising Autism Awareness in the United States, Facebook lets ideas spread from friend to friend to friend. There's no perfect formula for creating a Facebook revolution, but don't hesitate to share your beliefs on your timeline or express support for causes around the world.

Goin' to the Chapel

A small bit of Facebook trivia: There has, in many circles, arisen the idea of *Facebook Official (FBO)* — the act of moving from *single* to *in a relationship* and listing the person that you're in a relationship with on your timeline. For any fledgling couple, this is a big deal for their personal lives; however, becoming Facebook Official also serves notice to friends and anyone who happens upon one's timeline: I'm taken.

Because of this relationship function, Facebook has become the fastest way to spread a wedding announcement to extended friend groups. Of course, people still call their parents and their closest friends, but *everyone* can find out and share in the happiness via News Feed. Congratulatory timeline posts ensue, as do copious numbers of photos with *the ring* tagged front and center.

After the wedding has taken place, Facebook becomes a wonderland of virtual congratulations as well as photos of the big day. And in case anyone missed it, they can share in the after-party online.

Hey, Facebook Me!

Before Facebook, in both romantic and platonic contexts, it was hard to get from "Nice to meet you" to "Will you be my friend?" Now, the simple phrase, "Facebook me!" expresses this sentiment and so much more. "Facebook me!" can mean, *get in touch, look me up,* or *I want you to know more about me* but in a pressure-free way. It doesn't mean *take me to dinner,* or *let's be best friends forever and ever.* It's simply a way to acknowledge a budding friendship.

"Facebook me!" can also be how good friends say, "Keep up with my life; I want you to know about it," which acknowledges that people are busy and that it's difficult to find time to see each other or talk on the phone. However, even when people are incredibly busy, a quick check on Facebook can make you feel connected again and secure that your friend is doing well.

Chapter 18

Ten Frequently Asked Questions

Having worked for Facebook and worked on this book for several years, I know a lot about the specific complications, confusions, and pain points people come across while using Facebook. At dinner parties, group functions, family events, or even walking across the street wearing a Facebook hoodie, someone always has a suggestion or a question about how to use the site. It's understandable. Facebook is a complex and powerful tool with a ton of social nuances, many of which have yet to be standardized. There are a lot of different features, and Facebook changes a lot. Each year, Facebook modifies parts of the site, redesigns how certain pages look and feel, and adds features. To keep up on what's happening with Facebook, you can Like the official Facebook Page, and you'll get updates straight from the horse's mouth.

What follows are the questions I hear most often from friends and family (and the occasional message from a stranger who really needs help), often with strain in their voices or pain in their eyes. The goal of highlighting the more complicated questions is to save you the stress of encountering these issues yourself and wondering if you're the only one who just doesn't get it.

Is My Computer Infected with a Virus?

A virus is such a total bummer, and if your computer is infected with one, you have our deepest, most sincere sympathies. But first, make sure you really have one. One of the main ways that people discover they've picked up a virus through Facebook is when a friend receives a message from them that looks like spam. If this situation happens to you, your first step should be to change your password by clicking the Forgot Your Password link from the log-in page, or going to Account Settings. Often, viruses hack an account and change the associated e-mail address or password to take control. If you can't change your password, that's probably what happened. If that's the case, contact Facebook customer support immediately by going to the Security Help topic in the Help center: www.facebook.com/help/?page=420. Finally, you should run a virus scan of your computer to help remove any malware that might have ended up on your computer as a result.

Much more information about Facebook-related viruses can be found at www.facebook.com/security. You'll find recommended virus scanners, steps for fixing problems, and information about any new viruses as they crop up. By liking the Facebook security page, you can get information in your News Feed from the Facebook security team, which can help keep you on the lookout for any suspicious-looking links. That, in turn, brings us to the most important reminder about viruses.

The best way to deal with a virus is not to get it in the first place. The best way to *not* get a virus on Facebook is this: Don't click any links you don't trust. When a friend sends you a link through a message or a timeline post, make sure that the friend's message is significantly personal to your relationship, such as "Hey, Mom, remember how we were talking about that video of the woman on the subway the other day? Check out this video." If it's impersonal, such as, "Hi! Check out this link, you'll like it." That's a vague message that could easily be a virus in disguise. Second, check whether you recognize the domain name of the link. URLs for well-known sites such as www.youtube.com, www.facebook.com, www.flikr.com, and so on are likely legitimate. If you don't recognize the URL, don't click. Instead, write back to your friend and ask him if he meant to send you the message. If he did, no harm, no foul. If he didn't, you've just alerted him that he has a virus, and you should tell him about the Facebook security page and recommend a good virus scanner.

Do People Know When I Look at Their Timelines?

No. No. No. When people see stories about their friends pop up on their Home page, they sometimes get a little anxious that this means Facebook is tracking everything everyone does and publishing it to everyone else. That's not true. Consider two types of actions on Facebook: creating content and viewing it. Creating content means you've intentionally added something to Facebook for others to look at or read, such as uploading a photo or a video, commenting or Liking something, or posting a status. These types of actions are all publishable posts — that is, stories about them may end up on your timeline or in your friends' News Feeds — although you have direct control over who exactly gets to see these posts. The other type of action on Facebook is viewing content such as flipping through photos, watching a video, clicking a link your friend has Liked, or viewing someone's timeline. Unless someone is looking over your shoulder as you browse, these types of actions are strictly private. No one is ever directly notified about them, and no trace of the fact that you took that action is left on your timeline or in your friends' News Feeds. So now you can check people out to your heart's content.

I Have a Problem with My Account — Can You Help Me?

I wish I could. Unfortunately, I am but a user like yourself, and that means while I can help diagnose the issue, I can't usually treat it. Sometimes the problems are Facebook's fault, and sometimes they are user error, but either way, I don't really have the tools required to fix it. Most account problems can be resolved only by employees with special access to the specific tool required to fix an account. Here are a few of the account questions we've received recently, and the answers given:

✔ **I can't remember my password. Can you reset it for me?** Answer: No can do. Click the Forgot Your Password link on the login page to start the reset process, which entails Facebook sending a reset link to your e-mail account.

✔ **My account got deactivated because it said I was sending too many messages. Why? Can you fix it?** Answer: I recently had this happen to two friends: one who was using his account to promote his music career, and one who was distributing his poetry to many, many friends through messages. This is Facebook spam detection at work. When an account starts sending a lot of messages in quick succession, especially when those messages contain links, this looks a lot like spam to the system. In most cases, the person is warned first, but if the behavior continues, his account is disabled. The only way to have this action reversed is to write in through the Help pages and request reactivation. To write in, click Help Center from the Account menu — the white downward-facing arrow — from the blue bar on top. Search for an FAQ titled My Personal Facebook Account Is Disabled, and follow the instructions for contacting Facebook. This can sometimes take several days.

✔ **I changed my name to a fake one as a joke, and now I can't change it back, can you do it for me?** Again, a special tool is required. From the Name section of the Account Settings page, request a name change. These requests may take up to a week to fulfill. This example also serves as a heads-up to everyone else. Facebook allows only one name change before requiring people to write in and get permission for a change. This requirement preserves the authenticity of the accounts.

What Do I Do with Friend Requests I Don't Want to Accept?

This is a tough question. As far as I know, there isn't exactly a social convention for this yet, so the answer to this question is pretty personal. Just know that there are a number of actions you can take:

- **Many people just leave the request sitting there forever.** I don't recommend this action because it just clutters up your account — it's better to make a decision.

- **Click Not Now.** This is my favorite option. It sends the request to the hidden requests section of the Friends page, where you won't have to see it anymore. You can then go delete the request from that section of the Friends page. Although people are never directly notified that you've rejected their request, they may notice later that you're not friends and make the correct inference you did not accept. If you do ignore a request, you also need to prepare your follow-up if she asks you about why you ignored her request. Because there is no social convention for this situation just yet, most responses work well here, such as "I'm sorry, I like to keep my friend list down to only my closest friends," or "It's OK. I don't use Facebook often, anyway." You can try "Weird, Facebook must have messed up, I don't think I got it," but then you'll have to accept her request when she likely tries again.

- **If you don't want to accept because you don't want that person having access to your timeline, you can accept the request and then add him to a special restricted Friend List (see Chapter 5).** You can go into your Privacy settings and exclude that Friend List from seeing any parts of your timeline. Then anyone you add to that list will be restricted. In this way, you can accept the friend request without giving up access to your timeline.

- **If you don't want to accept because you don't want to read about that person in your News Feed, no problem!** Simply hit Accept. The first time she shows up in News Feed, hit the caron (downward-pointing triangle) at the upper-right of the story and choose Unsubscribe from <friend's name> or Hide All by <friend's name>. This action removes her from your News Feed for good until you choose to add her back.

What's the Difference between Facebook, MySpace, Twitter, and LinkedIn?

It's likely there are graduate students across the globe writing theses on this particular topic. Needless to say, it's a tough question to answer in a paragraph or casual conversation, so anything you read here is a gross generalization and subject to opinion:

✔ **MySpace has its origins as a tool for local bands to promote their music.** Because many people love music, many people flocked to MySpace (www.myspace.com) in order to connect with their favorite musical artists. A key rule of advertising is to go where the people are, and because so many people were going to MySpace, other businesses and celebrities got involved to garner public attention as well. To this day, MySpace is still oriented toward the relationships between people and media and people and celebrities. The site is designed in a way to make it maximally easy for popular figures to achieve wide distribution and large audiences, or even for everyday Janes and Joes to become popular figures.

✔ **LinkedIn is a tool geared to help people connect primarily for business purposes.** LinkedIn (www.linkedin.com) users try to connect with as many people as they can so that if and when they need a new job or they're looking for someone to hire, they can flip through a vast network of friends and friends of friends to find a reliable lead. People can write and request letters of recommendation for one another, and often recruiters reach out to LinkedIn users whether they're actively looking for a job or not.

✔ **Twitter allows people to engage in real-time sharing.** Whenever a Twitter member has something interesting to share, he blasts out some text, 140 characters or fewer, that everyone who is "following" him has the option to see. The Twitter post is actually very similar to a Facebook Status Update. What differentiates Twitter (www.twitter.com) from Facebook is its extreme simplicity and single focus on real-time exchange of ideas. Facebook is a place where you build longstanding relationships with people; you have access to their static content like their phone numbers and photos; you can message them privately or interact with them through groups and events. Twitter is a place where your friends (and anyone else) find out the information you're sharing at any given time, and vice versa. Popular uses of Twitter are link sharing for interesting websites and news, short opinions about current events, and enabling people to meet up when two people are out and about at the same time.

Will Facebook Start Charging Me to Use the Site?

Another simple answer: No.

This rumor is a particularly nasty one that makes the rounds every now and again via people's statuses. There are several variations, but they always seem to involve asking you to repost the status that Facebook is shutting down/going to start charging/running out of names. Don't fall victim to this ruse. Facebook has long maintained that it will always be free to users. Unless you're advertising something, Facebook will always have space for you for free.

How Do I Convince My Friends to Join Facebook?

Most methods for persuasion involve showing (rather than telling) your friend the value by sending him links to the photos you post on Facebook, putting his e-mail address on the invite of Event and group invitations, or even sending him links and messages (again, by putting his e-mail address on the To line) from the Facebook Inbox.

You can tell her anecdotally the ways in which Facebook has enriched your life. Maybe you're interacting with your kids more, you're keeping in touch with friends you thought were lost, or you have a place to put your thoughts and photos where your friends might actually see them. You can let her look over your shoulder as you use the site so that she can see the experience herself — ask her questions about whether there's anyone in particular she'd like to look up. The more information she sees about the people she cares about, the more likely she is to take the next step.

One common complaint from people who haven't joined the site is that they "don't have time for yet another computer thing." To this concern, one common response is that Facebook is an efficiency tool that often saves a person time compared to using old-school methods. Messaging can often replace e-mail, and events are easier to coordinate over Facebook. Sharing phone numbers is easier. Sending and receiving links is easier. Finding rides to the airport, restaurant recommendations, and who is heading to the park on Saturday are all faster and easier than trying to use e-mail, phone, or other methods of communication.

Finally, for some people, it's just not their time. No matter what you say, they'll stick their fingers in their ears and sing la-la-la until you start talking about sports or the weather or the circus coming to town next week. You can't force them to Facebook; you have to let Facebook come to them. Over the years, I have watched many a nonbeliever eventually cross over and discover the value. Patience may be your only weapon for these diehards.

What if 1 Don't Want Everyone Knowing My Business?

To those who ask that question and don't have time to read Chapter 5 of this book, which goes into great detail about how to be a private person on Facebook, I simply try to impart the following message: You can be an extremely private person and still derive nearly all the same value out of Facebook as anyone else. All you have to do is learn how to use the Privacy controls and lock down all your information and access to your timeline, ensuring that only those you trust can see your info. From there, you can interact in all the same ways as anyone else without feeling like your privacy is being compromised.

Note: Besides learning the Privacy settings and taking the initial time to adjust yours until they feel just right, you will have to do a little extra work to be private on Facebook and still derive comparable value. You'll likely have to put in extra effort connecting with friends, because the more locked-down your information is, the harder you make it for not-yet-Facebook-friends to find your timeline, and the harder it is for your friends to find you, identify you, and connect with you. As long as you're willing to do the work of seeking out your friends and connecting with them, however, your experience should be nearly identical with everyone else's.

1 Heard Facebook Owns Everything 1 Put on its Site — True?

In a legal sense, yes. You also own everything you put on Facebook, and whenever you delete any of your content, it will be deleted by Facebook. What Facebook doesn't own (but you do) is the right to transfer ownership of any of your content to anyone else. So it's completely illegal for anyone else to take your content from Facebook and use it for their own or any commercial use. In early 2009, many Facebook users banded together to express concern about their content and who owns it. In response, Facebook published a Statement of Rights and Responsibilities that makes a commitment about what Facebook will and won't do with your information. These commitments were voted on by every Facebook user who chose to participate, and the commitments govern the company's use of any material you add to the site. Read about these rights and responsibilities in greater detail at www. facebook.com/terms.

Does Facebook Have a Feature That Lets Me Lock Myself Out for a Few Hours?

Short answer: not really.

Long answer: Many people do *deactivate* their accounts. Deactivation is a way of shutting down your account temporarily. It means that no one will see your timeline or be able to interact with you on Facebook. Some people will deactivate their accounts, their reason being "I spend too much time using Facebook." The benefit of such an action is that you're guaranteed not to get notifications about messages, picture tags, timeline posts, or anything else. The downside is that it will cause a lot of confusion among your friends who suddenly can't message you, tag you, or write on your timeline. If they have your e-mail address, they're likely to bug you anyway to ask why you disappeared from Facebook.

The reason it's not a real solution is because all you have to do to reactivate at any time is to enter your password (just like signing in), and you're completely back to normal. So if you're remotely curious how your social group has evolved without you, you might have trouble truly staying away. Which brings us to our next suggestion: Have some self-control. Just like many good things in life, the key to keeping them good is moderation. French fries are delicious, but too many give you a tummy ache. Dancing is a blast — 'til your feet are covered with blisters. Television is educational and entertaining until it's 3 a.m., you're watching your fifth infomercial, you forgot to feed the cat and put out the trash, and you find yourself wondering what life is all about. Facebook is no different. It's a brilliant utility when used to make your life easier and your social interactions richer. When you find yourself flipping through two-year-old vacation photos of a friend of a friend of a friend of a friend, it's time to blink a few times, step away from the mouse, and go out for ice cream, or dancing, or whatever else it is that gives you joy.

Chapter 19

Ten Tips for Parents of Teens on Facebook

. . . .

In This Chapter

▶ Talk to them about Internet safety

▶ Teach them how to report abuse and block people

▶ Learn to use Privacy settings

. . . .

*I*t's hard to put the word *teenager* together with the phrase *social networking* and not get just the teensiest bit anxious. There are a lot of horror stories out there about cyberbullying and online predators. Any parent is likely to be a bit worried.

However, it's unreasonable to think you can keep your teen away from Facebook, much less the Internet. That's where their friends are and that's where they want to be. So here are some tips I hope will be useful in navigating the waters of Facebook and the Internet at large.

I should acknowledge here that I'm neither a parent nor a teenager myself, so I don't pretend to know everything about what's going on in your family or in your teen's life. Think of these tips as a useful jumping-off place for figuring out how to keep your teen safe online.

Talk to Them about General Internet Safety

Here are some general Internet safety tips that apply no matter what kind of website you're using:

✔ Don't share any personally identifying info (address, phone number, credit card info, and so on) with anyone you don't know.

✔ Create different passwords for all of the sites you use. Passwords should also be difficult to guess and contain a mix of numbers, letters, and symbols.

✔ Don't share your passwords with anyone, even boyfriends/girlfriends or best friends (this is one that teenagers tend to struggle with).

✔ Only click links you trust; be wary of scammy-sounding advertisements. They are usually scams.

Beware of Strangers

On Facebook, in general, people are who they say they are and tend to have only one account that links to their real e-mail address and contains only real information about them. Unfortunately, like the real world, Facebook isn't completely free of malicious people who lie to take advantage of someone else.

The good news is that it's fairly easy to keep your experience free of people like this by only accepting Friend Requests from people you actually know in real life. Talk to your teen about the importance of sharing information only with people they actually know, and telling you when someone they don't know contacts them.

Teach Them How to Report Abuse

Virtually every piece of content on Facebook has a report link. These include photos, videos, messages, timelines, groups, posts, and events. If you or your child comes across content that is abusive or offensive, report it by clicking any of the Report links located near these pieces of content. Facebook investigates all abuse reports and removes content that violates its Statement of Rights and Responsibilities. You can report timelines for being fake or posts for being harassing.

The only caveat is that some stuff that may be offensive to you or your teen may not be considered offensive by Facebook's staff. For example, you can't report a photo for being unflattering — you can only ask that the person who posted it take it down.

Teach Them How to Block People

Certain kinds of behaviors can eventually lead to someone being kicked off of Facebook, but you (and your teen) might not want to wait around until the offender is out for good. If someone is bothering your teen (or you) and won't leave them alone, don't hesitate to block them from the Privacy pages. Blocking someone almost has the effect of making it seem like they are not on Facebook. Neither of you will be able to see each other in searches, message each other, or look at each other's timelines.

Personally, I block strangers early and often. I receive my share of junk mail, and anytime a stranger sends me a weird link or comments on my looks, I both report and block the person. It just gives me peace of mind to do so. Links to block people can be found within the group of actions links on the lower left of the timeline, or you can type in names or e-mail addresses into the Block Users section of the Manage Blocking privacy page.

Learn to Use Privacy Settings

This book contains an entire chapter on privacy. Teens in the United States on Facebook actually have very specific privacy rules that are different from most users. Their Everyone posts are not actually distributed to Everyone via search or otherwise, and generally adults see a limited version of their timelines regardless of their settings.

That being said, you can rest easier if you go through your teen's privacy settings with them and agree on settings that allow them to share more safely. In general, keeping things only shared with Friends is a quick way to make sure that fewer people are seeing your child's information and that at all times, you both have a complete list of who those people are. If you have a question about anything, hopefully Chapter 5 can help.

Talk about Posts and Consequences

Even with good privacy settings, teenagers often struggle with the idea that once something is shared, it's hard to undo. This is extremely true of things like Facebook photos or posts. Encourage your teen to think about how something might be seen and interpreted by people who aren't their closest friends. Would they want a college admissions officer to see that photo? Would they want their boss to read that post? Both of these situations have happened and had real consequences: The college admissions officer might decide you aren't really Hahvard material, or the boss may fire you for complaining on Facebook about her way of speaking. The things that happen on Facebook don't always stay on Facebook; they have a way of spreading. Remind your teen to think before they post.

Remember the Golden Rule

As much as many parents worry about their kids being the victims of cyber-bullying, you have to also consider that kids can be the perpetrators of cyber-bullying. Talk to your kids about the behaviors that might affect others, whether known or unknown. This includes things like creating hateful Facebook groups targeting a teacher or peer, as well as going into a forum somewhere else on the Internet and posting something inflammatory or offensive under the protection of anonymity (although, on the Internet, anonymity doesn't usually last).

The golden rule applies to your child just as much in adolescence as when they were in kindergarten: Do unto others as you would have them do unto you. Would you want someone saying something bad about you online? How would you feel if you posted something really personal, and people made fun of you? Part of being part of Facebook (and other online communities) is being a good citizen. That makes Facebook Nation a safe place for all.

Respect Their Boundaries

After you've got them set up on Facebook and talked about all the general ideas for Internet and Facebook safety, you need to give them some space. As one of my teenage cousins said to me, "They should be my friend, and that's it."

Some kids are really comfortable interacting with their parents; others think it is the most embarrassing thing in the world. Hey, that's okay. When you were a teen, did you like it when your parents came along with you and your friends when you went out? Did you like it when they listened in on your phone calls or read your diary? That's what it can feel like to some teenagers when they are asked to be friends with their parents: like you are invading their space.

You can talk to them about some of the things you see on Facebook (both the good and the bad; trust me, there are both!), but commenting on their stuff or posting on their timeline are things that are likely to get you unfriended. As long as you let them know they can come tell you whenever they are having some sort of problem (and that they always tell you when they are contacted by a stranger), it's important to let them know that you trust them to make smart choices.

Don't Send Friend Requests to their Friends

If their friends friend you, it's probably okay to accept those requests (though you may want to check with your teen first; see the previous section, "Respect Their Boundaries"). However, it's generally considered weird and pushy to reach out to their friends yourself.

Make Space for Your Own Social Life, and Your Family Life, on Facebook

If you joined Facebook just to understand what was going on in your teen's life, that's great. But now, having read this book, I hope you can see that there's a lot Facebook can offer you and your friends, with or without your children present. Share photos. Coordinate events with your friends. Post statuses about what's going on with you. It doesn't always have to be about them.

One way to keep your social life separate from your teen's social life, but still have a little interaction on Facebook, is to create a Group for your family. You can add lots of different family members and everyone can share the sort of stuff family likes to know: holiday newsletter–type stuff. It creates a space where it's okay for you and your son or daughter to interact on Facebook. Hopefully it's a way to bring you both a little closer.

One parent I spoke to mentioned that he likes to send his teen messages on Facebook letting her know he loves her. It's just another way for them to connect where his daughter is comfortable, and it has strengthened their relationship.

Index